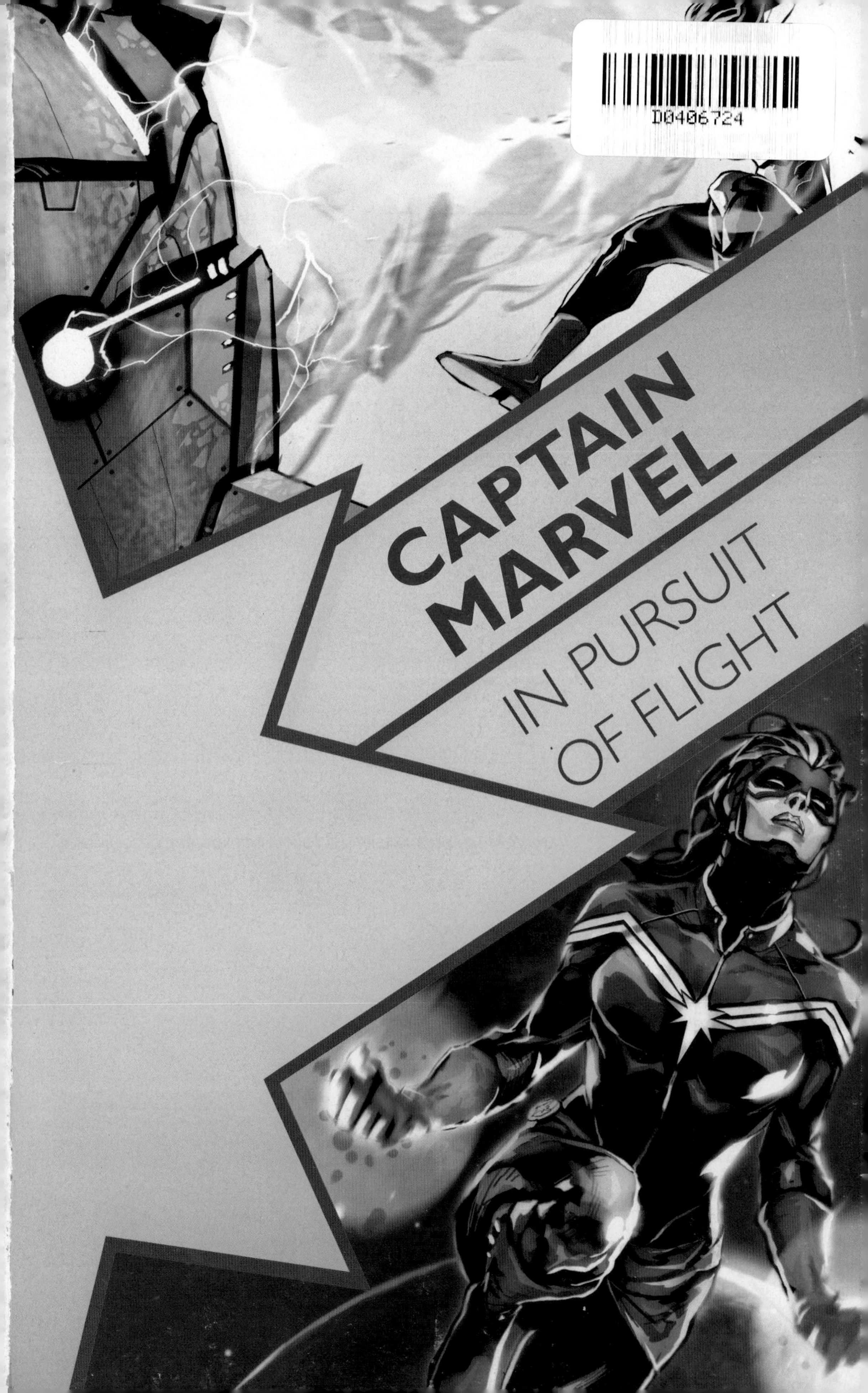
CAPTAIN MARVEL
IN PURSUIT OF FLIGHT

WRITER KELLY SUE DeCONNICK

ARTIST (ISSUES #1-4) DEXTER SOY

WITH RICHARD ELSON (ARTIST, #4 PGS. 17-18), WIL QUINTANA (COLOR ARTIST, #4 PGS. 17-18), KARL KESEL (ARTIST, #4 PG. 19), JAVIER RODRIGUEZ (COLOR ARTIST, #4 PG. 19), AL BARRIONUEVO (ARTIST, #5 PGS. 16-20) & WIL QUINTANA (COLOR ARTIST, #5 PGS. 16-20)

ARTIST (ISSUES #5-6) EMMA RIOS

WITH ÁLVARO LÓPEZ (INKER, #6)

COLOR ARTIST (ISSUES #5-6) JORDIE BELLAIRE

LETTERER VC'S JOE CARAMAGNA

COVER ART ED McGUINNESS, DEXTER VINES & JAVIER RODRIGUEZ (#1-4) AND TERRY DODSON & RACHEL DODSON (#5-6)

ASSISTANT EDITOR ELLIE PYLE

EDITOR SANA AMANAT

SENIOR EDITOR STEPHEN WACKER

CAPTAIN MARVEL COSTUME DESIGNED BY JAMIE McKELVIE
SPECIAL THANKS TO MAKI YAMANE & SIGRID ELLIS

COLLECTION EDITOR & DESIGN: CORY LEVINE
ASSISTANT EDITORS: ALEX STARBUCK & NELSON RIBEIRO
EDITORS, SPECIAL PROJECTS: JENNIFER GRÜNWALD & MARK D. BEAZLEY
SENIOR EDITOR, SPECIAL PROJECTS: JEFF YOUNGQUIST
SVP OF PRINT & DIGITAL PUBLISHING SALES: DAVID GABRIEL

EDITOR IN CHIEF: AXEL ALONSO
CHIEF CREATIVE OFFICER: JOE QUESADA
PUBLISHER: DAN BUCKLEY
EXECUTIVE PRODUCER: ALAN FINE

"FOR CIVILIAN PILOT AND RET. AIR FORCE MSGT. ROBERT L. DECONNICK, II.
I LOVE YOU, DADDY."
— KELLY SUE

CAPTAIN MARVEL VOL. 1: IN PURSUIT OF FLIGHT. Contains material originally published in magazine form as CAPTAIN MARVEL #1-6. Third printing 2014. ISBN# 978-0-7851-6549-1. Published by MARVEL WORLDWIDE, INC., a subsidiary of MARVEL ENTERTAINMENT, LLC. OFFICE OF PUBLICATION: 135 West 50th Street, New York, NY 10020. Copyright © 2012 Marvel Characters, Inc. All rights reserved. All characters featured in this issue and the distinctive names and likenesses thereof, and all related indicia are trademarks of Marvel Characters, Inc. No similarity between any of the names, characters, persons, and/or institutions in this magazine with those of any living or dead person or institution is intended, and any such similarity which may exist is purely coincidental. Printed in the U.S.A. ALAN FINE, EVP - Office of the President, Marvel Worldwide, Inc. and EVP & CMO Marvel Characters B.V.; DAN BUCKLEY, Publisher & President - Print, Animation & Digital Divisions; JOE QUESADA, Chief Creative Officer; TOM BREVOORT, SVP of Publishing; DAVID BOGART, SVP of Operations & Procurement, Publishing; C.B. CEBULSKI, SVP of Creator & Content Development; DAVID GABRIEL, SVP of Print & Digital Publishing Sales; JIM O'KEEFE, VP of Operations & Logistics; DAN CARR, Executive Director of Publishing Technology; SUSAN CRESPI, Editorial Operations Manager; ALEX MORALES, Publishing Operations Manager; STAN LEE, Chairman Emeritus. For information regarding advertising in Marvel Comics or on Marvel.com, please contact Niza Disla, Director of Marvel Partnerships, at ndisla@marvel.com. For Marvel subscription inquiries, please call 800-217-9158. Manufactured between 12/11/2013 and 1/13/2014 by R.R. DONNELLEY, INC., SALEM, VA, USA.

10 9 8 7 6 5 4 3

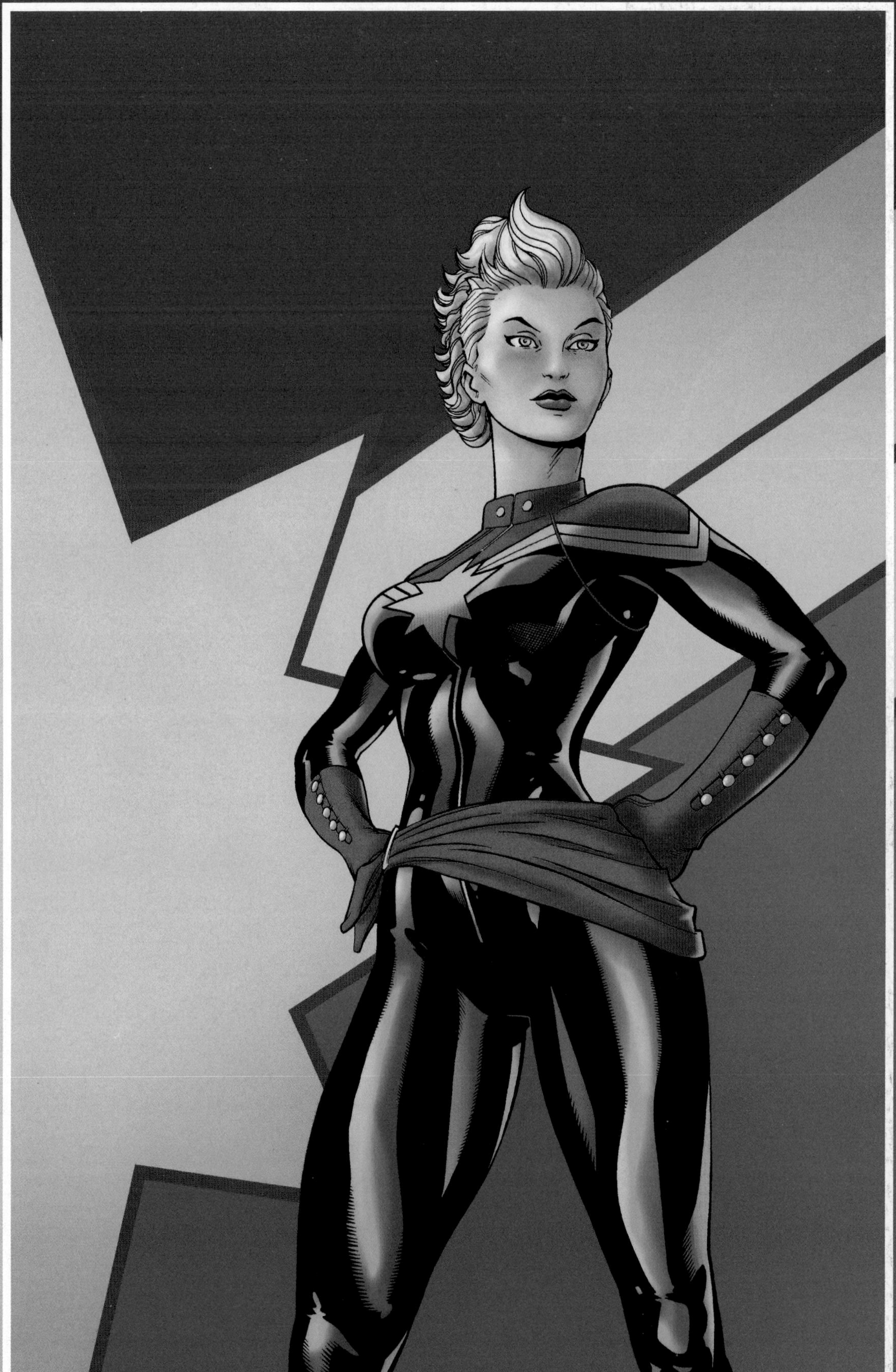

ONE

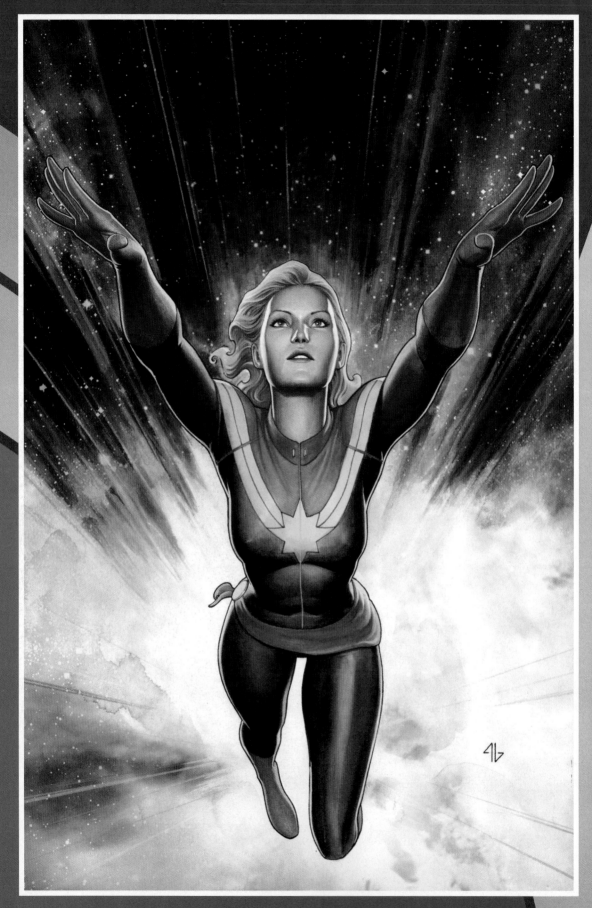

ONE VARIANT BY ADI GRANOV

FINAL

DAILY BUGLE®

SINCE 1897
$1.00 (in NYC)
$1.50 (outside city)

SPECIAL COMMEMORATIVE ISSUE!

INSIDE: BLONDE BOMBSHELL BRAVES BOSTON! DAREDEVIL SPOTTINGS CONFIRMED IN LATVERIA! LIZARDS LOOSE IN MANHATTAN! MORE...

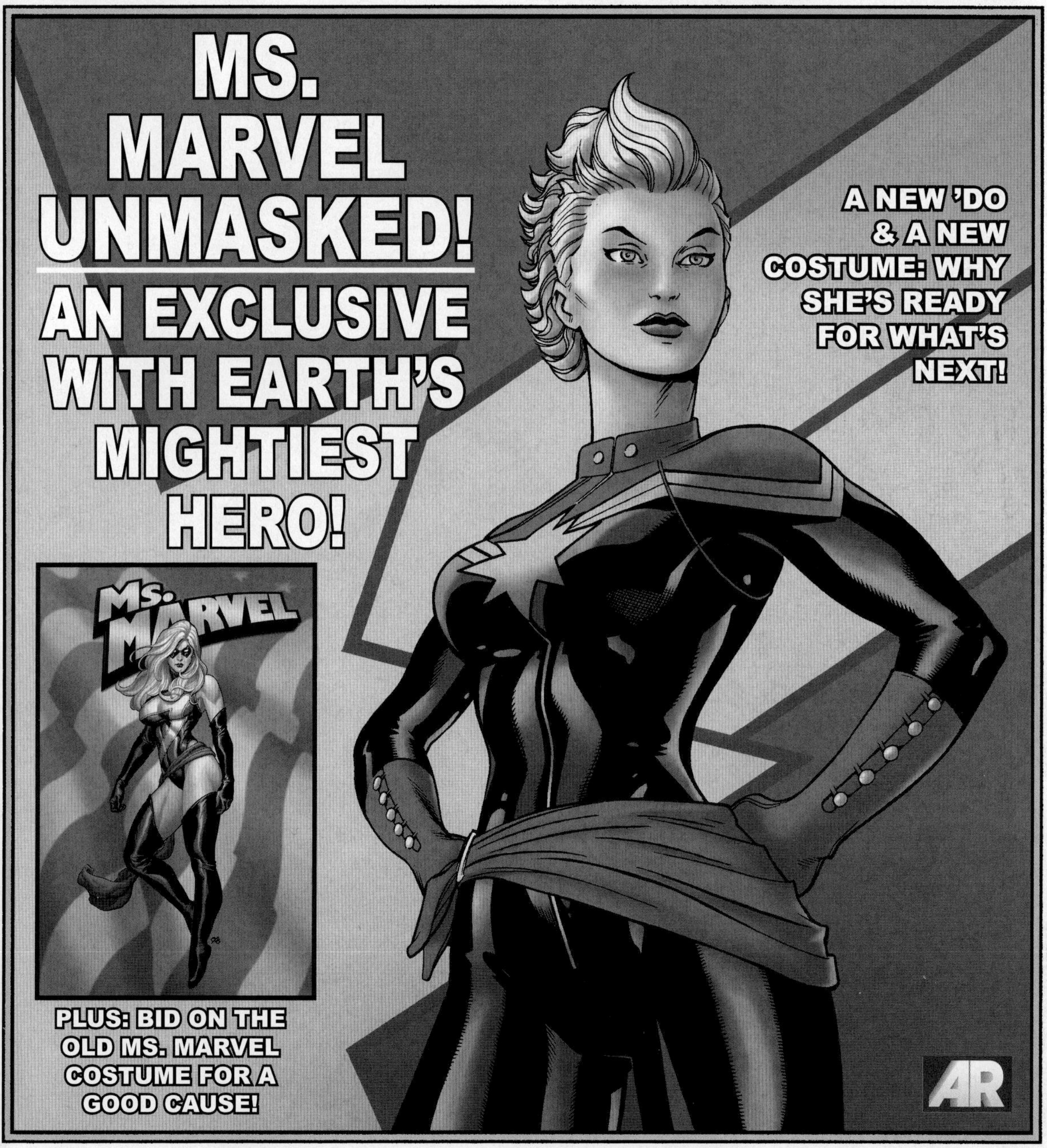
MS. MARVEL UNMASKED!
AN EXCLUSIVE WITH EARTH'S MIGHTIEST HERO!
A NEW 'DO & A NEW COSTUME: WHY SHE'S READY FOR WHAT'S NEXT!
MS. MARVEL
PLUS: BID ON THE OLD MS. MARVEL COSTUME FOR A GOOD CAUSE!
AR

When you see this: AR, open up the MARVEL AR APP (available on applicable Apple ® iOS or Android TM devices) and use your camera-enabled device to unlock extra-special exclusive features!

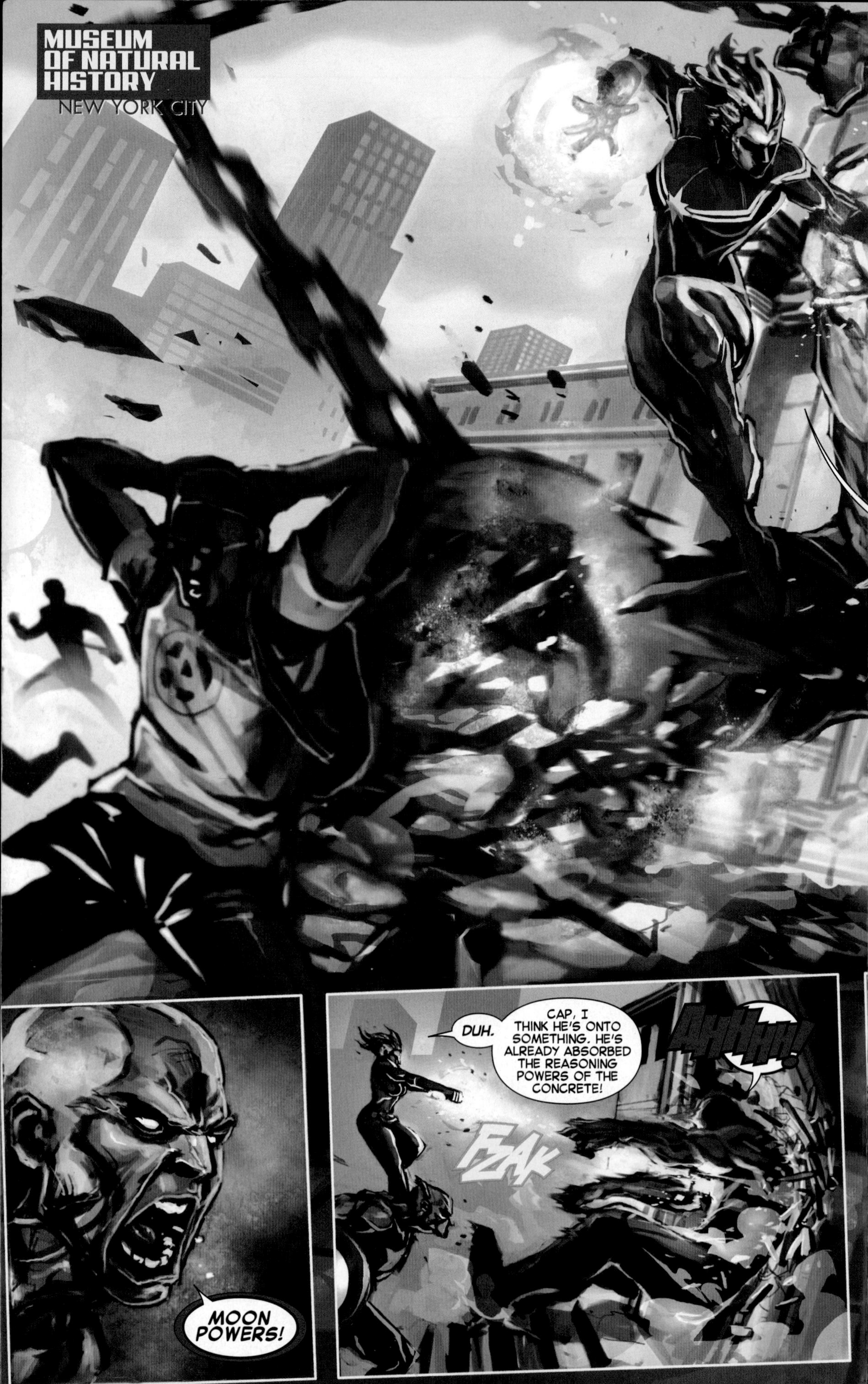
MUSEUM OF NATURAL HISTORY
NEW YORK CITY
MOON POWERS!
DUH.
CAP, I THINK HE'S ONTO SOMETHING. HE'S ALREADY ABSORBED THE REASONING POWERS OF THE CONCRETE!
AHHHH!
FZAK

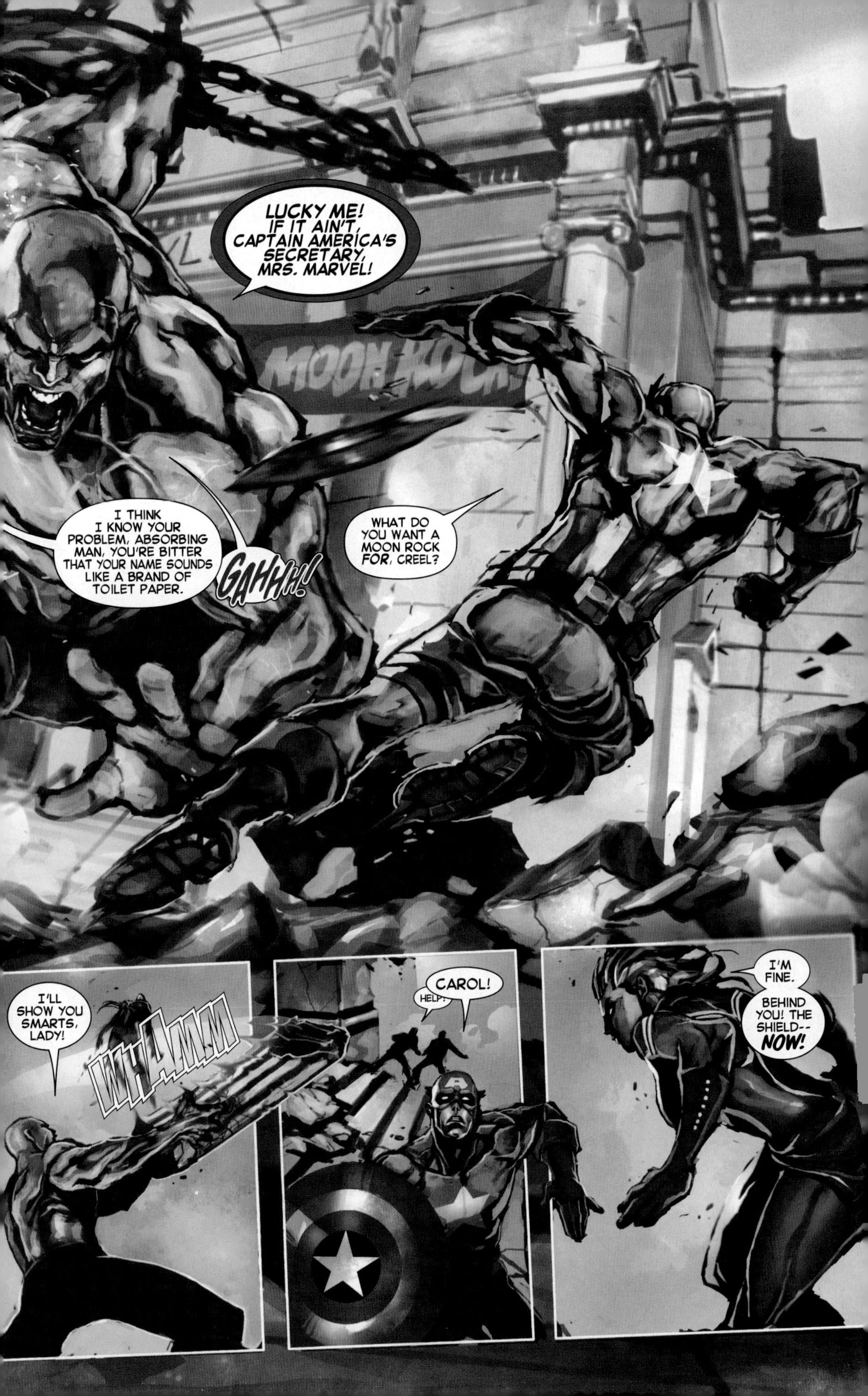
LUCKY ME! IF IT AIN'T, CAPTAIN AMERICA'S SECRETARY, MRS. MARVEL!
MOON ROCK
I THINK I KNOW YOUR PROBLEM, ABSORBING MAN, YOU'RE BITTER THAT YOUR NAME SOUNDS LIKE A BRAND OF TOILET PAPER.
GAHHH!
WHAT DO YOU WANT A MOON ROCK FOR, CREEL?
I'LL SHOW YOU SMARTS, LADY!
WHAMM
HELP!
CAROL!
I'M FINE.
BEHIND YOU! THE SHIELD-- NOW!

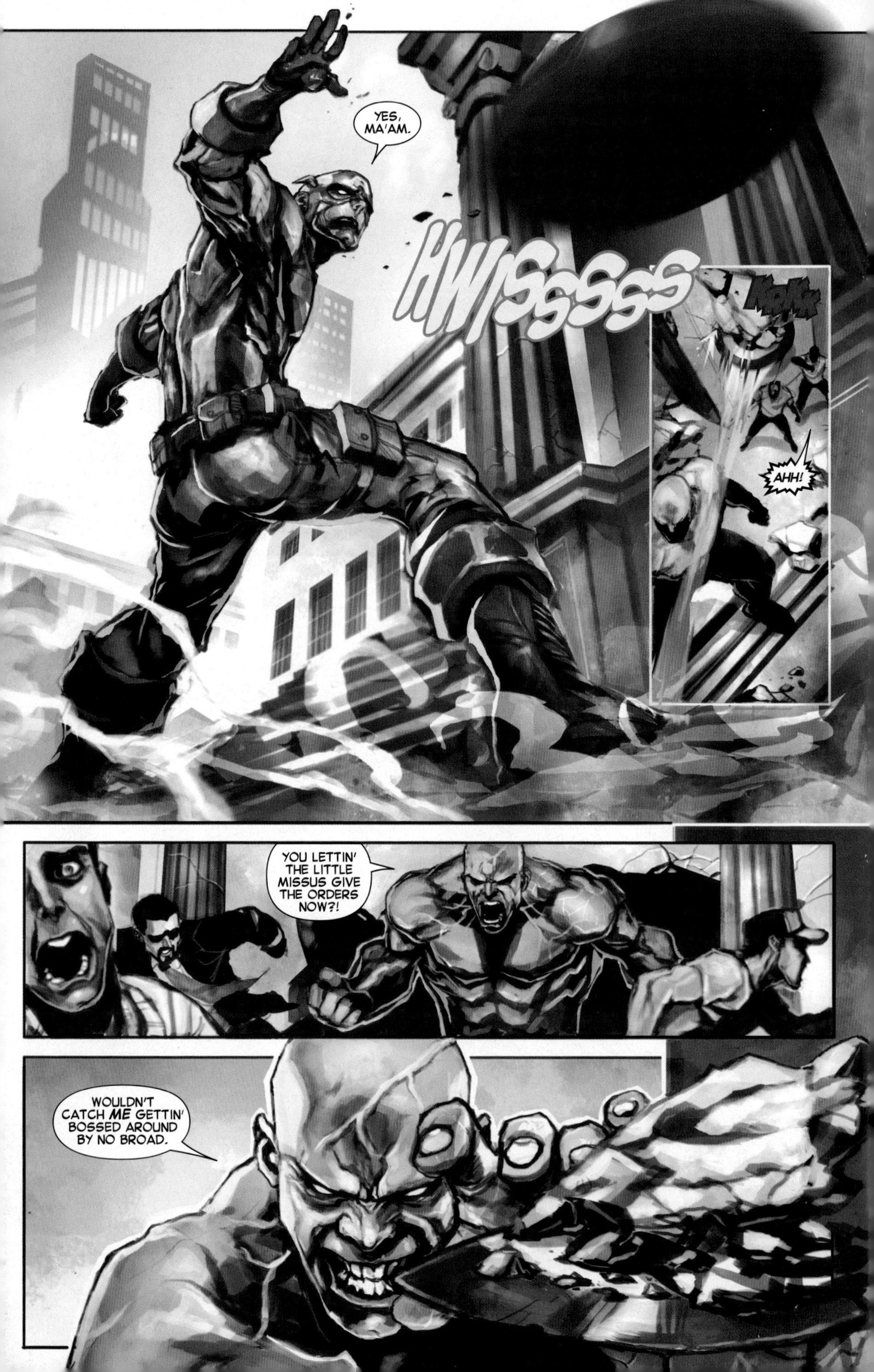
YES, MA'AM.
HWISSSSS
AHH!
YOU LETTIN' THE LITTLE MISSUS GIVE THE ORDERS NOW?!
WOULDN'T CATCH ME GETTIN' BOSSED AROUND BY NO BROAD.

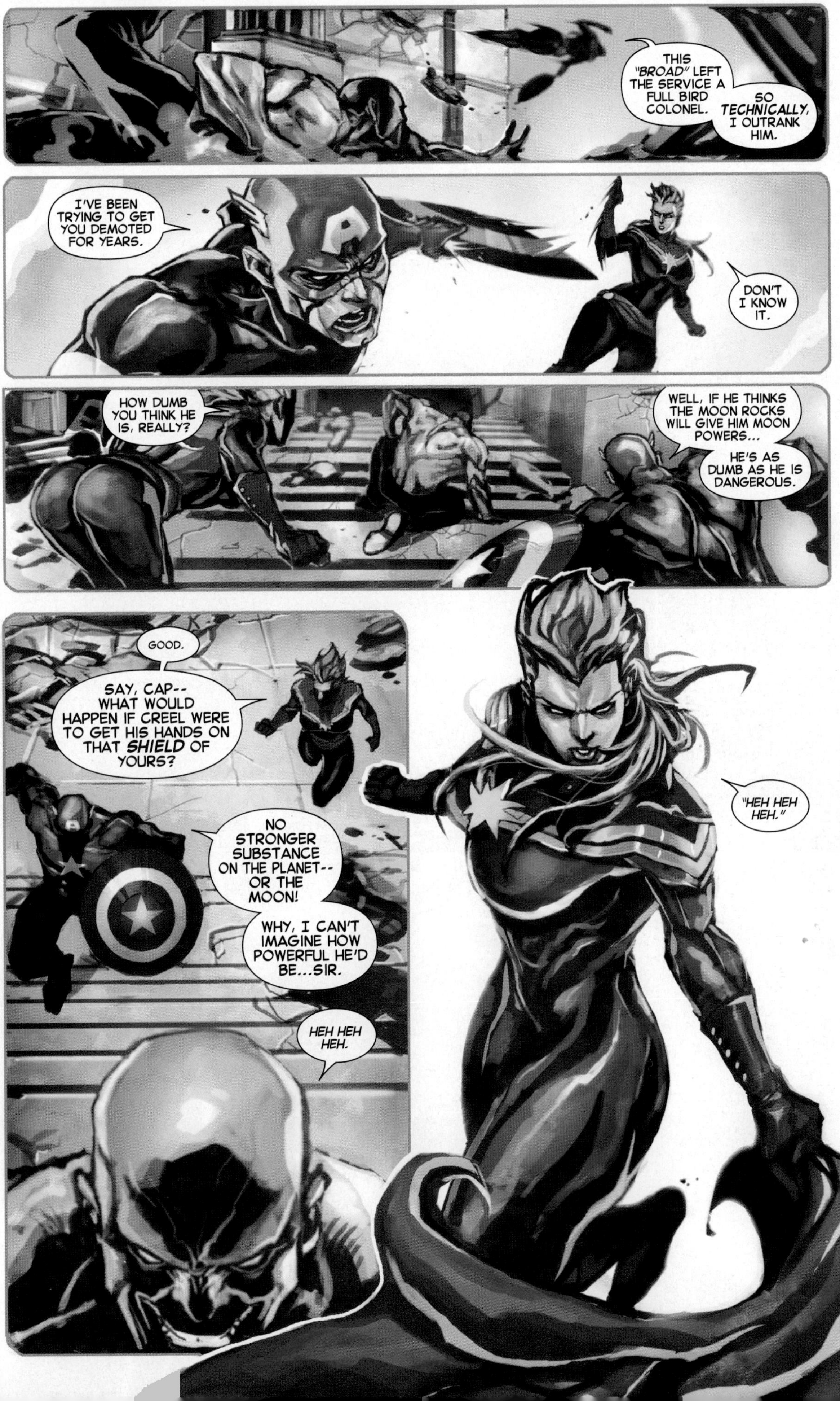
THIS "BROAD" LEFT THE SERVICE A FULL BIRD COLONEL.
SO TECHNICALLY, I OUTRANK HIM.
I'VE BEEN TRYING TO GET YOU DEMOTED FOR YEARS.
DON'T I KNOW IT.
HOW DUMB YOU THINK HE IS, REALLY?
WELL, IF HE THINKS THE MOON ROCKS WILL GIVE HIM MOON POWERS...
HE'S AS DUMB AS HE IS DANGEROUS.
GOOD.
SAY, CAP-- WHAT WOULD HAPPEN IF CREEL WERE TO GET HIS HANDS ON THAT SHIELD OF YOURS?
NO STRONGER SUBSTANCE ON THE PLANET-- OR THE MOON!
WHY, I CAN'T IMAGINE HOW POWERFUL HE'D BE...SIR.
HEH HEH HEH.
"HEH HEH HEH."

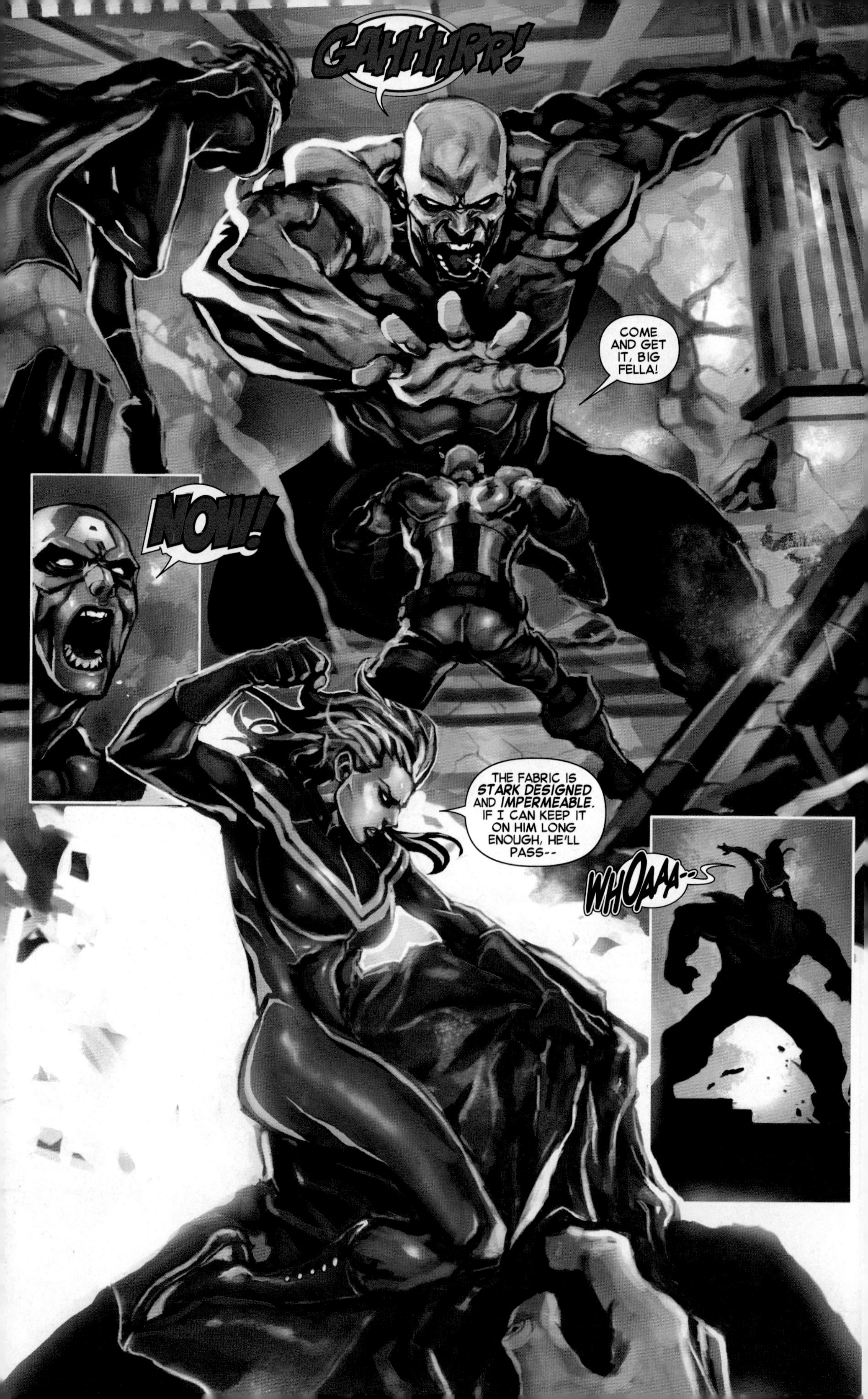
GAHHHRR!
COME AND GET IT, BIG FELLA!
NOW!
THE FABRIC IS STARK DESIGNED AND IMPERMEABLE. IF I CAN KEEP IT ON HIM LONG ENOUGH, HE'LL PASS--
WHOAAA--

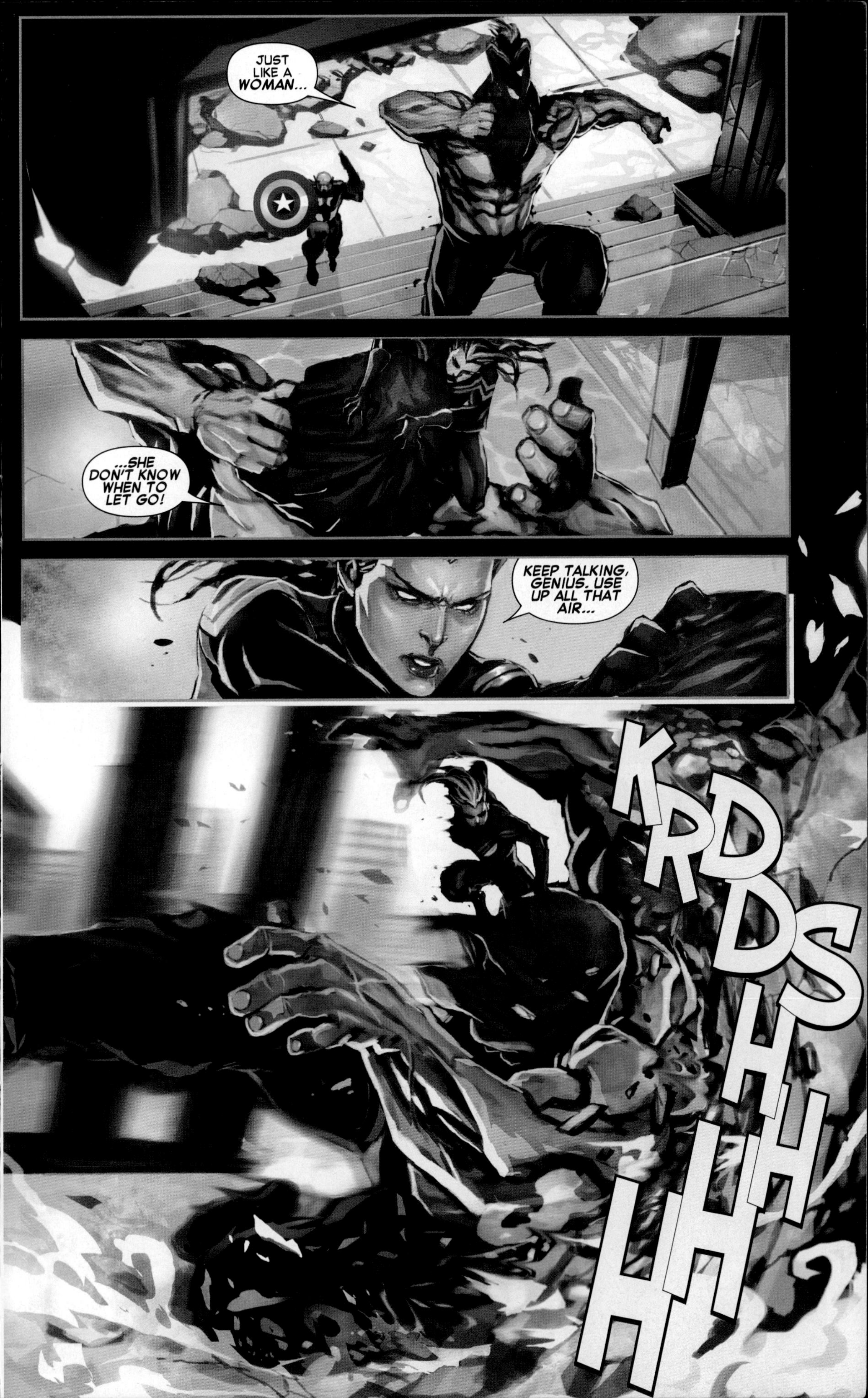

JUST LIKE A WOMAN...
...SHE DON'T KNOW WHEN TO LET GO!
KEEP TALKING, GENIUS. USE UP ALL THAT AIR...
KRRDDSHHHHHHH

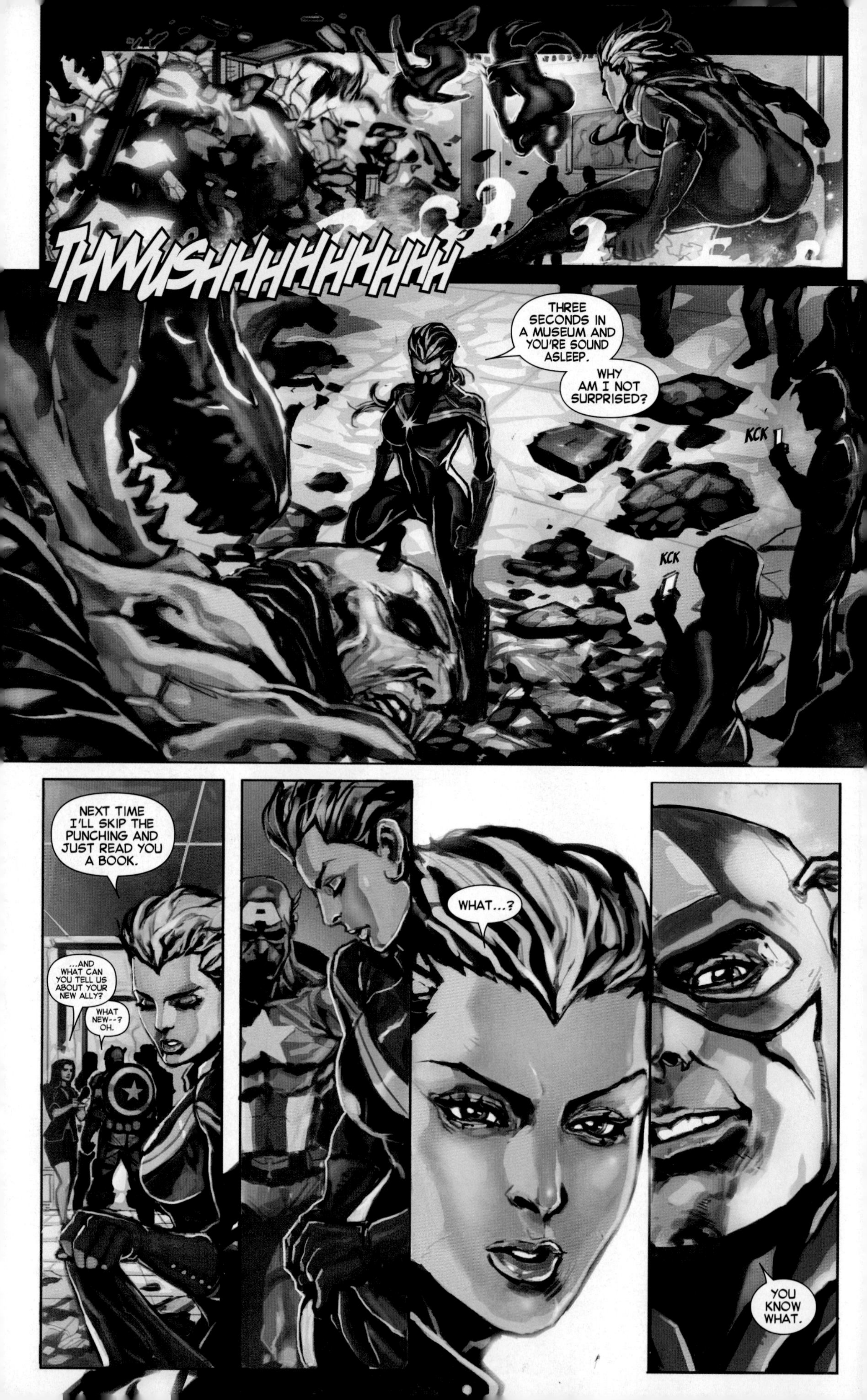
THWUSHHHHHHHHH
THREE SECONDS IN A MUSEUM AND YOU'RE SOUND ASLEEP.
WHY AM I NOT SURPRISED?
KCK
KCK
NEXT TIME I'LL SKIP THE PUNCHING AND JUST READ YOU A BOOK.
...AND WHAT CAN YOU TELL US ABOUT YOUR NEW ALLY?
WHAT NEW--? OH.
WHAT...?
YOU KNOW WHAT.

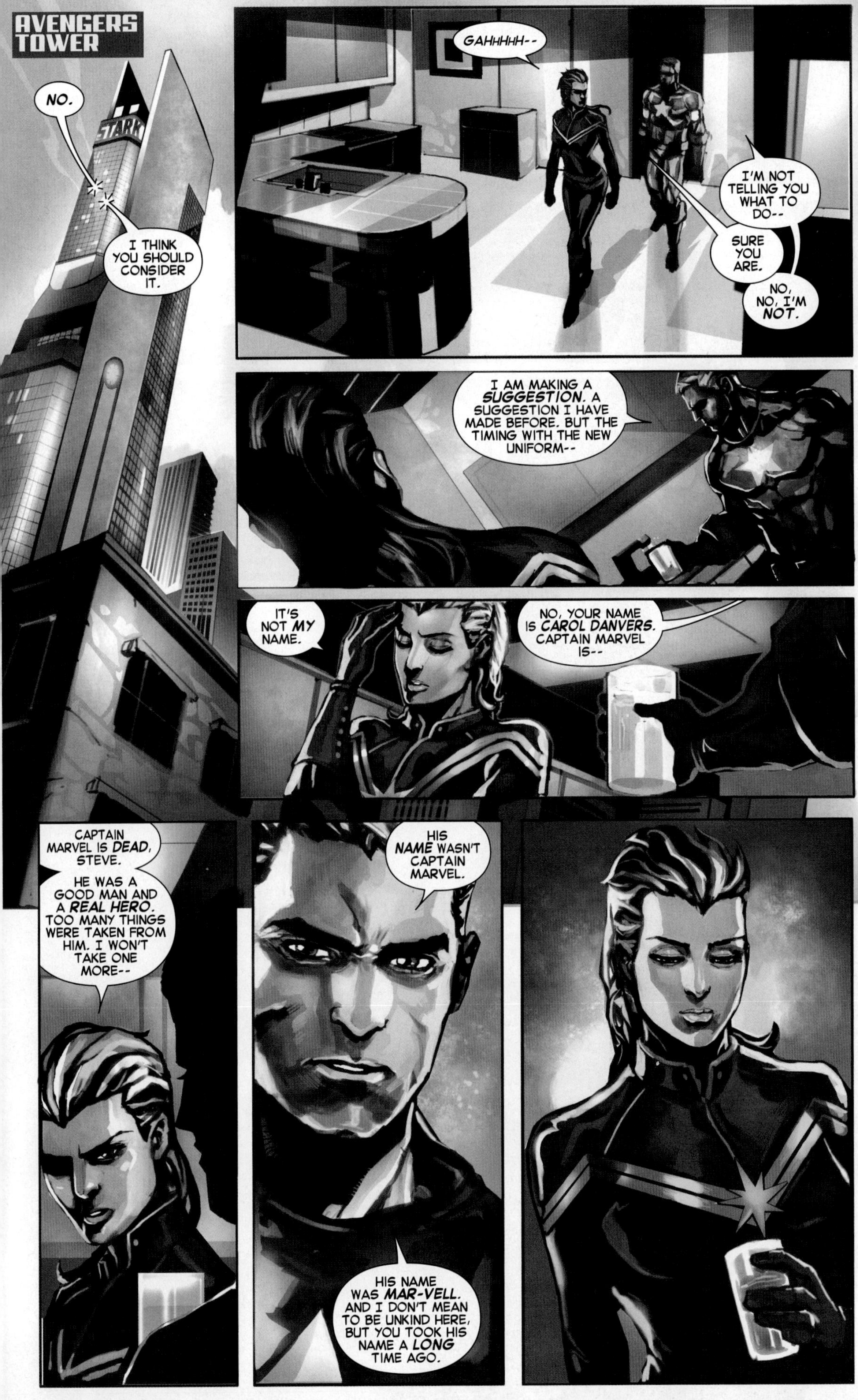
AVENGERS TOWER
NO.
I THINK YOU SHOULD CONSIDER IT.
STARK
GAHHHHH--
I'M NOT TELLING YOU WHAT TO DO--
SURE YOU ARE.
NO, NO, I'M NOT.
I AM MAKING A SUGGESTION. A SUGGESTION I HAVE MADE BEFORE. BUT THE TIMING WITH THE NEW UNIFORM--
IT'S NOT MY NAME.
NO, YOUR NAME IS CAROL DANVERS. CAPTAIN MARVEL IS--
CAPTAIN MARVEL IS DEAD, STEVE.
HE WAS A GOOD MAN AND A REAL HERO. TOO MANY THINGS WERE TAKEN FROM HIM. I WON'T TAKE ONE MORE--
HIS NAME WASN'T CAPTAIN MARVEL.
HIS NAME WAS MAR-VELL. AND I DON'T MEAN TO BE UNKIND HERE, BUT YOU TOOK HIS NAME A LONG TIME AGO.

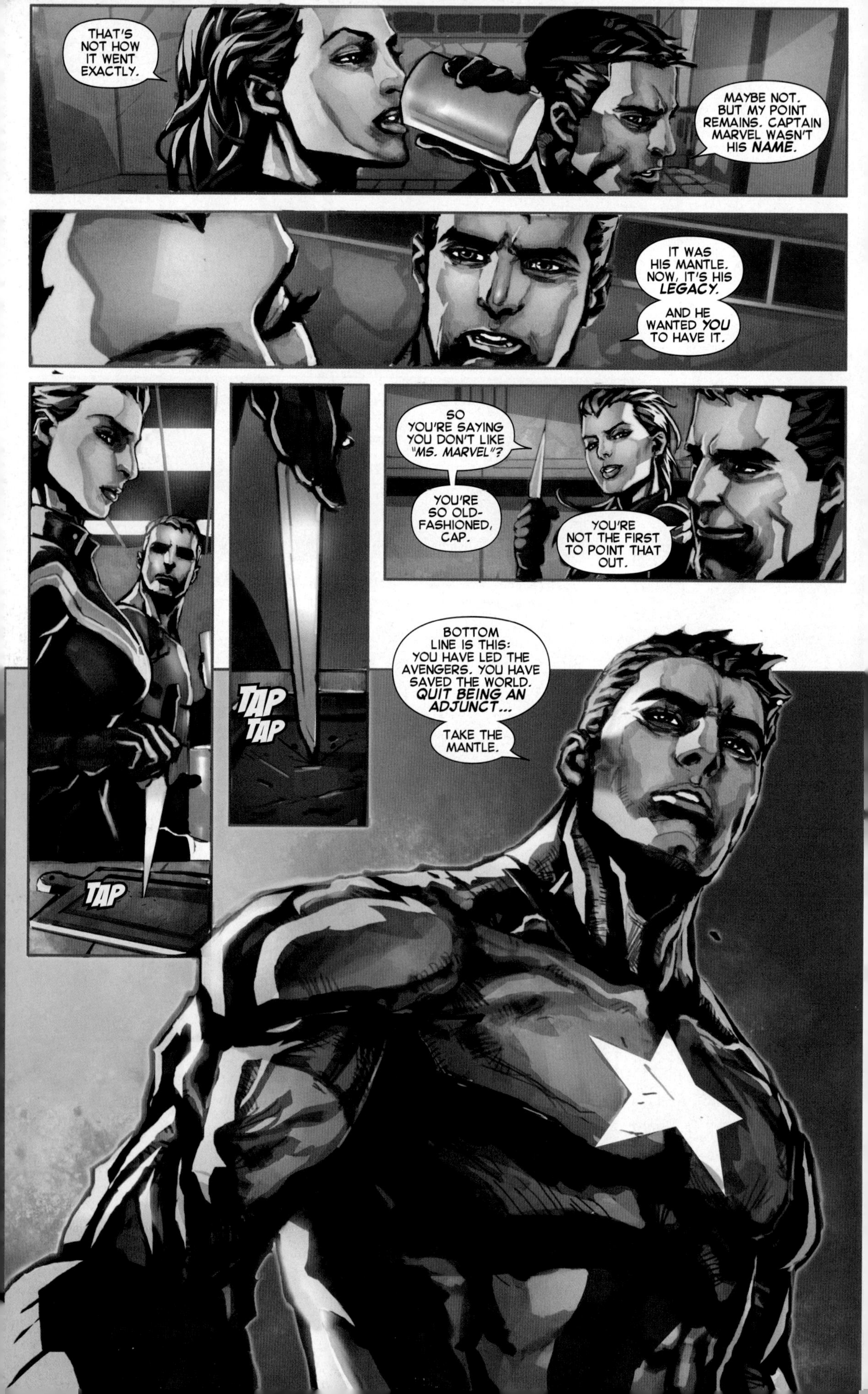
THAT'S NOT HOW IT WENT EXACTLY.
MAYBE NOT. BUT MY POINT REMAINS. CAPTAIN MARVEL WASN'T HIS NAME.
IT WAS HIS MANTLE. NOW, IT'S HIS LEGACY.
AND HE WANTED YOU TO HAVE IT.
TAP
TAP TAP
SO YOU'RE SAYING YOU DON'T LIKE "MS. MARVEL"?
YOU'RE SO OLD-FASHIONED, CAP.
YOU'RE NOT THE FIRST TO POINT THAT OUT.
BOTTOM LINE IS THIS: YOU HAVE LED THE AVENGERS. YOU HAVE SAVED THE WORLD. QUIT BEING AN ADJUNCT...
TAKE THE MANTLE.

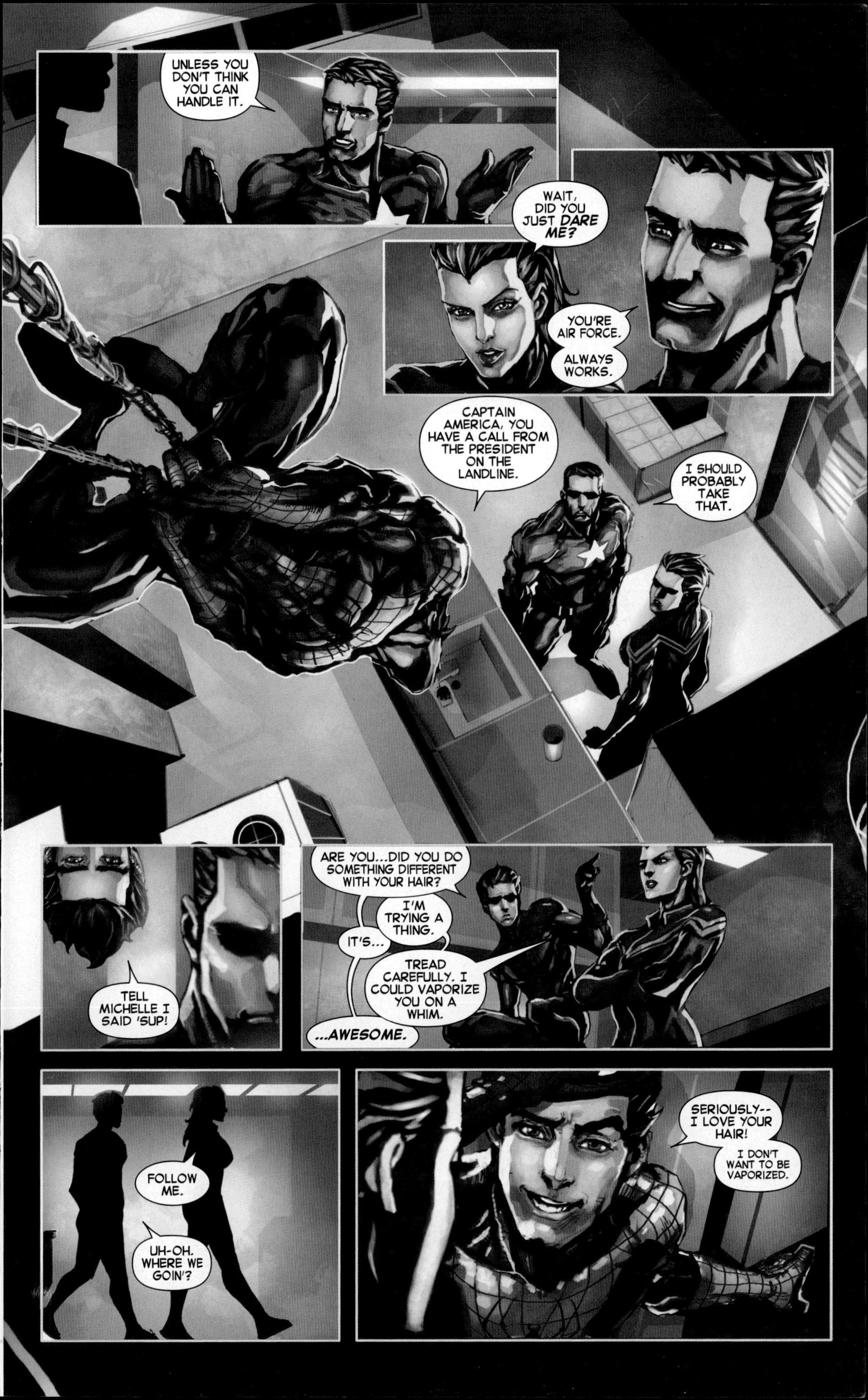
UNLESS YOU DON'T THINK YOU CAN HANDLE IT.
WAIT, DID YOU JUST *DARE ME?*
YOU'RE AIR FORCE.
ALWAYS WORKS.
CAPTAIN AMERICA, YOU HAVE A CALL FROM THE PRESIDENT ON THE LANDLINE.
I SHOULD PROBABLY TAKE THAT.
TELL MICHELLE I SAID 'SUP!
ARE YOU...DID YOU DO SOMETHING DIFFERENT WITH YOUR HAIR?
I'M TRYING A THING.
IT'S...
TREAD CAREFULLY. I COULD VAPORIZE YOU ON A WHIM.
...AWESOME.
FOLLOW ME.
UH-OH. WHERE WE GOIN'?
SERIOUSLY-- I LOVE YOUR HAIR!
I DON'T WANT TO BE VAPORIZED.

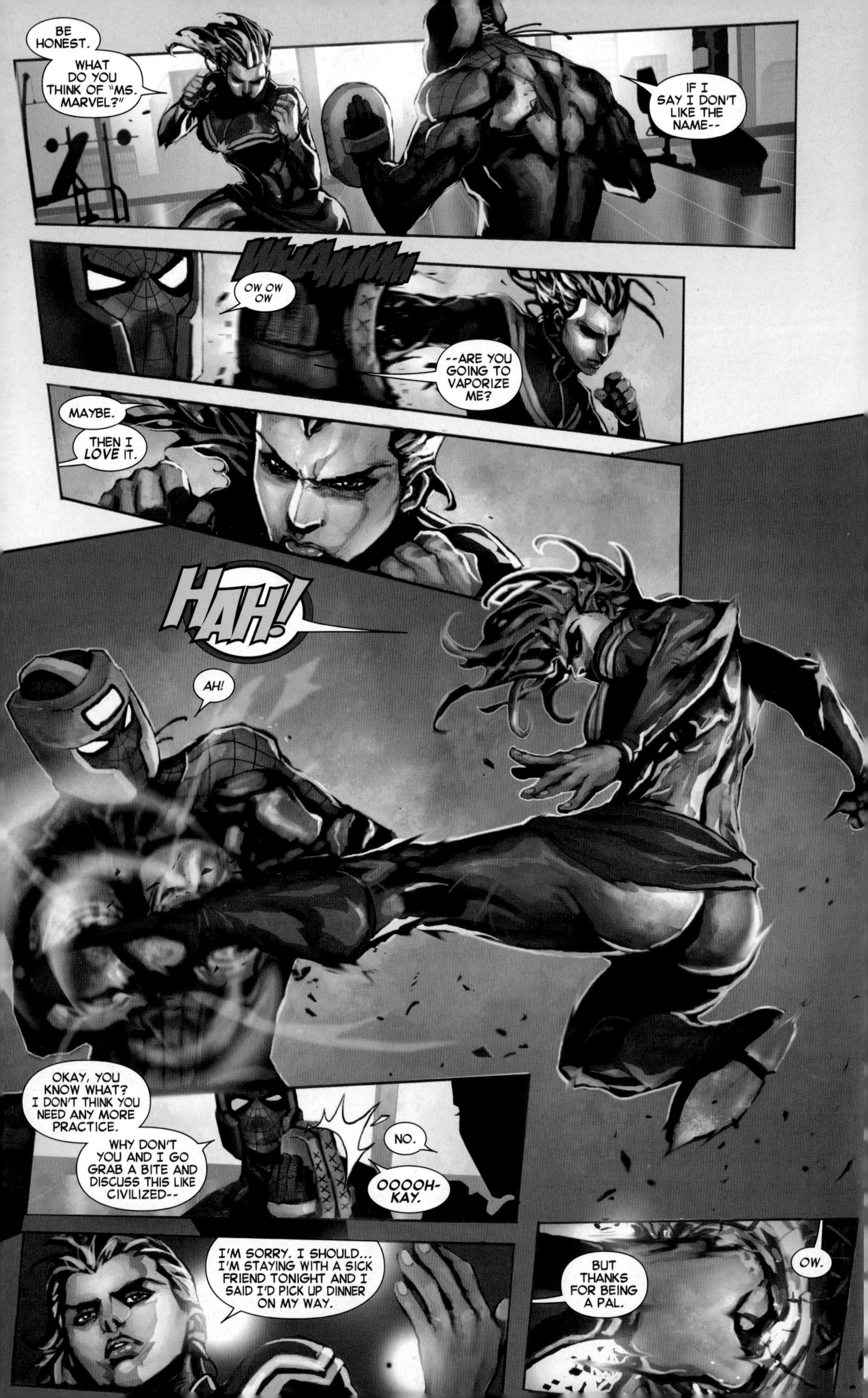
BE HONEST.
WHAT DO YOU THINK OF "MS. MARVEL?"
IF I SAY I DON'T LIKE THE NAME--
OW OW OW
--ARE YOU GOING TO VAPORIZE ME?
MAYBE.
THEN I LOVE IT.
HAH!
AH!
OKAY, YOU KNOW WHAT? I DON'T THINK YOU NEED ANY MORE PRACTICE.
WHY DON'T YOU AND I GO GRAB A BITE AND DISCUSS THIS LIKE CIVILIZED--
NO.
OOOOH-KAY.
I'M SORRY. I SHOULD... I'M STAYING WITH A SICK FRIEND TONIGHT AND I SAID I'D PICK UP DINNER ON MY WAY.
BUT THANKS FOR BEING A PAL.
OW.

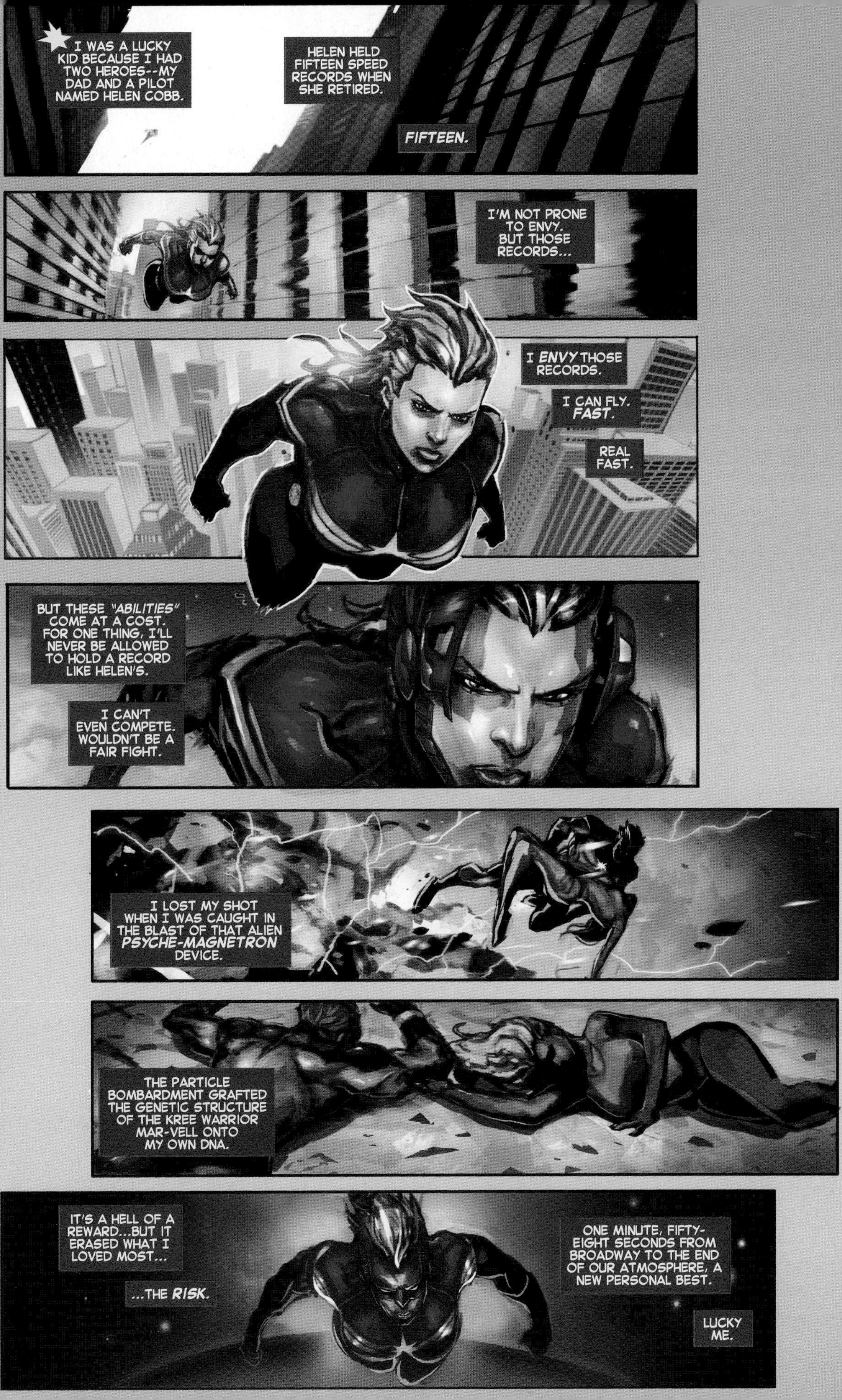
I WAS A LUCKY KID BECAUSE I HAD TWO HEROES--MY DAD AND A PILOT NAMED HELEN COBB.
HELEN HELD FIFTEEN SPEED RECORDS WHEN SHE RETIRED.
FIFTEEN.
I'M NOT PRONE TO ENVY. BUT THOSE RECORDS...
I ENVY THOSE RECORDS.
I CAN FLY. FAST.
REAL FAST.
BUT THESE "ABILITIES" COME AT A COST. FOR ONE THING, I'LL NEVER BE ALLOWED TO HOLD A RECORD LIKE HELEN'S.
I CAN'T EVEN COMPETE. WOULDN'T BE A FAIR FIGHT.
I LOST MY SHOT WHEN I WAS CAUGHT IN THE BLAST OF THAT ALIEN PSYCHE-MAGNETRON DEVICE.
THE PARTICLE BOMBARDMENT GRAFTED THE GENETIC STRUCTURE OF THE KREE WARRIOR MAR-VELL ONTO MY OWN DNA.
IT'S A HELL OF A REWARD...BUT IT ERASED WHAT I LOVED MOST...
...THE RISK.
ONE MINUTE, FIFTY-EIGHT SECONDS FROM BROADWAY TO THE END OF OUR ATMOSPHERE, A NEW PERSONAL BEST.
LUCKY ME.

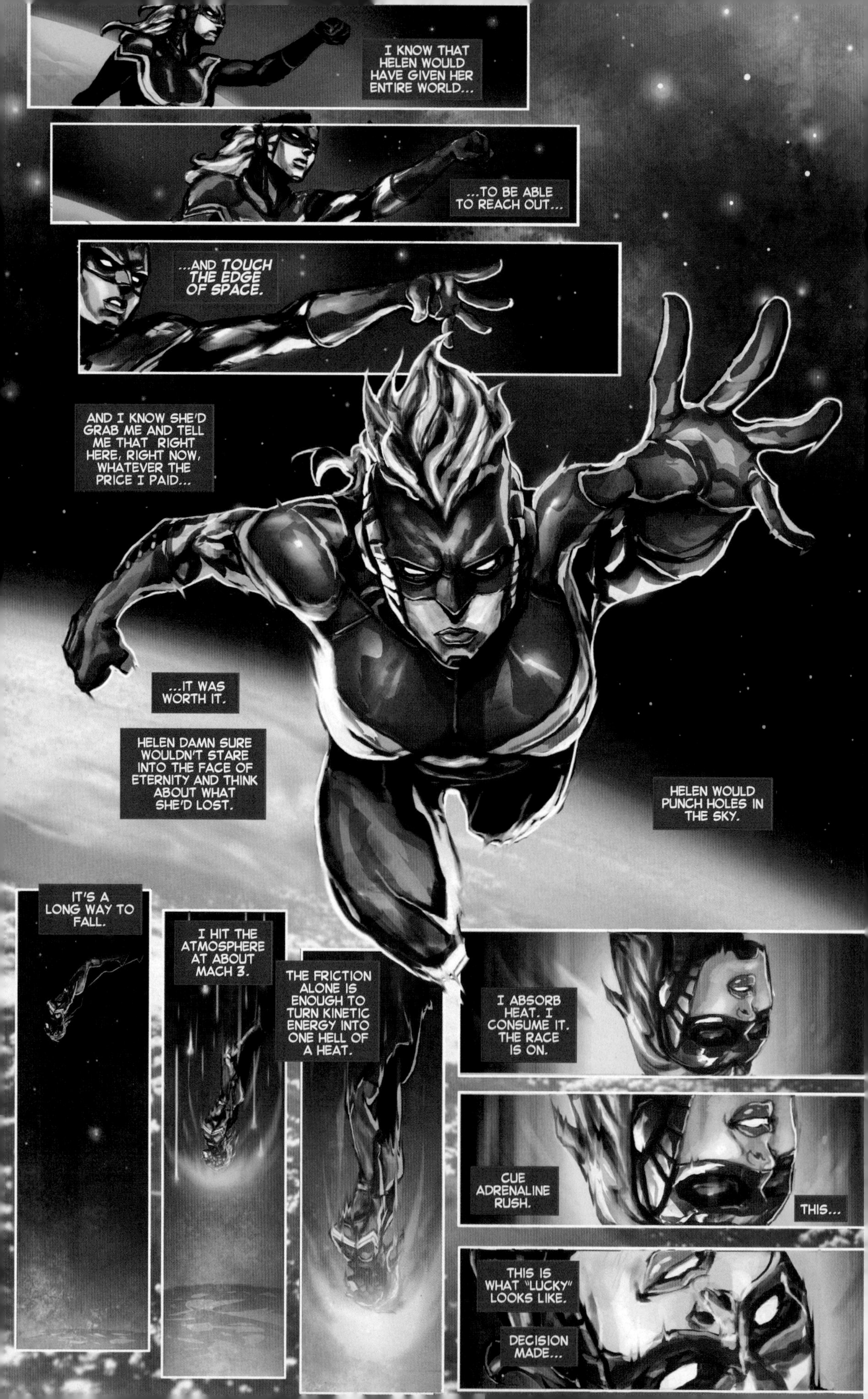
I KNOW THAT HELEN WOULD HAVE GIVEN HER ENTIRE WORLD...
...TO BE ABLE TO REACH OUT...
...AND TOUCH THE EDGE OF SPACE.
AND I KNOW SHE'D GRAB ME AND TELL ME THAT RIGHT HERE, RIGHT NOW, WHATEVER THE PRICE I PAID...
...IT WAS WORTH IT.
HELEN DAMN SURE WOULDN'T STARE INTO THE FACE OF ETERNITY AND THINK ABOUT WHAT SHE'D LOST.
HELEN WOULD PUNCH HOLES IN THE SKY.
IT'S A LONG WAY TO FALL.
I HIT THE ATMOSPHERE AT ABOUT MACH 3.
THE FRICTION ALONE IS ENOUGH TO TURN KINETIC ENERGY INTO ONE HELL OF A HEAT.
I ABSORB HEAT. I CONSUME IT. THE RACE IS ON.
CUE ADRENALINE RUSH.
THIS...
THIS IS WHAT "LUCKY" LOOKS LIKE.
DECISION MADE...

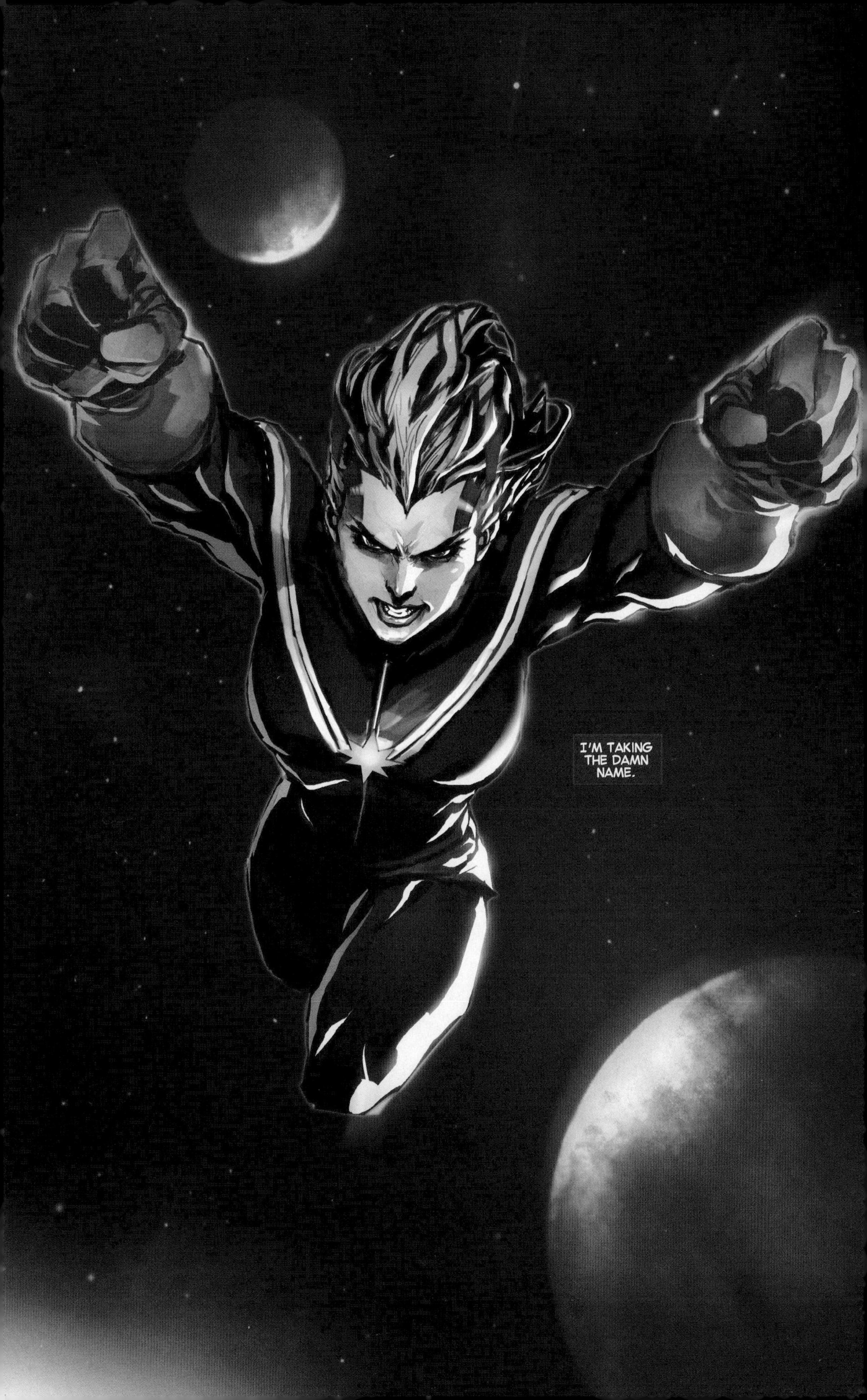
I'M TAKING THE DAMN NAME.

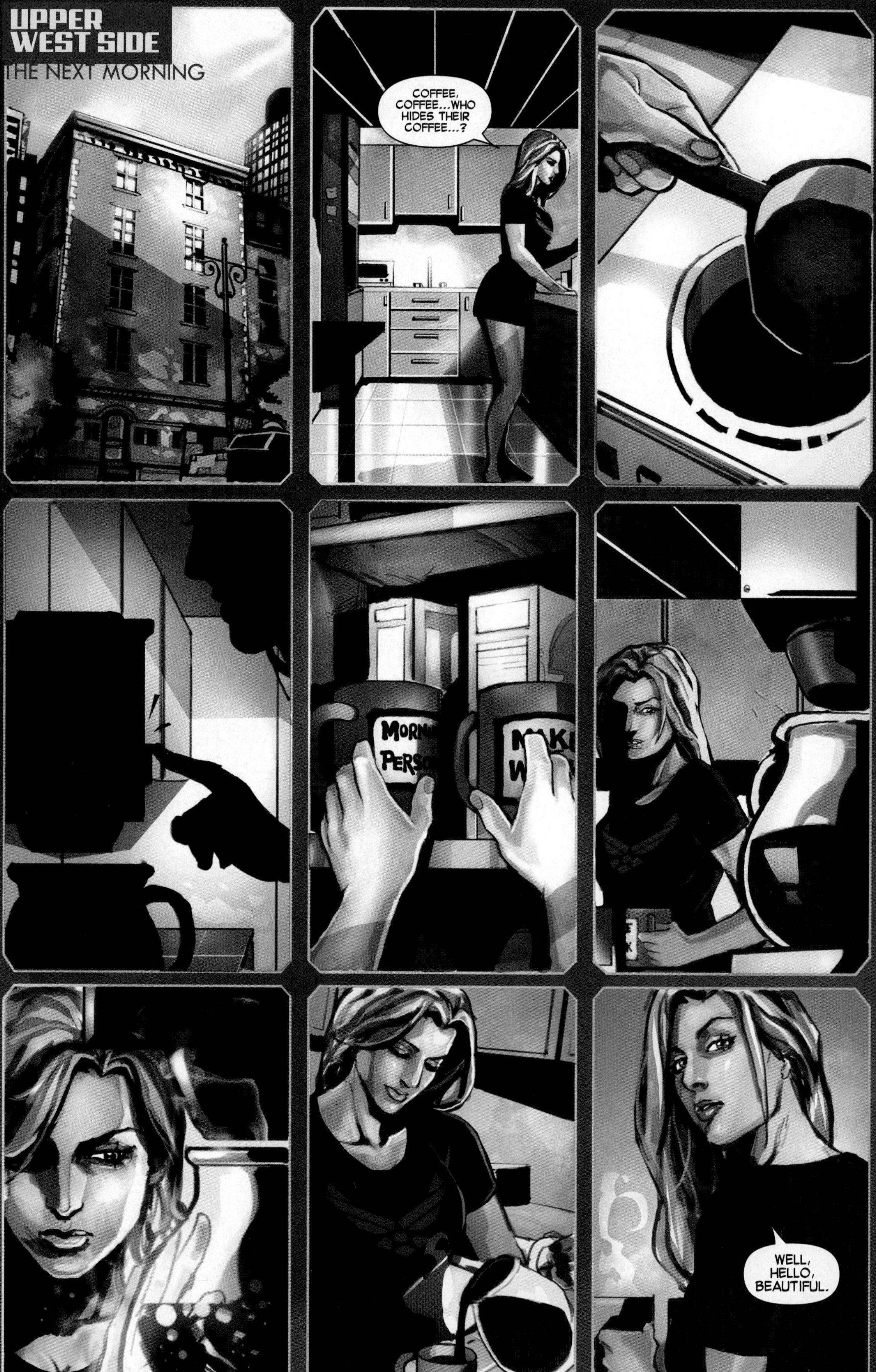
UPPER WEST SIDE
THE NEXT MORNING
COFFEE, COFFEE...WHO HIDES THEIR COFFEE...?
WELL, HELLO, BEAUTIFUL.

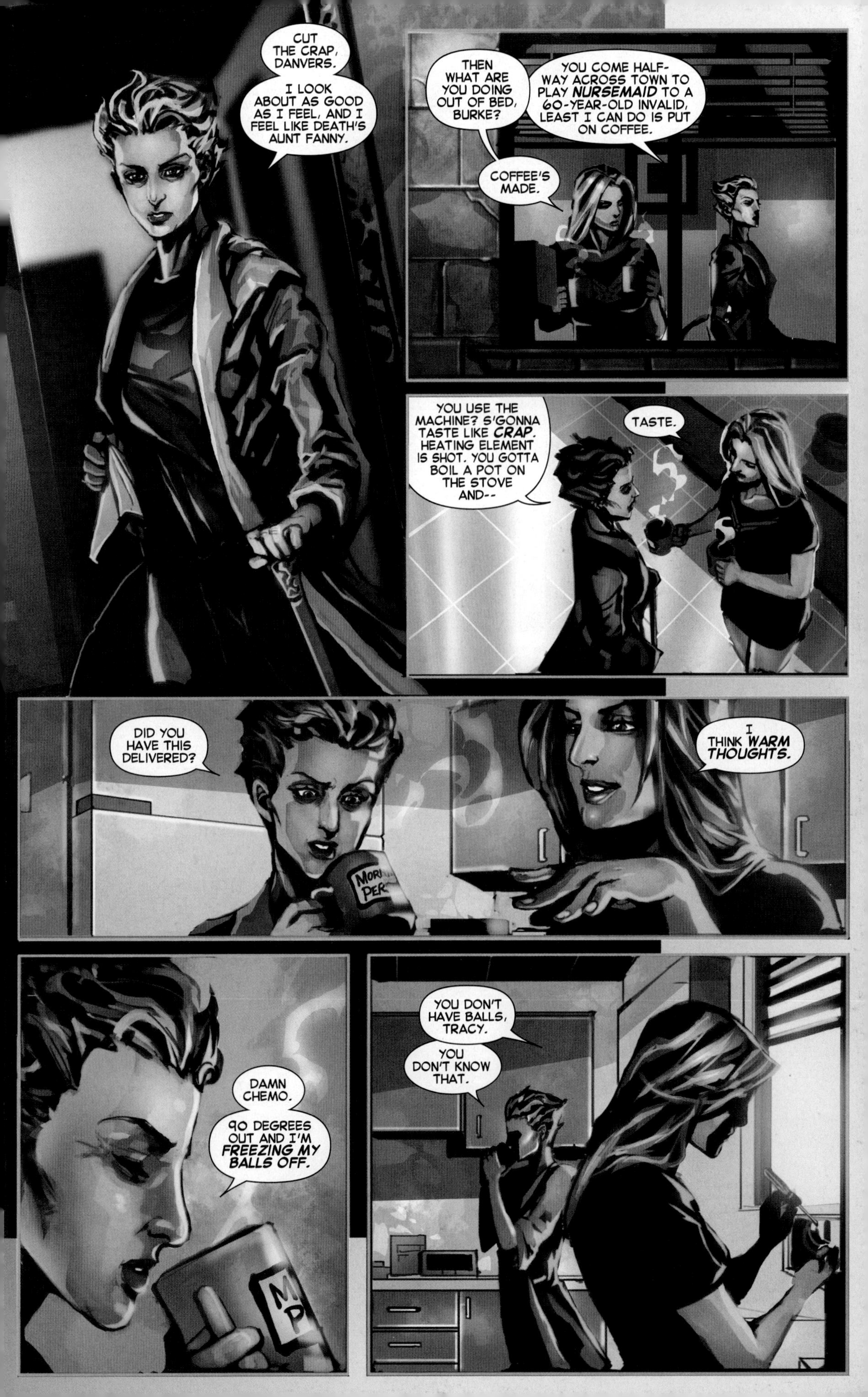
CUT THE CRAP, DANVERS.
I LOOK ABOUT AS GOOD AS I FEEL, AND I FEEL LIKE DEATH'S AUNT FANNY.
THEN WHAT ARE YOU DOING OUT OF BED, BURKE?
YOU COME HALF-WAY ACROSS TOWN TO PLAY NURSEMAID TO A 60-YEAR-OLD INVALID, LEAST I CAN DO IS PUT ON COFFEE.
COFFEE'S MADE.
YOU USE THE MACHINE? S'GONNA TASTE LIKE CRAP. HEATING ELEMENT IS SHOT. YOU GOTTA BOIL A POT ON THE STOVE AND--
TASTE.
DID YOU HAVE THIS DELIVERED?
I THINK WARM THOUGHTS.
DAMN CHEMO.
90 DEGREES OUT AND I'M FREEZING MY BALLS OFF.
YOU DON'T HAVE BALLS, TRACY.
YOU DON'T KNOW THAT.

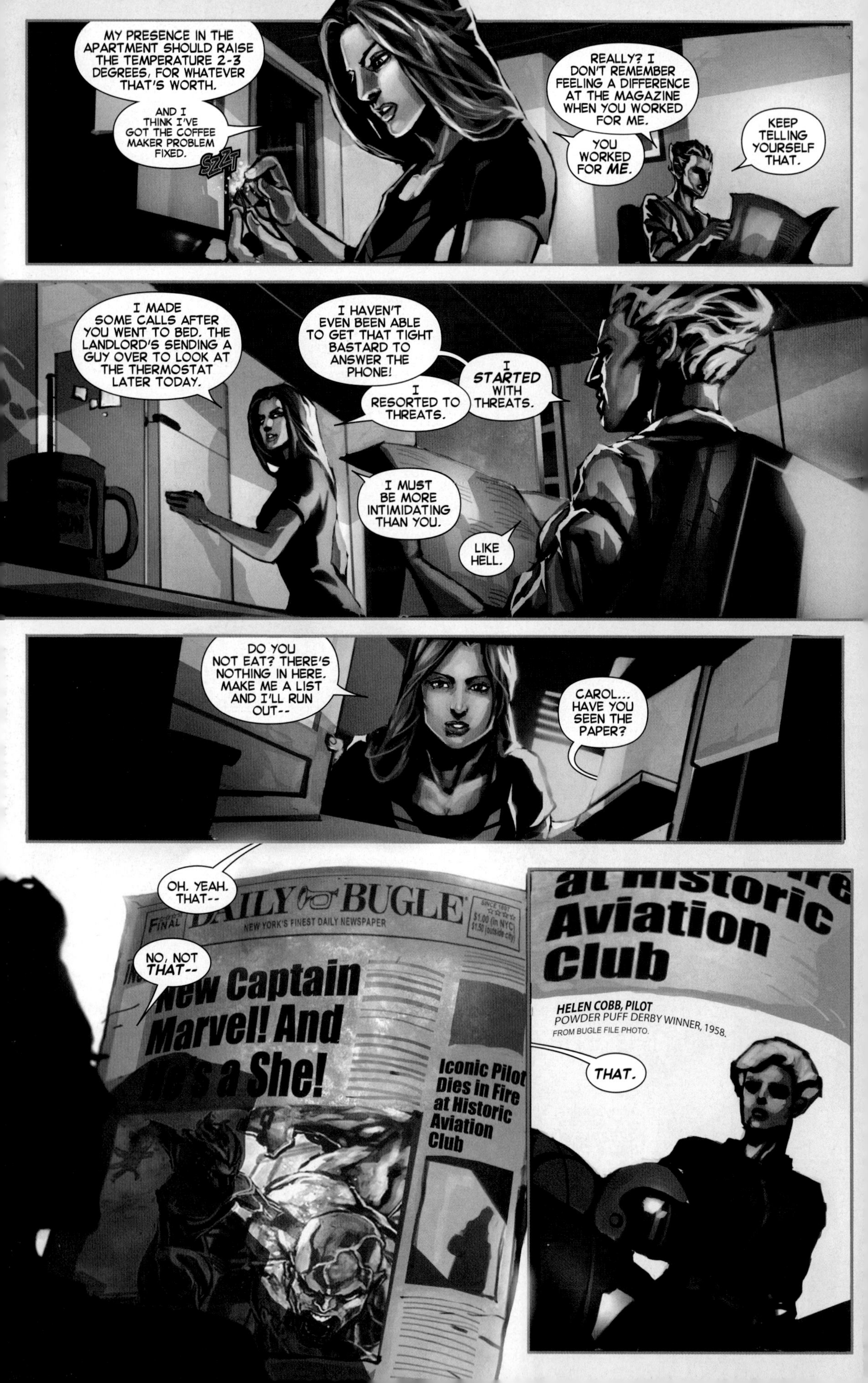
MY PRESENCE IN THE APARTMENT SHOULD RAISE THE TEMPERATURE 2-3 DEGREES, FOR WHATEVER THAT'S WORTH.
AND I THINK I'VE GOT THE COFFEE MAKER PROBLEM FIXED.
SZZT
REALLY? I DON'T REMEMBER FEELING A DIFFERENCE AT THE MAGAZINE WHEN YOU WORKED FOR ME.
YOU WORKED FOR ME.
KEEP TELLING YOURSELF THAT.
I MADE SOME CALLS AFTER YOU WENT TO BED. THE LANDLORD'S SENDING A GUY OVER TO LOOK AT THE THERMOSTAT LATER TODAY.
I HAVEN'T EVEN BEEN ABLE TO GET THAT TIGHT BASTARD TO ANSWER THE PHONE!
I RESORTED TO THREATS.
I STARTED WITH THREATS.
I MUST BE MORE INTIMIDATING THAN YOU.
LIKE HELL.
DO YOU NOT EAT? THERE'S NOTHING IN HERE. MAKE ME A LIST AND I'LL RUN OUT--
CAROL... HAVE YOU SEEN THE PAPER?
OH. YEAH. THAT--
DAILY BUGLE
FINAL
NEW YORK'S FINEST DAILY NEWSPAPER
SINCE 1897
$1.00 (in NYC) $1.50 (outside city)
NO, NOT THAT--
New Captain Marvel! And He's a She!
Iconic Pilot Dies in Fire at Historic Aviation Club
at Historic Aviation Club
HELEN COBB, PILOT
POWDER PUFF DERBY WINNER, 1958.
FROM BUGLE FILE PHOTO.
THAT.

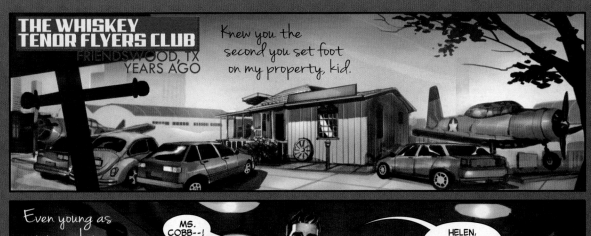

THE WHISKEY TENOR FLYERS CLUB
FRIENDSWOOD, TX
YEARS AGO

Knew you, the second you set foot on my property, kid.

Even young as you were, how could I not?

MS. COBB--!

HELEN, THEN. I GOT SOMEBODY HERE DYING TO MEET YOU.

--STEVIE DANVERS! DON'T YOU CALL ME THAT, BOY.

I BETTER TURN AROUND AND SEE *DEAN MARTIN* RETURNED FROM THE GRAVE, AIRMAN.

Folks want to blame someone for gals like us. "Her daddy was unkind" or "some fella broke her heart"...

Hogwash.

CLOSE. MY SISTER.

QUIET ONE. SHE ALWAYS THIS GOOD WITH PEOPLE?

PRETTY MUCH. CAROL! C'MON, YOU'RE EMBARRASSING YOUR KID BROTHER.

You and me've always been like this. Always a little removed. Always...

I'M SORRY, I WAS--

--dreaming.

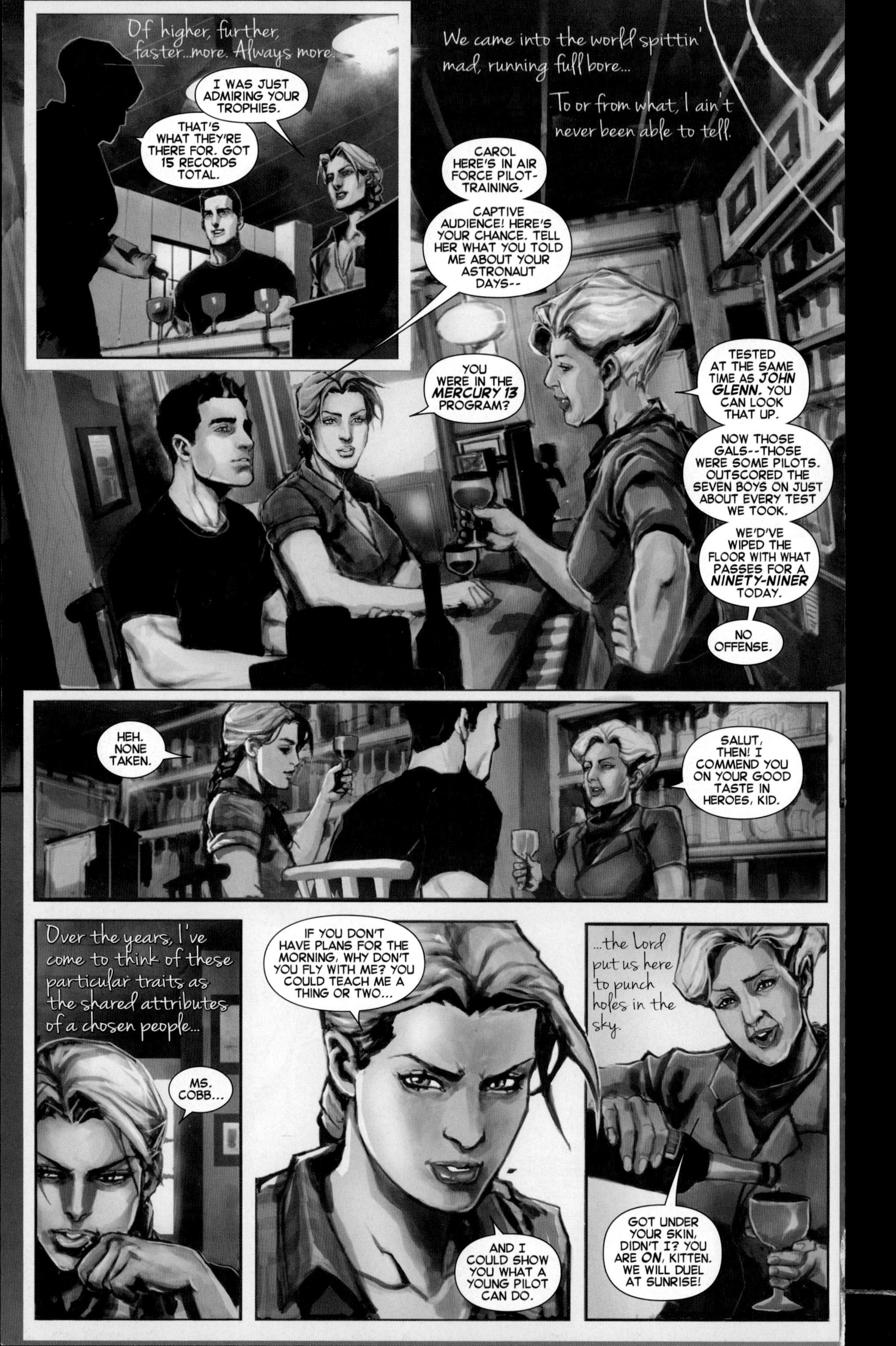

Of higher, further, faster...more. Always more.
I WAS JUST ADMIRING YOUR TROPHIES.
THAT'S WHAT THEY'RE THERE FOR. GOT 15 RECORDS TOTAL.
We came into the world spittin' mad, running full bore...
To or from what, I ain't never been able to tell.
CAROL HERE'S IN AIR FORCE PILOT-TRAINING.
CAPTIVE AUDIENCE! HERE'S YOUR CHANCE. TELL HER WHAT YOU TOLD ME ABOUT YOUR ASTRONAUT DAYS--
YOU WERE IN THE MERCURY 13 PROGRAM?
TESTED AT THE SAME TIME AS JOHN GLENN. YOU CAN LOOK THAT UP.
NOW THOSE GALS--THOSE WERE SOME PILOTS. OUTSCORED THE SEVEN BOYS ON JUST ABOUT EVERY TEST WE TOOK.
WE'D'VE WIPED THE FLOOR WITH WHAT PASSES FOR A NINETY-NINER TODAY.
NO OFFENSE.
HEH. NONE TAKEN.
SALUT, THEN! I COMMEND YOU ON YOUR GOOD TASTE IN HEROES, KID.
Over the years, I've come to think of these particular traits as the shared attributes of a chosen people...
MS. COBB...
IF YOU DON'T HAVE PLANS FOR THE MORNING, WHY DON'T YOU FLY WITH ME? YOU COULD TEACH ME A THING OR TWO...
AND I COULD SHOW YOU WHAT A YOUNG PILOT CAN DO.
...the Lord put us here to punch holes in the sky.
GOT UNDER YOUR SKIN, DIDN'T I? YOU ARE ON, KITTEN. WE WILL DUEL AT SUNRISE!

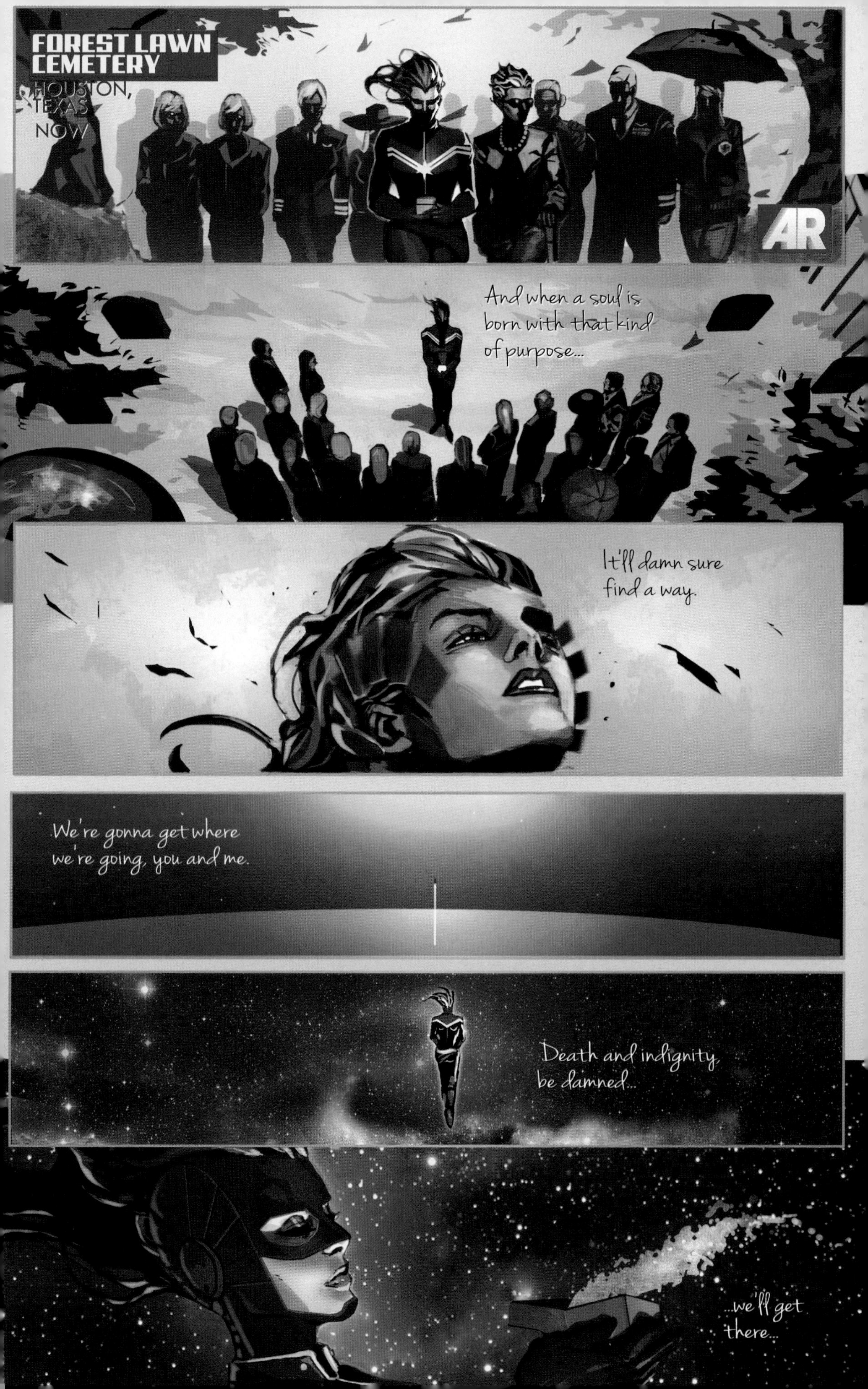

FOREST LAWN CEMETERY
HOUSTON, TEXAS
NOW
AR
And when a soul is born with that kind of purpose...
It'll damn sure find a way.
We're gonna get where we're going, you and me.
Death and indignity be damned...
...we'll get there...

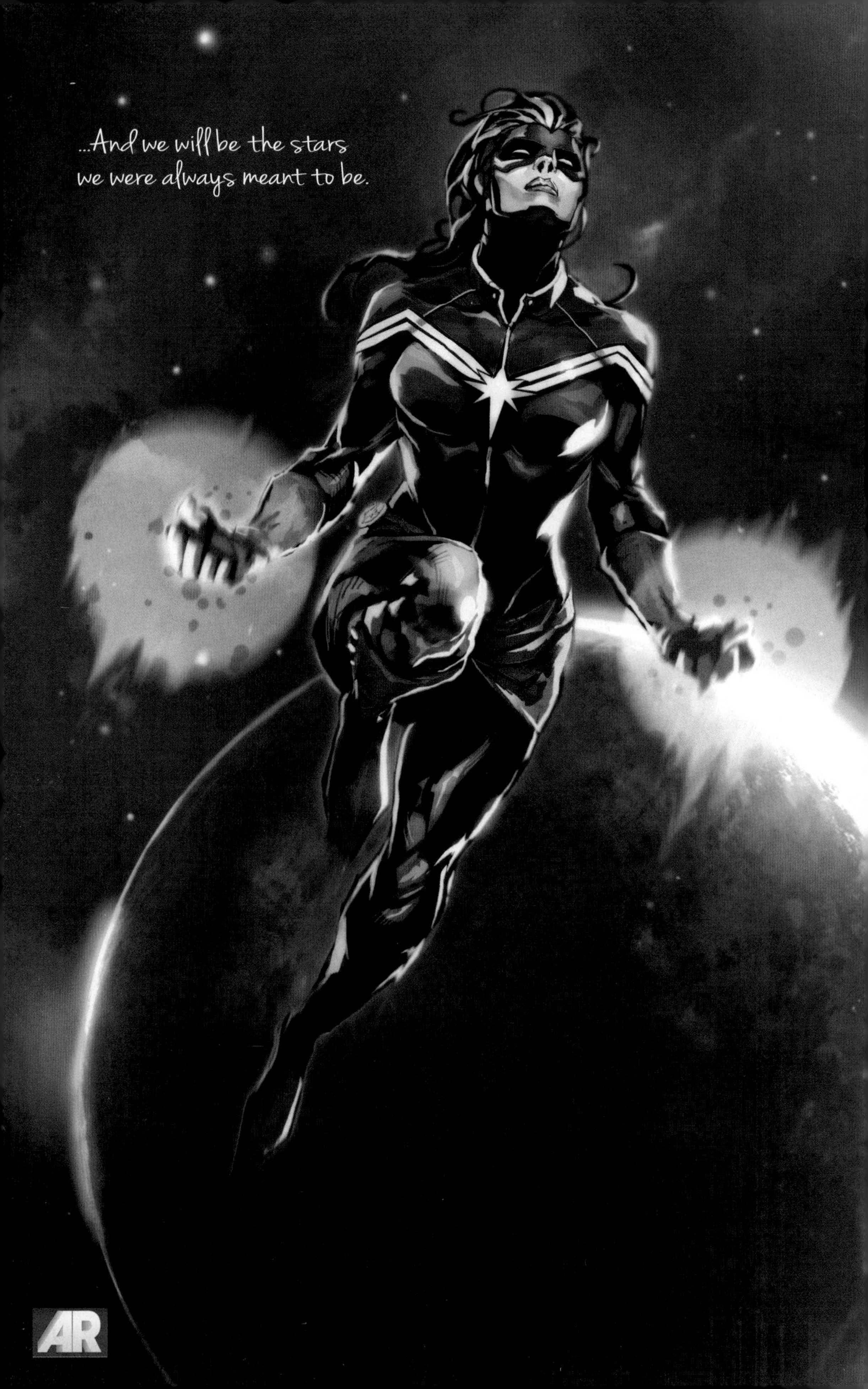
...And we will be the stars we were always meant to be.

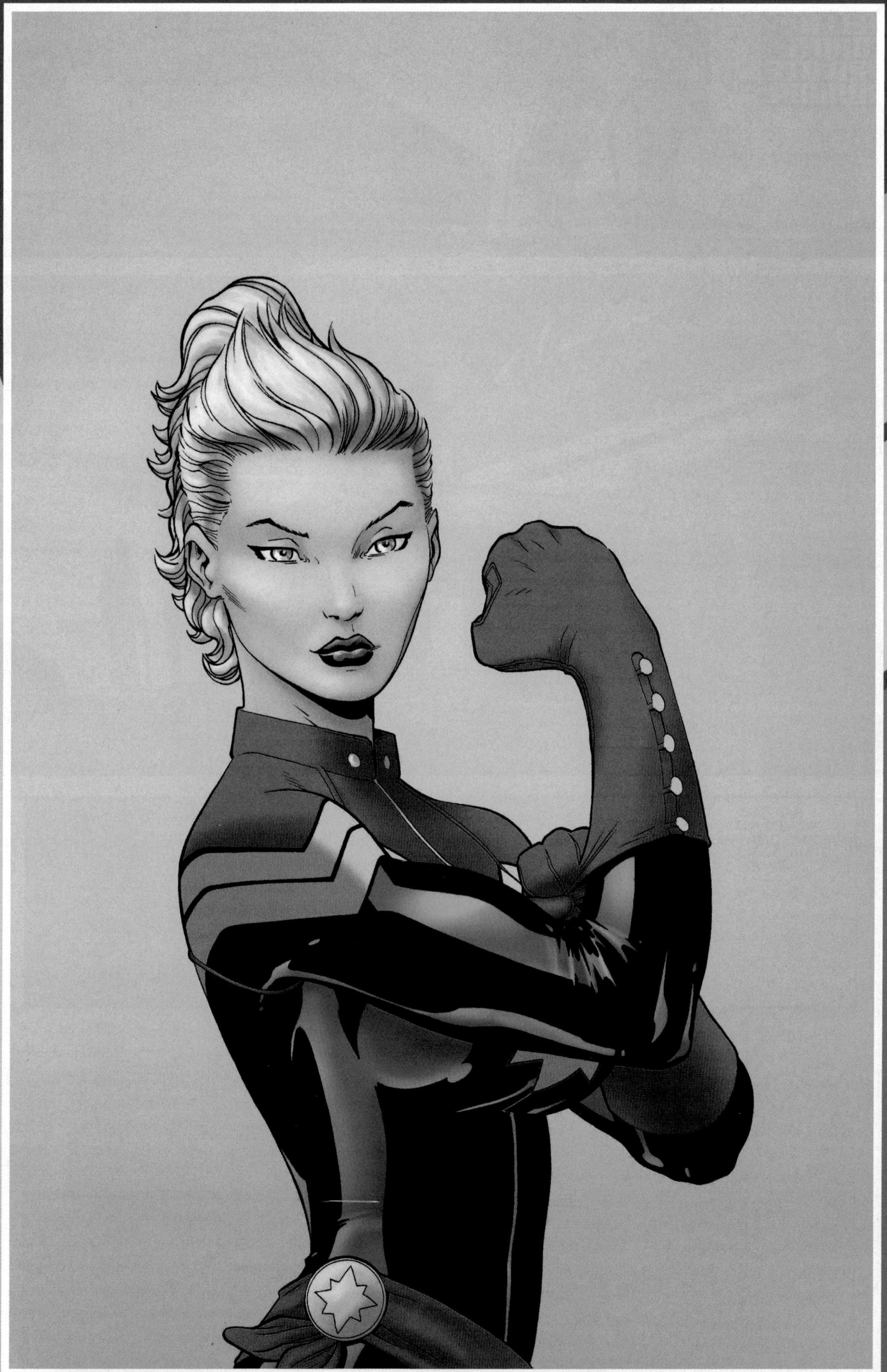

TWO

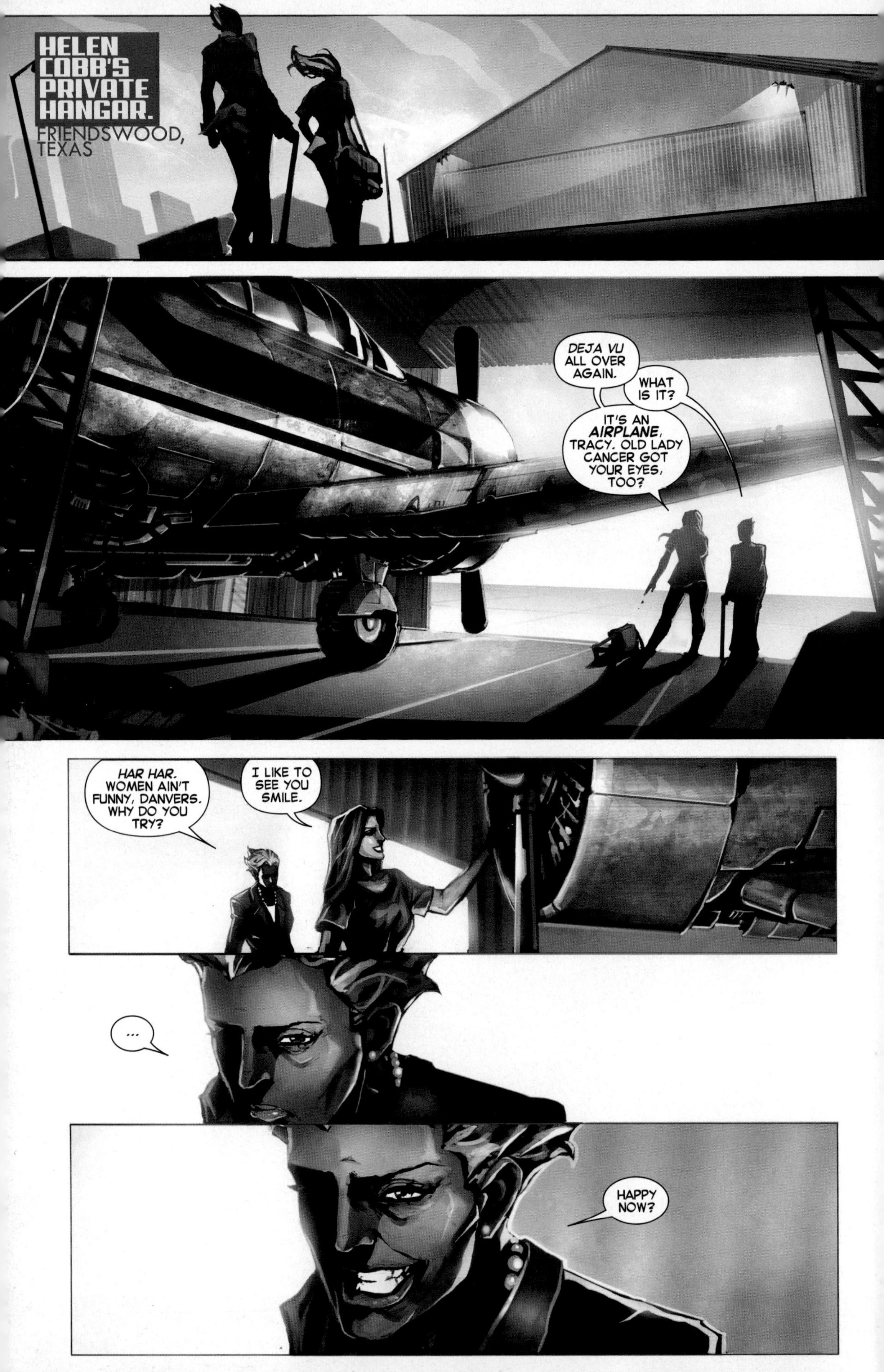
HELEN COBB'S PRIVATE HANGAR.
FRIENDSWOOD, TEXAS
DEJA VU ALL OVER AGAIN.
WHAT IS IT?
IT'S AN AIRPLANE, TRACY. OLD LADY CANCER GOT YOUR EYES, TOO?
HAR HAR. WOMEN AIN'T FUNNY, DANVERS. WHY DO YOU TRY?
I LIKE TO SEE YOU SMILE.
...
HAPPY NOW?

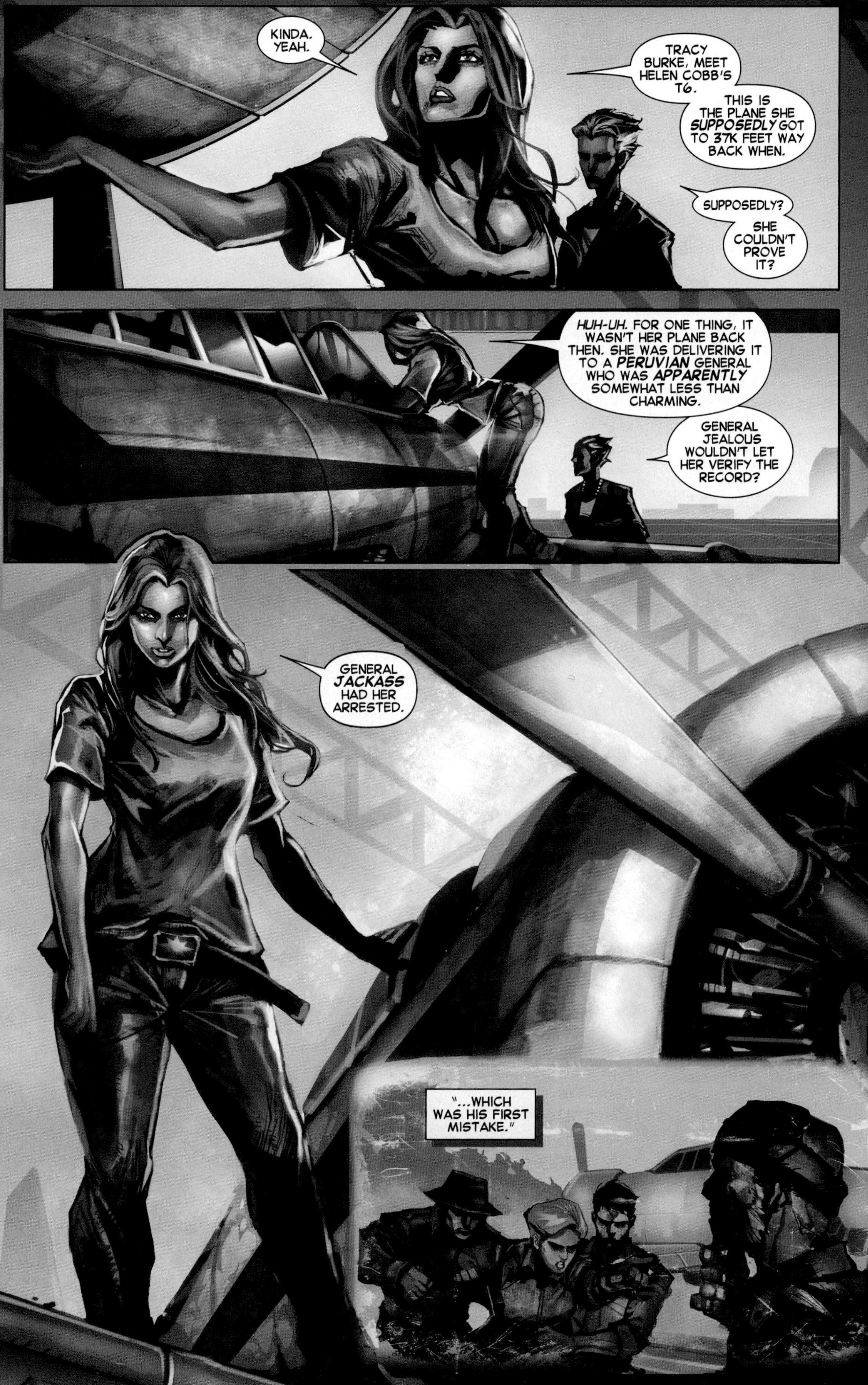

KINDA. YEAH.
TRACY BURKE, MEET HELEN COBB'S T6.
THIS IS THE PLANE SHE *SUPPOSEDLY* GOT TO 37K FEET WAY BACK WHEN.
SUPPOSEDLY?
SHE COULDN'T PROVE IT?
HUH-UH. FOR ONE THING, IT WASN'T HER PLANE BACK THEN. SHE WAS DELIVERING IT TO A *PERUVIAN* GENERAL WHO WAS *APPARENTLY* SOMEWHAT LESS THAN CHARMING.
GENERAL JEALOUS WOULDN'T LET HER VERIFY THE RECORD?
GENERAL *JACKASS* HAD HER ARRESTED.
"...WHICH WAS HIS FIRST MISTAKE."

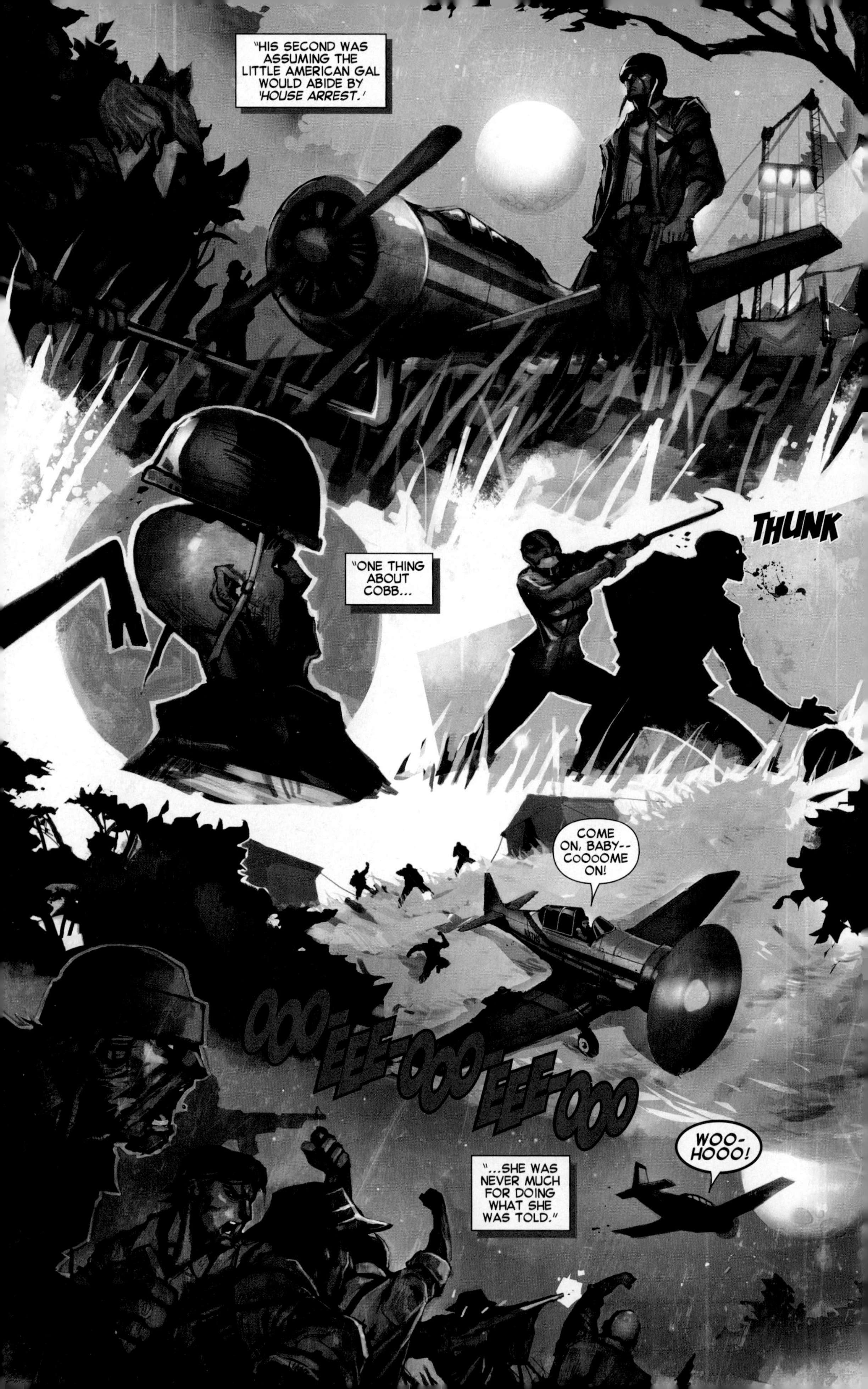
"HIS SECOND WAS ASSUMING THE LITTLE AMERICAN GAL WOULD ABIDE BY 'HOUSE ARREST.'
"ONE THING ABOUT COBB...
THUNK
COME ON, BABY-- COOOOME ON!
OOO EEE-OOO EEE-OOO
"...SHE WAS NEVER MUCH FOR DOING WHAT SHE WAS TOLD."
WOO-HOOO!

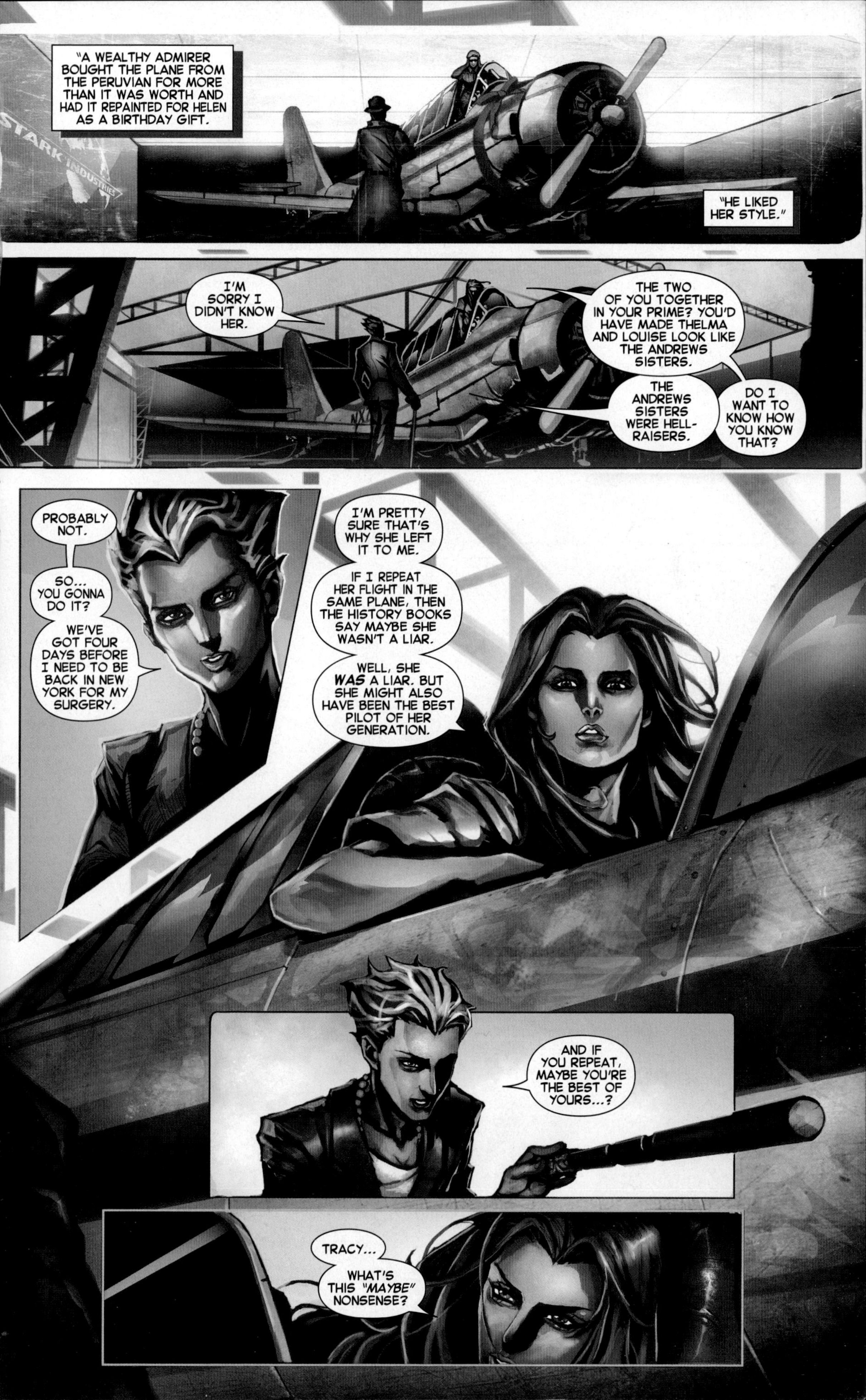
"A WEALTHY ADMIRER BOUGHT THE PLANE FROM THE PERUVIAN FOR MORE THAN IT WAS WORTH AND HAD IT REPAINTED FOR HELEN AS A BIRTHDAY GIFT.
STARK INDUSTRIES
"HE LIKED HER STYLE."
I'M SORRY I DIDN'T KNOW HER.
THE TWO OF YOU TOGETHER IN YOUR PRIME? YOU'D HAVE MADE THELMA AND LOUISE LOOK LIKE THE ANDREWS SISTERS.
THE ANDREWS SISTERS WERE HELL-RAISERS.
DO I WANT TO KNOW HOW YOU KNOW THAT?
PROBABLY NOT.
I'M PRETTY SURE THAT'S WHY SHE LEFT IT TO ME.
SO... YOU GONNA DO IT?
WE'VE GOT FOUR DAYS BEFORE I NEED TO BE BACK IN NEW YORK FOR MY SURGERY.
IF I REPEAT HER FLIGHT IN THE SAME PLANE, THEN THE HISTORY BOOKS SAY MAYBE SHE WASN'T A LIAR.
WELL, SHE *WAS* A LIAR. BUT SHE MIGHT ALSO HAVE BEEN THE BEST PILOT OF HER GENERATION.
AND IF YOU REPEAT, MAYBE YOU'RE THE BEST OF YOURS...?
TRACY...
WHAT'S THIS "*MAYBE*" NONSENSE?

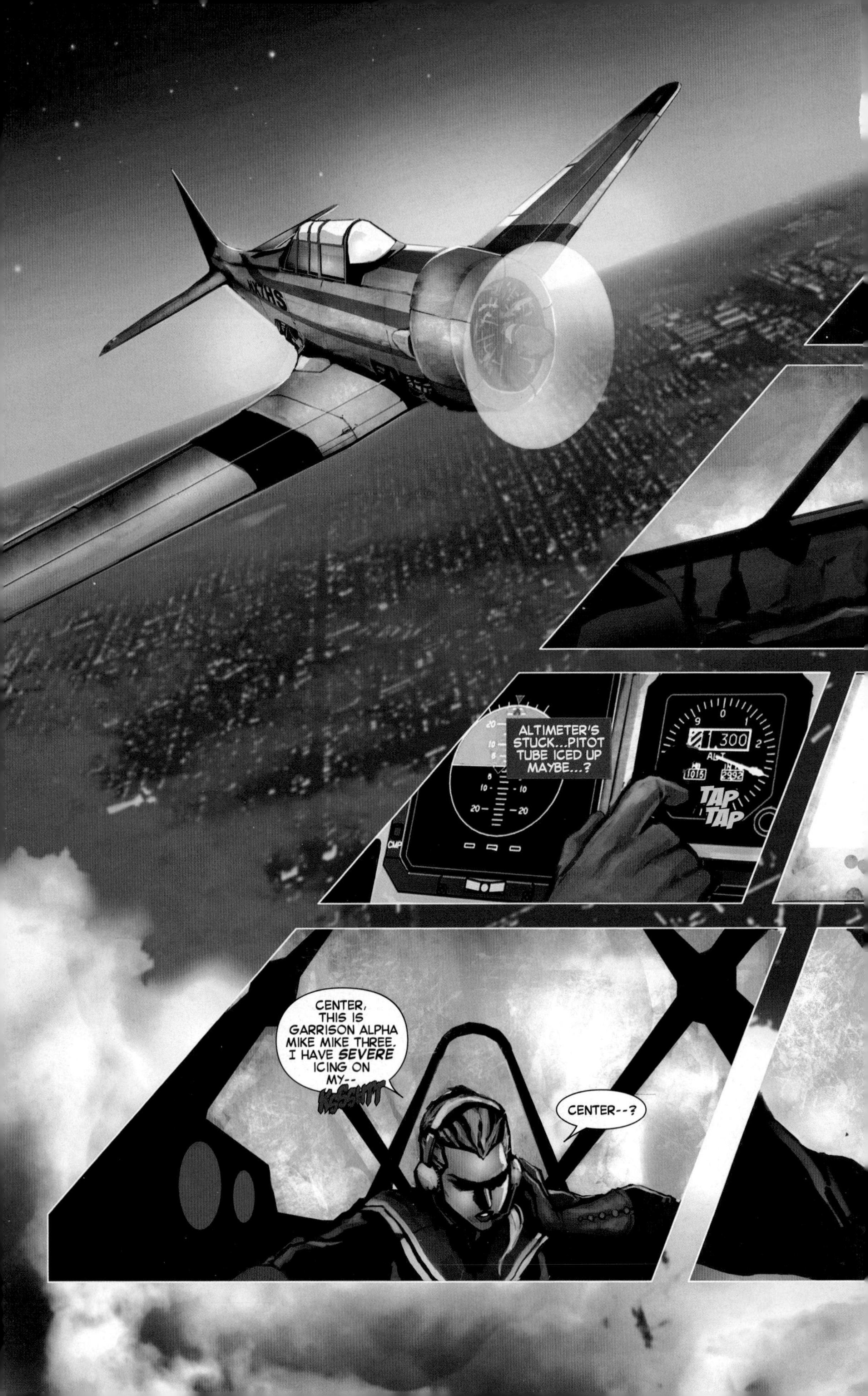
ALTIMETER'S STUCK...PITOT TUBE ICED UP MAYBE...?
TAP TAP
CENTER, THIS IS GARRISON ALPHA MIKE MIKE THREE. I HAVE *SEVERE* ICING ON MY--
KSSSHTT
CENTER--?

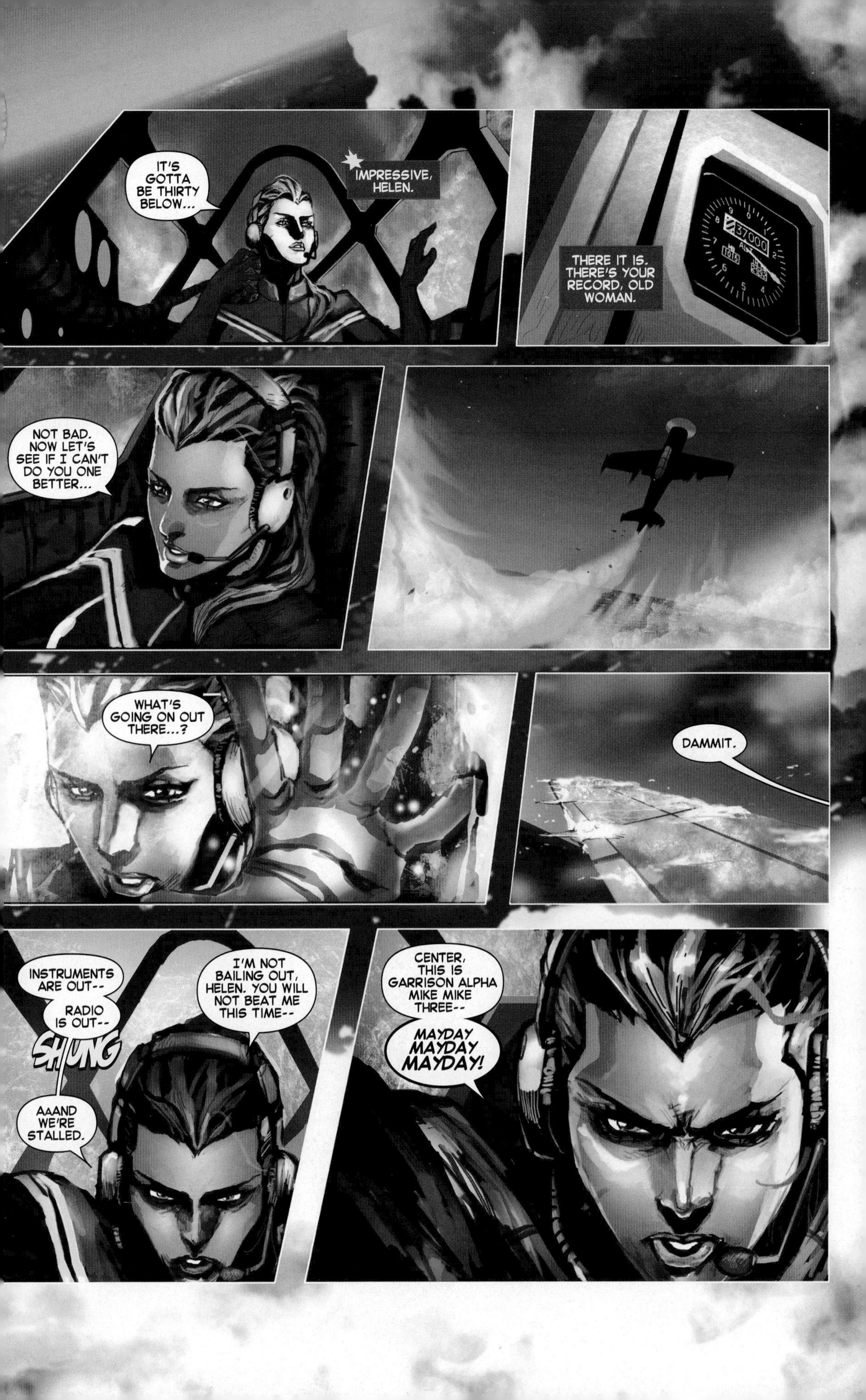
IT'S GOTTA BE THIRTY BELOW...
IMPRESSIVE, HELEN.
THERE IT IS. THERE'S YOUR RECORD, OLD WOMAN.
NOT BAD. NOW LET'S SEE IF I CAN'T DO YOU ONE BETTER...
WHAT'S GOING ON OUT THERE...?
DAMMIT.
INSTRUMENTS ARE OUT--
RADIO IS OUT--
SHUNG
AAAND WE'RE STALLED.
I'M NOT BAILING OUT, HELEN. YOU WILL NOT BEAT ME THIS TIME--
CENTER, THIS IS GARRISON ALPHA MIKE MIKE THREE--
MAYDAY MAYDAY MAYDAY!

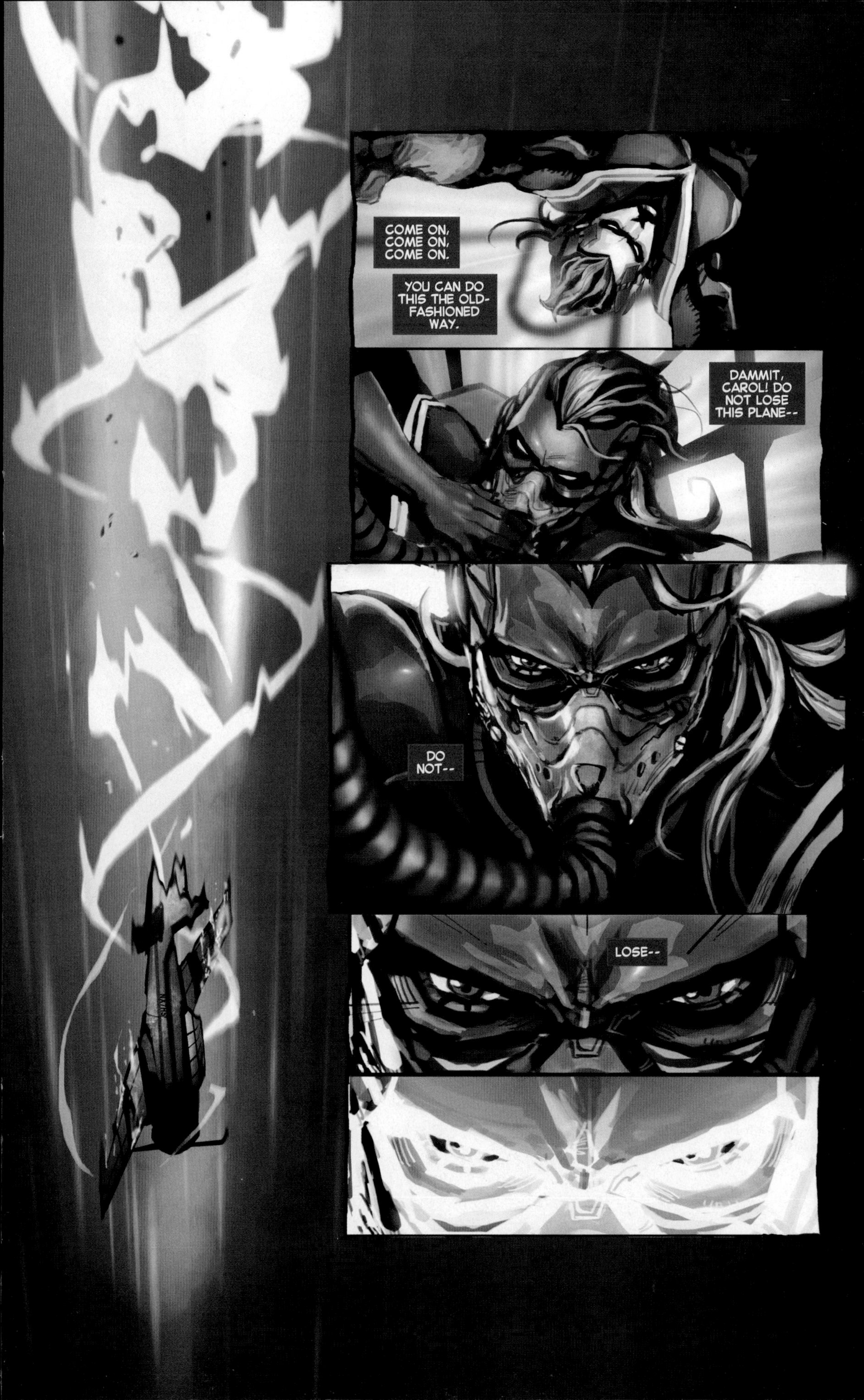
COME ON, COME ON, COME ON.
YOU CAN DO THIS THE OLD-FASHIONED WAY.
DAMMIT, CAROL! DO NOT LOSE THIS PLANE--
DO NOT--
LOSE--

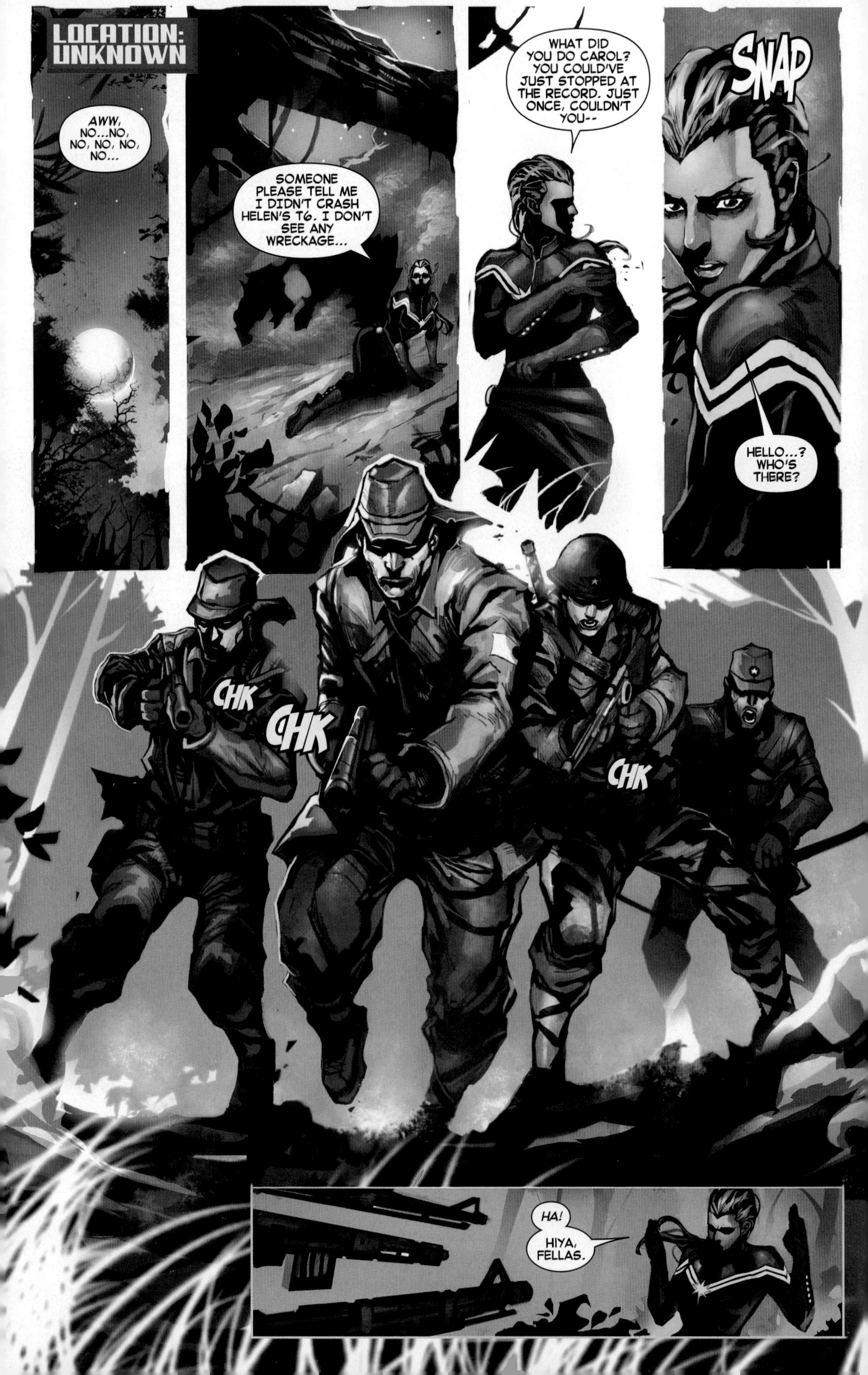
LOCATION: UNKNOWN
AWW, NO...NO, NO, NO, NO, NO...
SOMEONE PLEASE TELL ME I DIDN'T CRASH HELEN'S T6. I DON'T SEE ANY WRECKAGE...
WHAT DID YOU DO CAROL? YOU COULD'VE JUST STOPPED AT THE RECORD. JUST ONCE, COULDN'T YOU--
SNAP
HELLO...? WHO'S THERE?
CHK
CHK
CHK
HA!
HIYA, FELLAS.

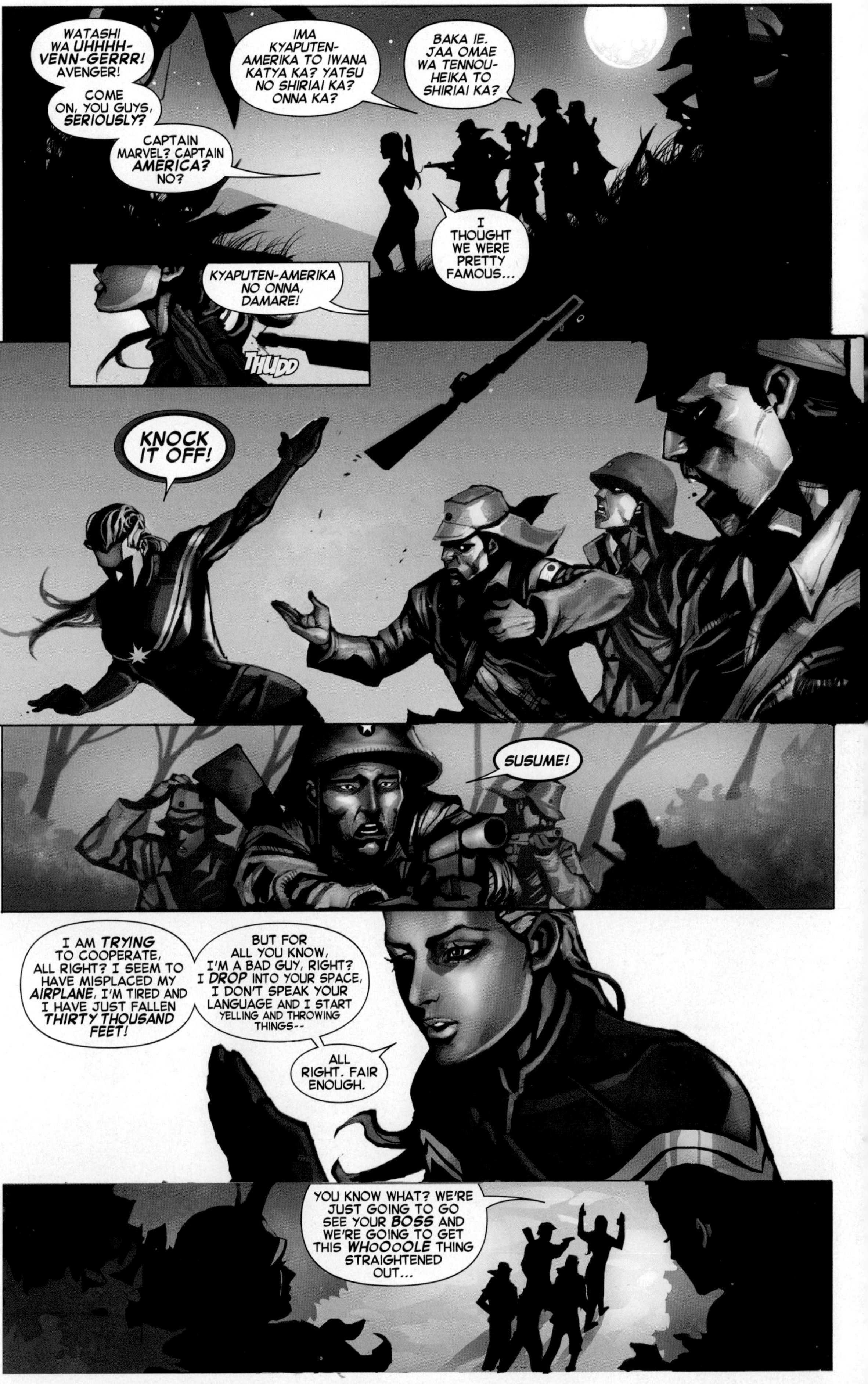
WATASHI WA UHHHH-VENN-GERRR! AVENGER!
COME ON, YOU GUYS, SERIOUSLY?
CAPTAIN MARVEL? CAPTAIN AMERICA? NO?
IMA KYAPUTEN-AMERIKA TO IWANA KATYA KA? YATSU NO SHIRIAI KA? ONNA KA?
BAKA IE. JAA OMAE WA TENNOU-HEIKA TO SHIRIAI KA?
I THOUGHT WE WERE PRETTY FAMOUS...
KYAPUTEN-AMERIKA NO ONNA, DAMARE!
THUDD
KNOCK IT OFF!
SUSUME!
I AM TRYING TO COOPERATE, ALL RIGHT? I SEEM TO HAVE MISPLACED MY AIRPLANE, I'M TIRED AND I HAVE JUST FALLEN THIRTY THOUSAND FEET!
BUT FOR ALL YOU KNOW, I'M A BAD GUY, RIGHT? I DROP INTO YOUR SPACE, I DON'T SPEAK YOUR LANGUAGE AND I START YELLING AND THROWING THINGS--
ALL RIGHT. FAIR ENOUGH.
YOU KNOW WHAT? WE'RE JUST GOING TO GO SEE YOUR BOSS AND WE'RE GOING TO GET THIS WHOOOOLE THING STRAIGHTENED OUT...

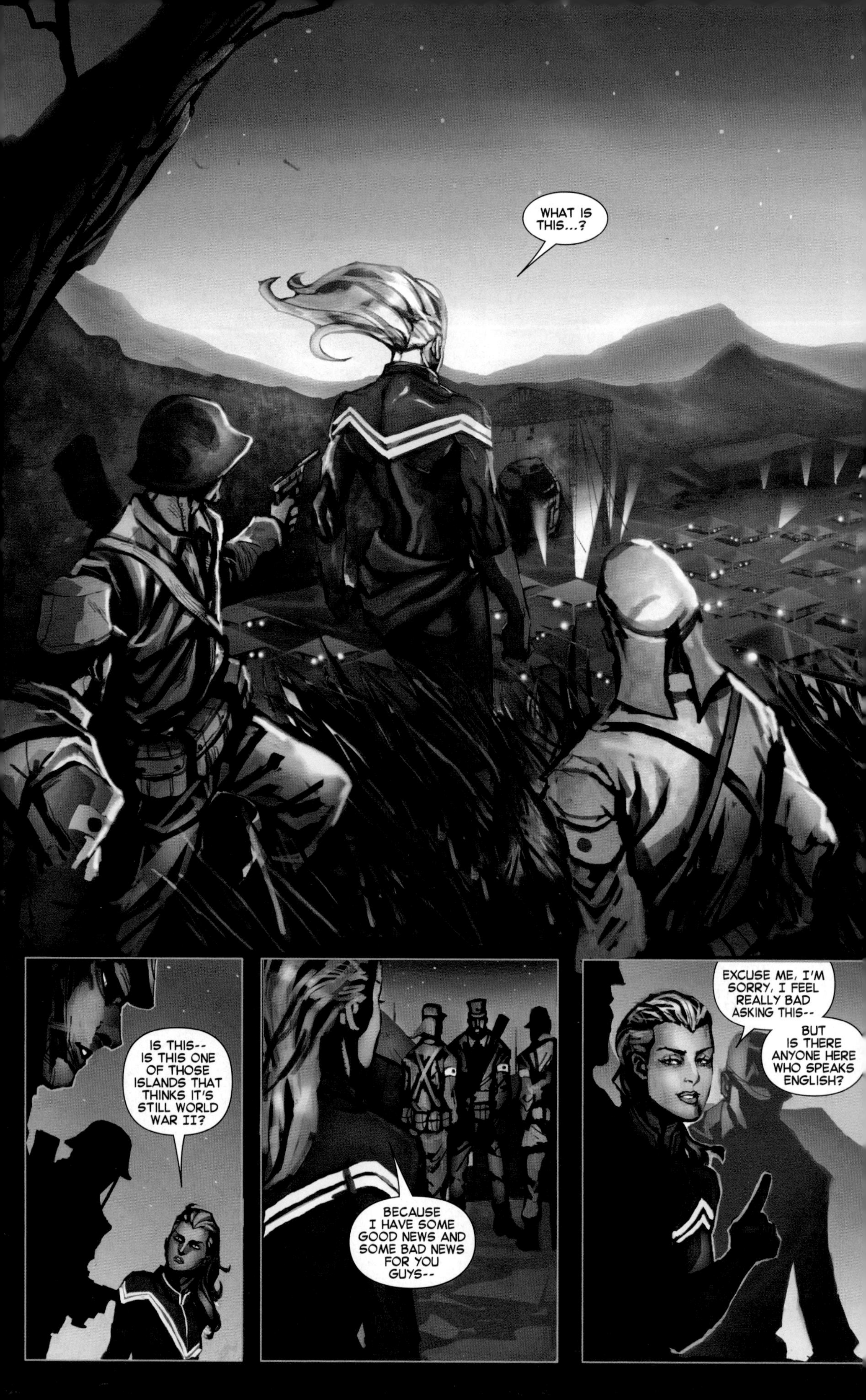
WHAT IS THIS...?
IS THIS-- IS THIS ONE OF THOSE ISLANDS THAT THINKS IT'S STILL WORLD WAR II?
BECAUSE I HAVE SOME GOOD NEWS AND SOME BAD NEWS FOR YOU GUYS--
EXCUSE ME, I'M SORRY, I FEEL REALLY BAD ASKING THIS--
BUT IS THERE ANYONE HERE WHO SPEAKS ENGLISH?

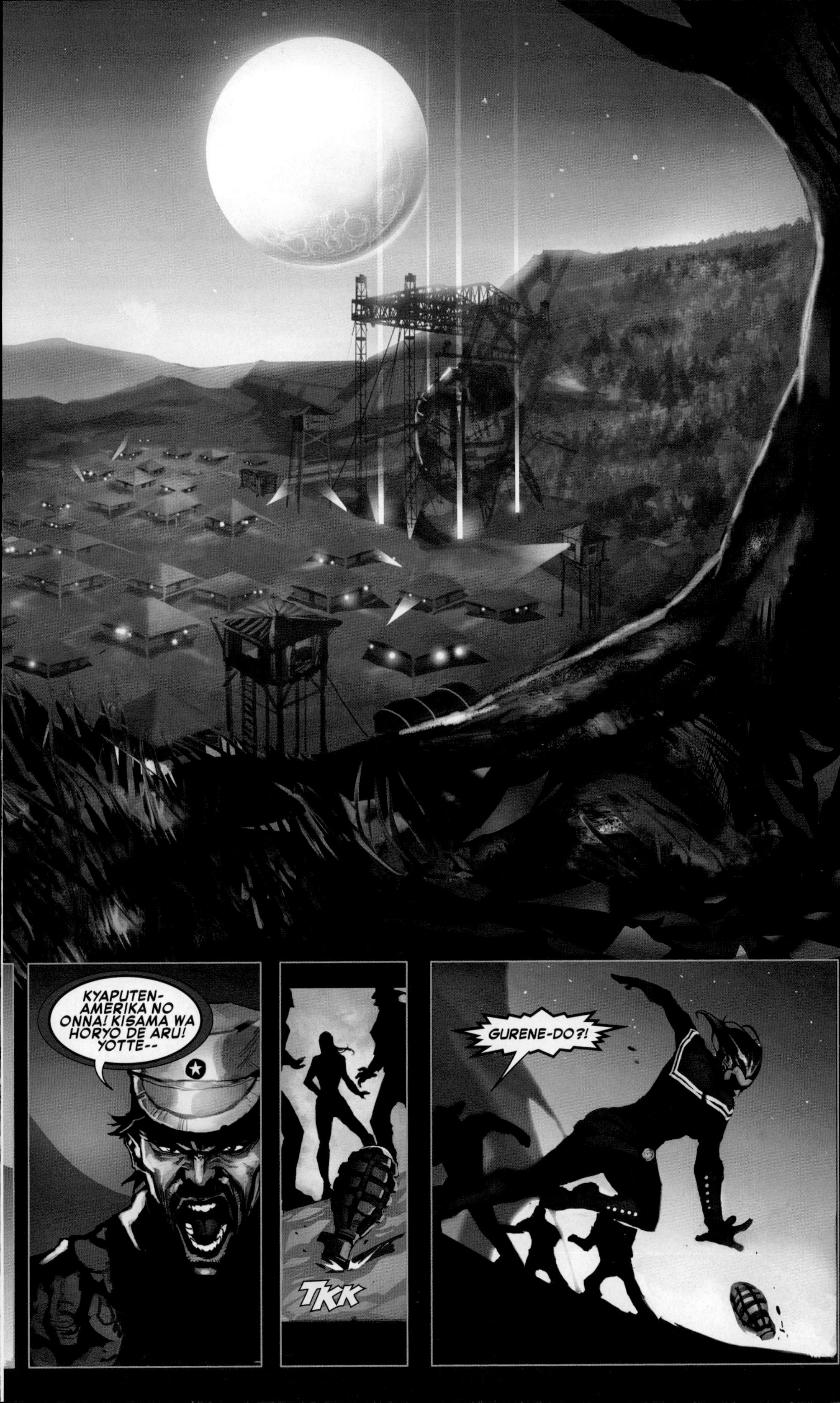
KYAPUTEN-AMERIKA NO ONNA! KISAMA WA HORYO DE ARU! YOTTE--
TKK
GURENE-DO?!

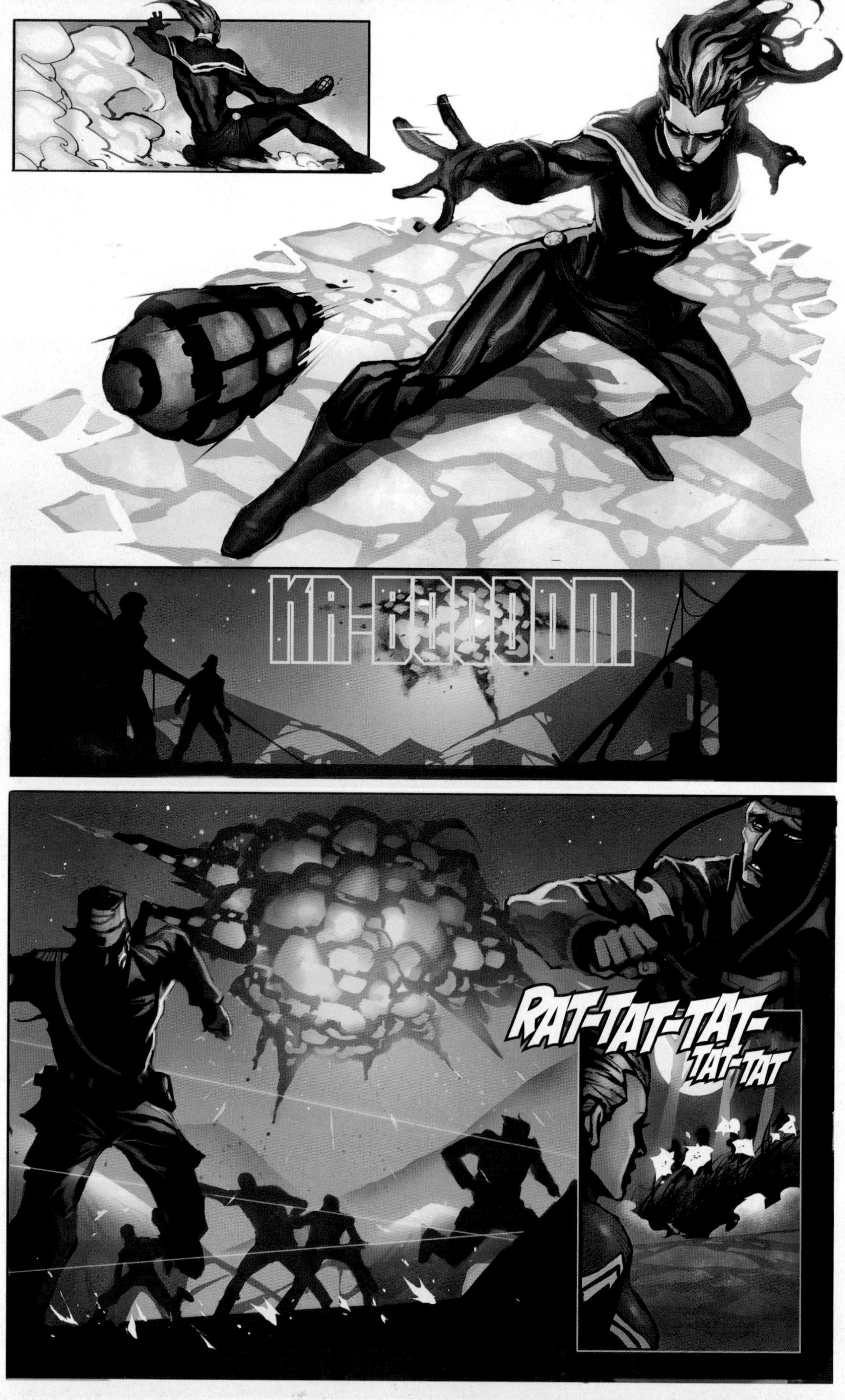
KA-BOOOOM
RAT-TAT-TAT-TAT-TAT

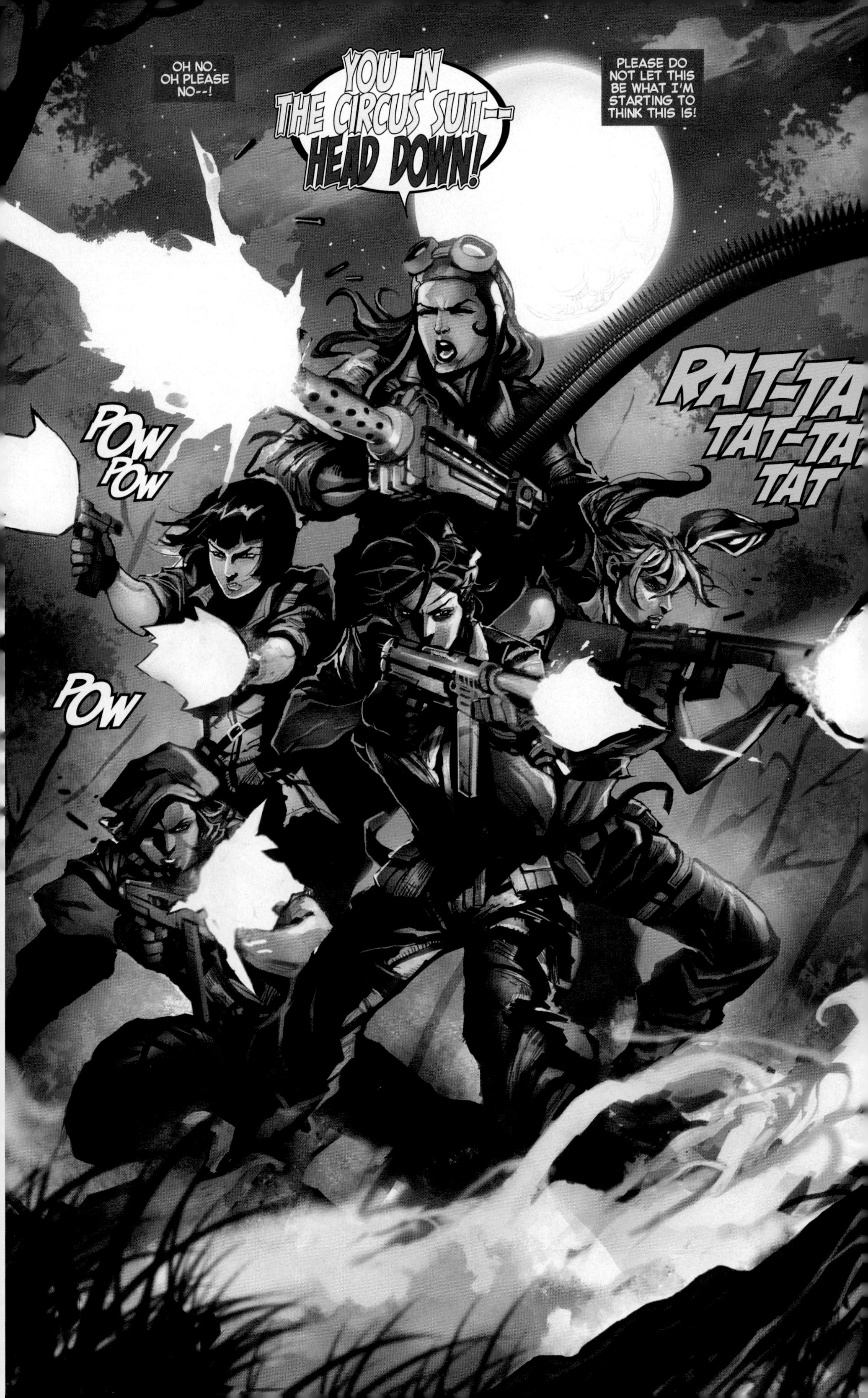
OH NO. OH PLEASE NO--!
YOU IN THE CIRCUS SUIT-- HEAD DOWN!
PLEASE DO NOT LET THIS BE WHAT I'M STARTING TO THINK THIS IS!
POW POW
POW
RAT-TA TAT-TA TAT

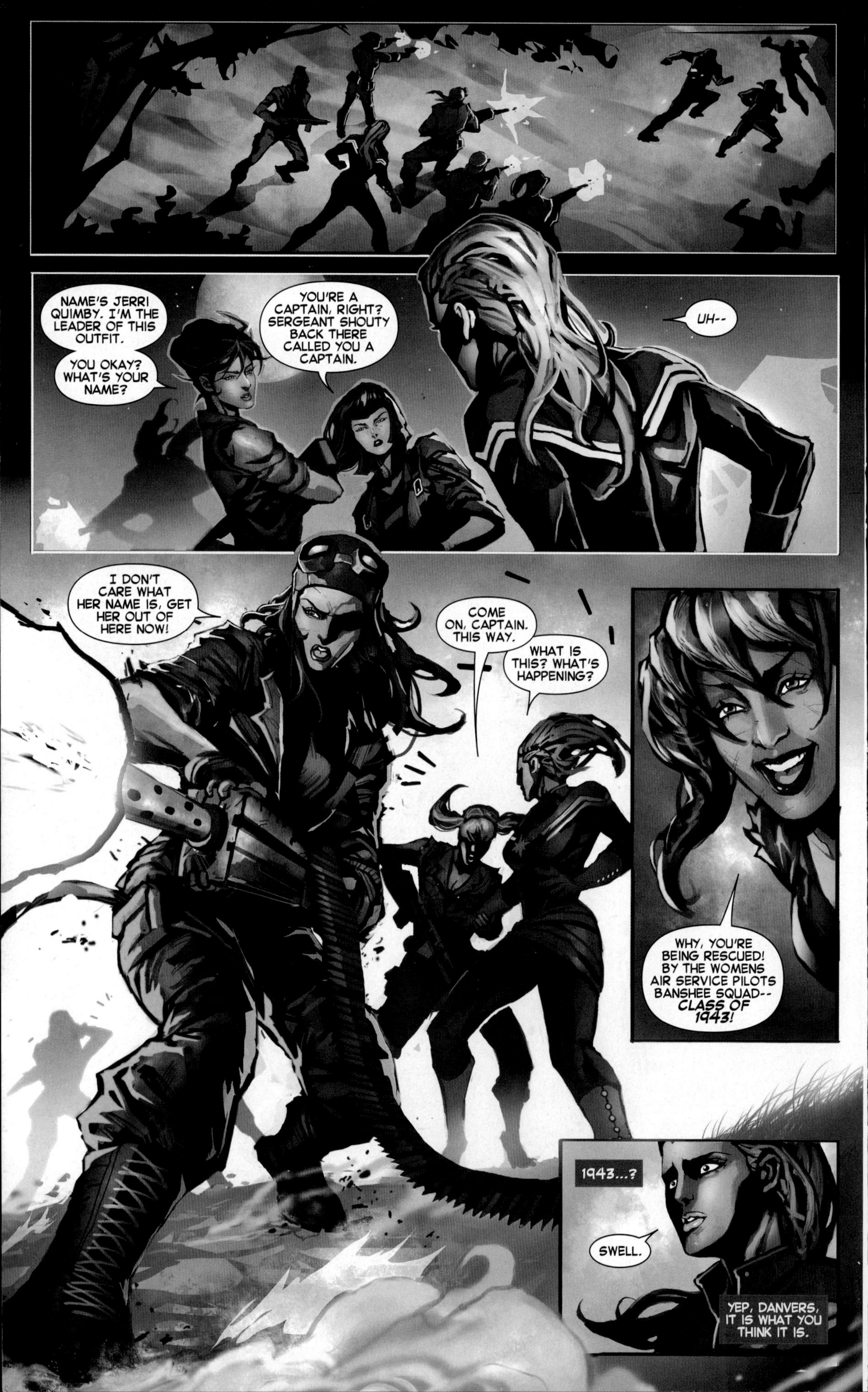
NAME'S JERRI QUIMBY. I'M THE LEADER OF THIS OUTFIT.
YOU OKAY? WHAT'S YOUR NAME?
YOU'RE A CAPTAIN, RIGHT? SERGEANT SHOUTY BACK THERE CALLED YOU A CAPTAIN.
UH--
I DON'T CARE WHAT HER NAME IS, GET HER OUT OF HERE NOW!
COME ON, CAPTAIN. THIS WAY.
WHAT IS THIS? WHAT'S HAPPENING?
WHY, YOU'RE BEING RESCUED! BY THE WOMENS AIR SERVICE PILOTS BANSHEE SQUAD-- CLASS OF 1943!
1943...?
SWELL.
YEP, DANVERS, IT IS WHAT YOU THINK IT IS.

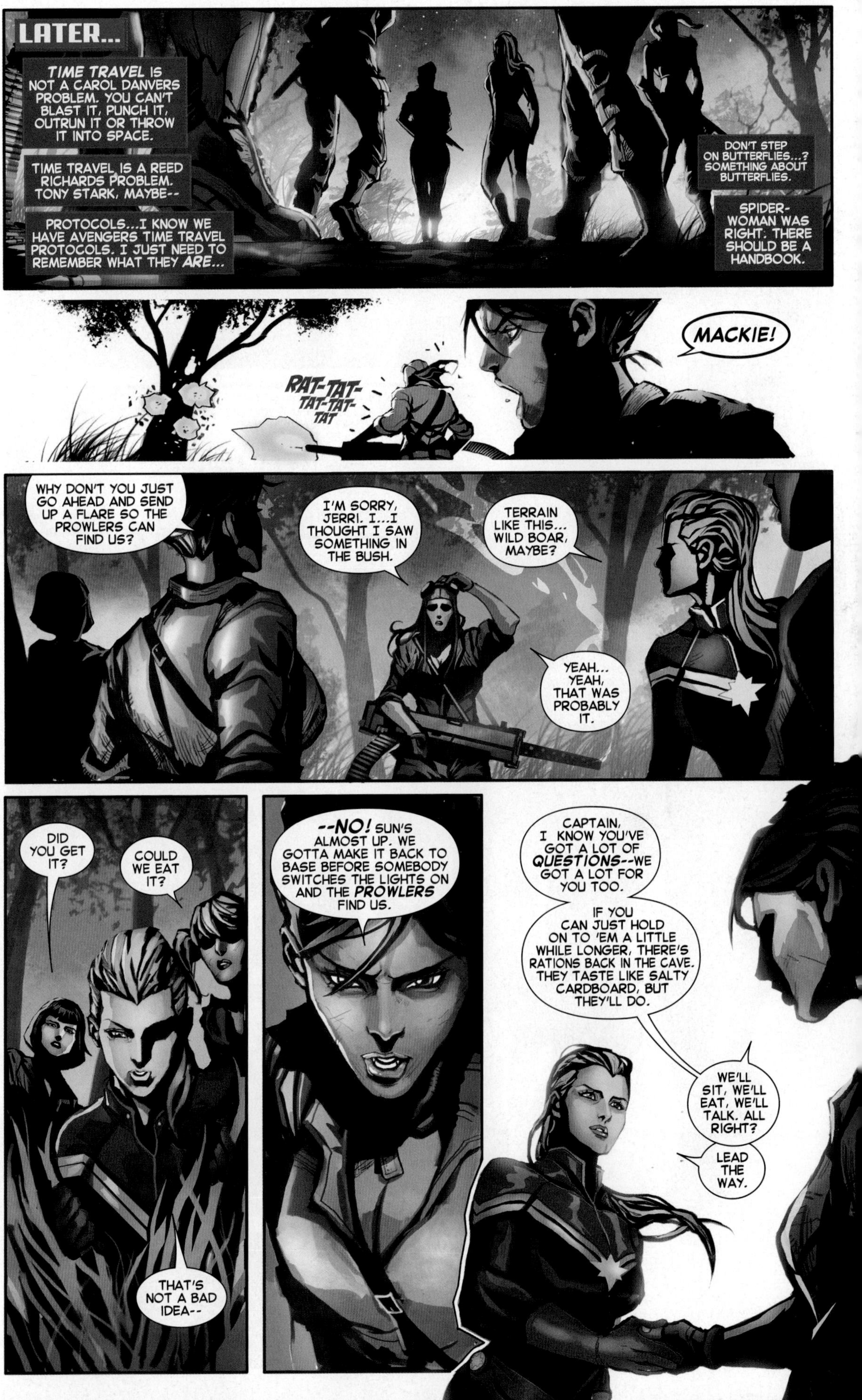
LATER...
TIME TRAVEL IS NOT A CAROL DANVERS PROBLEM. YOU CAN'T BLAST IT, PUNCH IT, OUTRUN IT OR THROW IT INTO SPACE.
TIME TRAVEL IS A REED RICHARDS PROBLEM. TONY STARK, MAYBE--
PROTOCOLS...I KNOW WE HAVE AVENGERS TIME TRAVEL PROTOCOLS. I JUST NEED TO REMEMBER WHAT THEY ARE...
DON'T STEP ON BUTTERFLIES...? SOMETHING ABOUT BUTTERFLIES.
SPIDER-WOMAN WAS RIGHT: THERE SHOULD BE A HANDBOOK.
RAT-TAT-TAT-TAT-TAT
MACKIE!
WHY DON'T YOU JUST GO AHEAD AND SEND UP A FLARE SO THE PROWLERS CAN FIND US?
I'M SORRY, JERRI. I...I THOUGHT I SAW SOMETHING IN THE BUSH.
TERRAIN LIKE THIS... WILD BOAR, MAYBE?
YEAH... YEAH, THAT WAS PROBABLY IT.
DID YOU GET IT?
COULD WE EAT IT?
THAT'S NOT A BAD IDEA--
--NO! SUN'S ALMOST UP. WE GOTTA MAKE IT BACK TO BASE BEFORE SOMEBODY SWITCHES THE LIGHTS ON AND THE PROWLERS FIND US.
CAPTAIN, I KNOW YOU'VE GOT A LOT OF QUESTIONS--WE GOT A LOT FOR YOU TOO.
IF YOU CAN JUST HOLD ON TO 'EM A LITTLE WHILE LONGER, THERE'S RATIONS BACK IN THE CAVE. THEY TASTE LIKE SALTY CARDBOARD, BUT THEY'LL DO.
WE'LL SIT, WE'LL EAT, WE'LL TALK. ALL RIGHT?
LEAD THE WAY.

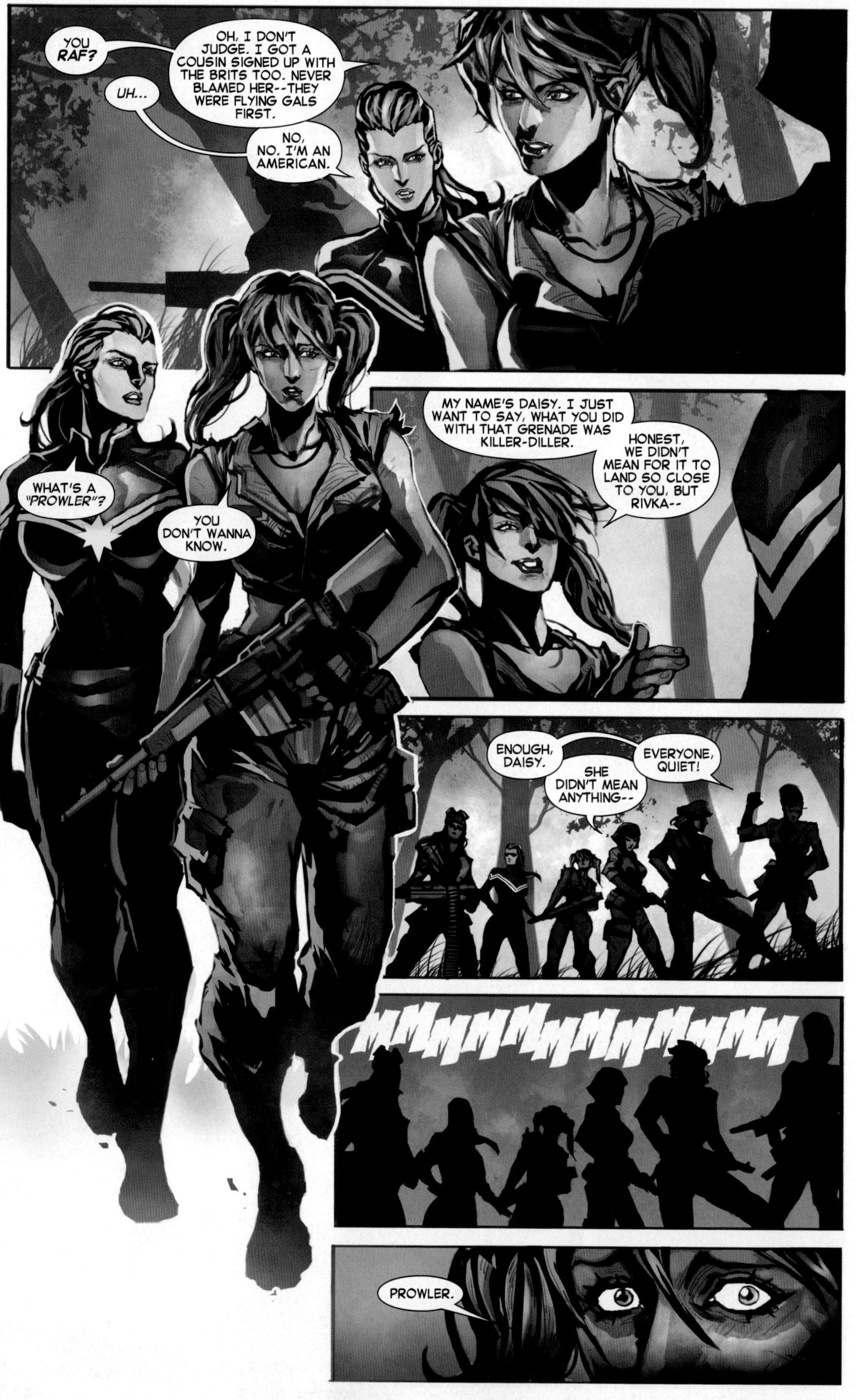

YOU RAF?
OH, I DON'T JUDGE. I GOT A COUSIN SIGNED UP WITH THE BRITS TOO. NEVER BLAMED HER--THEY WERE FLYING GALS FIRST.
UH...
NO, NO. I'M AN AMERICAN.
WHAT'S A "PROWLER"?
YOU DON'T WANNA KNOW.
MY NAME'S DAISY. I JUST WANT TO SAY, WHAT YOU DID WITH THAT GRENADE WAS KILLER-DILLER.
HONEST, WE DIDN'T MEAN FOR IT TO LAND SO CLOSE TO YOU, BUT RIVKA--
ENOUGH, DAISY.
SHE DIDN'T MEAN ANYTHING--
EVERYONE, QUIET!
MMMMMMMMMMMMMMMMM
PROWLER.

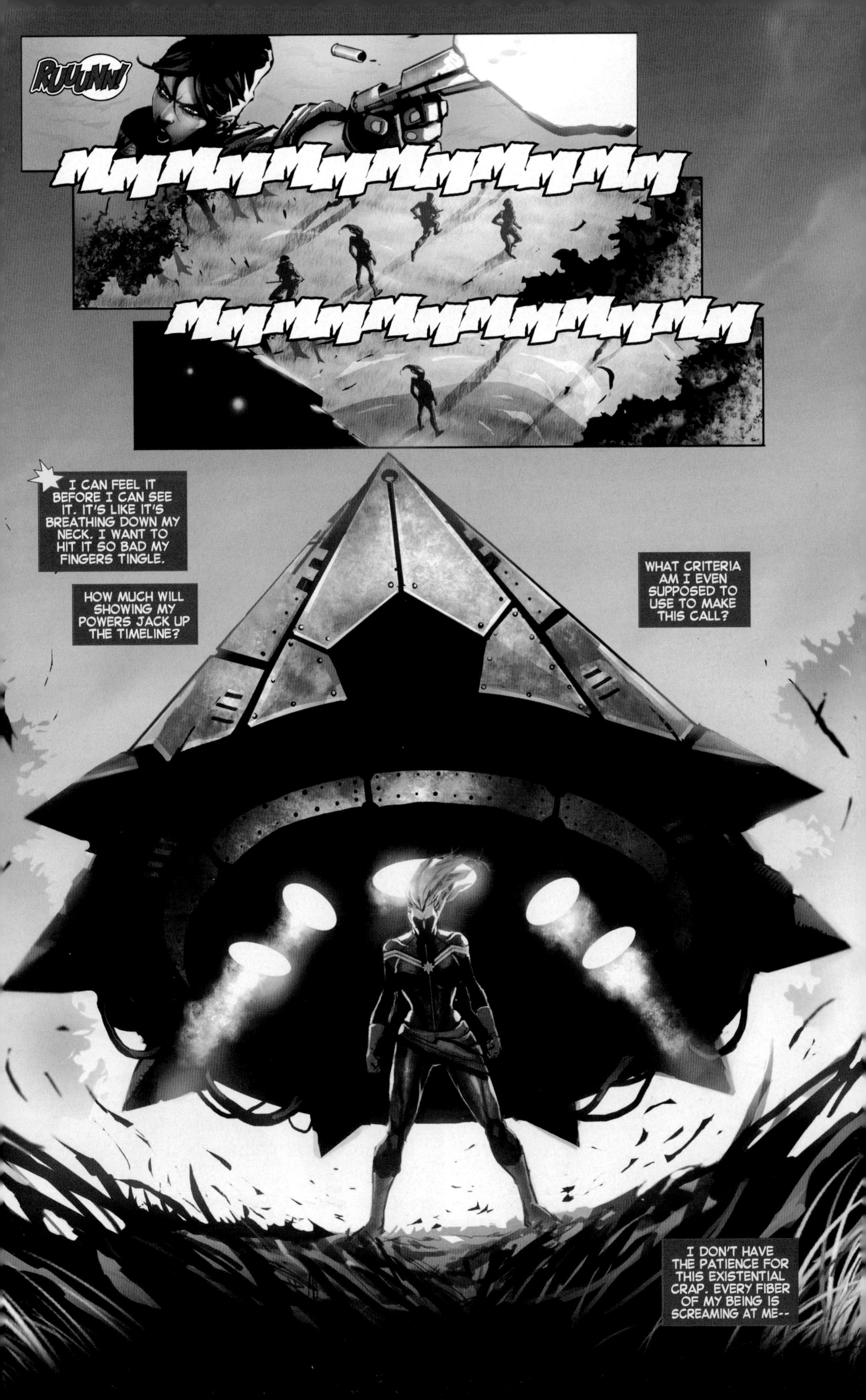
RUUUNN!
MMMMMMMMMMMMMMMMMMMMMM
MMMMMMMMMMMMMMMMMMMMMMMM
I CAN FEEL IT BEFORE I CAN SEE IT. IT'S LIKE IT'S BREATHING DOWN MY NECK. I WANT TO HIT IT SO BAD MY FINGERS TINGLE.
HOW MUCH WILL SHOWING MY POWERS JACK UP THE TIMELINE?
WHAT CRITERIA AM I EVEN SUPPOSED TO USE TO MAKE THIS CALL?
I DON'T HAVE THE PATIENCE FOR THIS EXISTENTIAL CRAP. EVERY FIBER OF MY BEING IS SCREAMING AT ME--

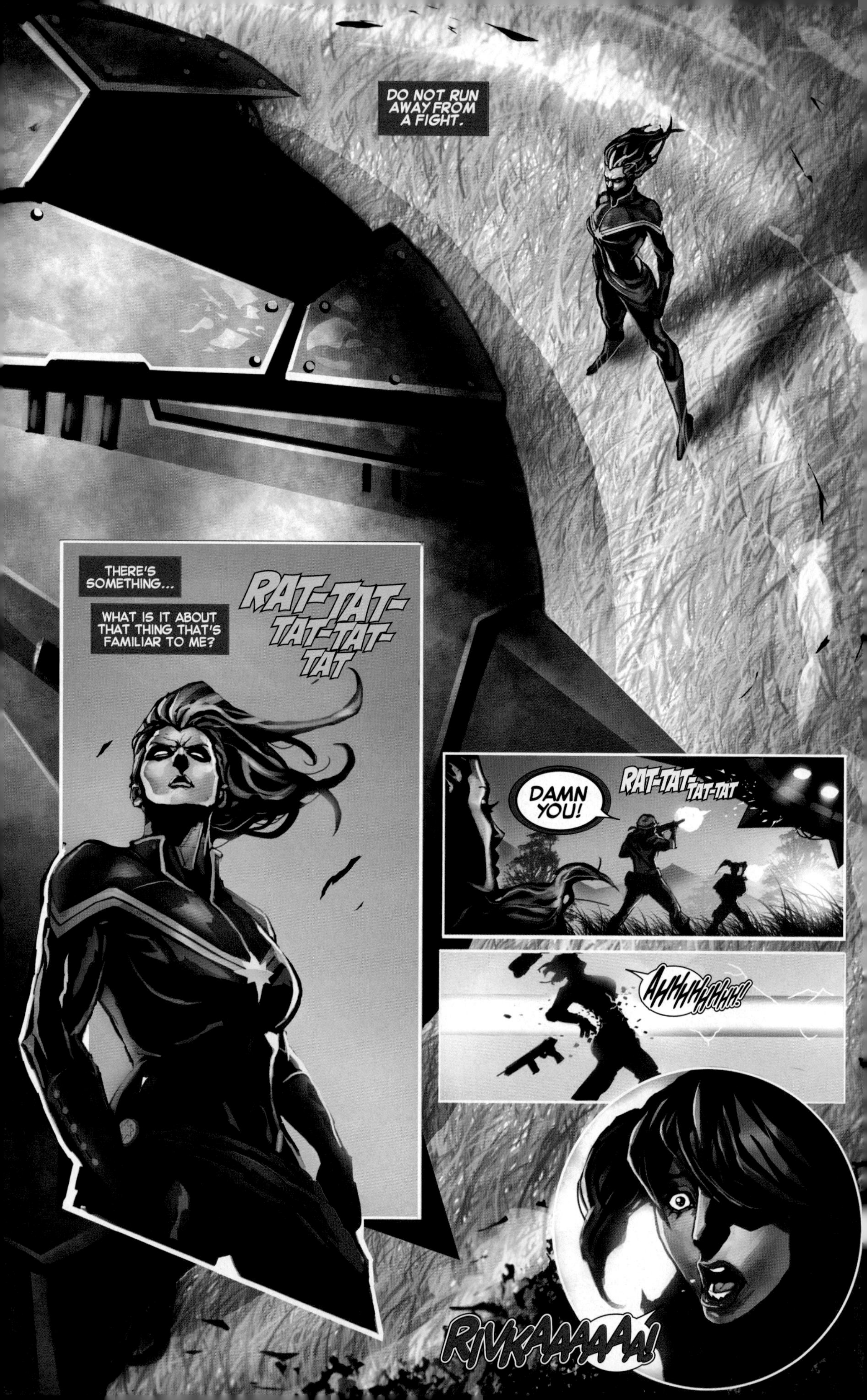
DO NOT RUN AWAY FROM A FIGHT.
THERE'S SOMETHING...
WHAT IS IT ABOUT THAT THING THAT'S FAMILIAR TO ME?
RAT-TAT-TAT-TAT-TAT
DAMN YOU!
RAT-TAT-TAT-TAT
AHHHHHHH!
RINKAAAAAA!

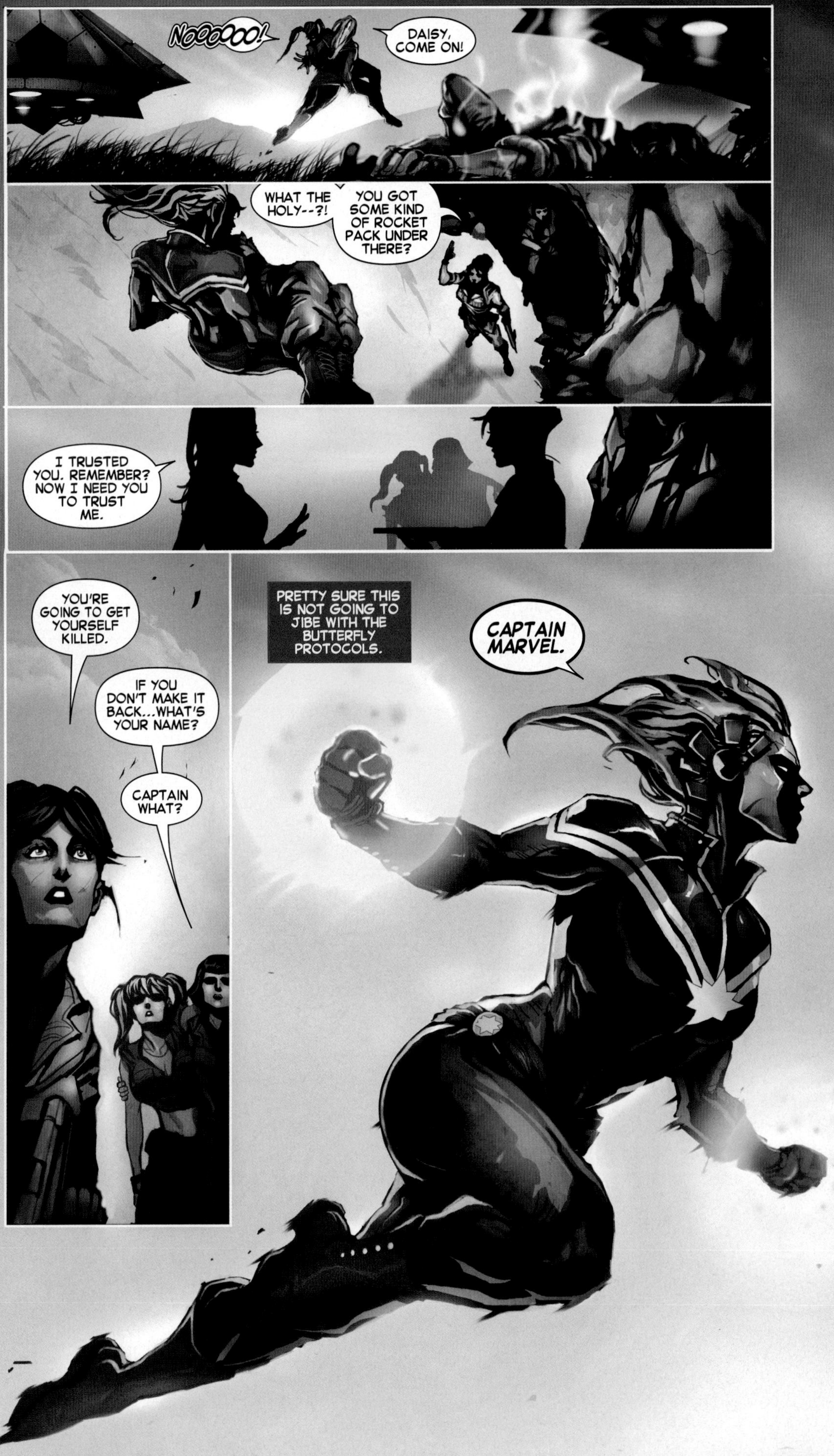
NOOOOOO!
DAISY, COME ON!
WHAT THE HOLY--?!
YOU GOT SOME KIND OF ROCKET PACK UNDER THERE?
I TRUSTED YOU. REMEMBER? NOW I NEED YOU TO TRUST ME.
YOU'RE GOING TO GET YOURSELF KILLED.
IF YOU DON'T MAKE IT BACK...WHAT'S YOUR NAME?
CAPTAIN WHAT?
PRETTY SURE THIS IS NOT GOING TO JIBE WITH THE BUTTERFLY PROTOCOLS.
CAPTAIN MARVEL.

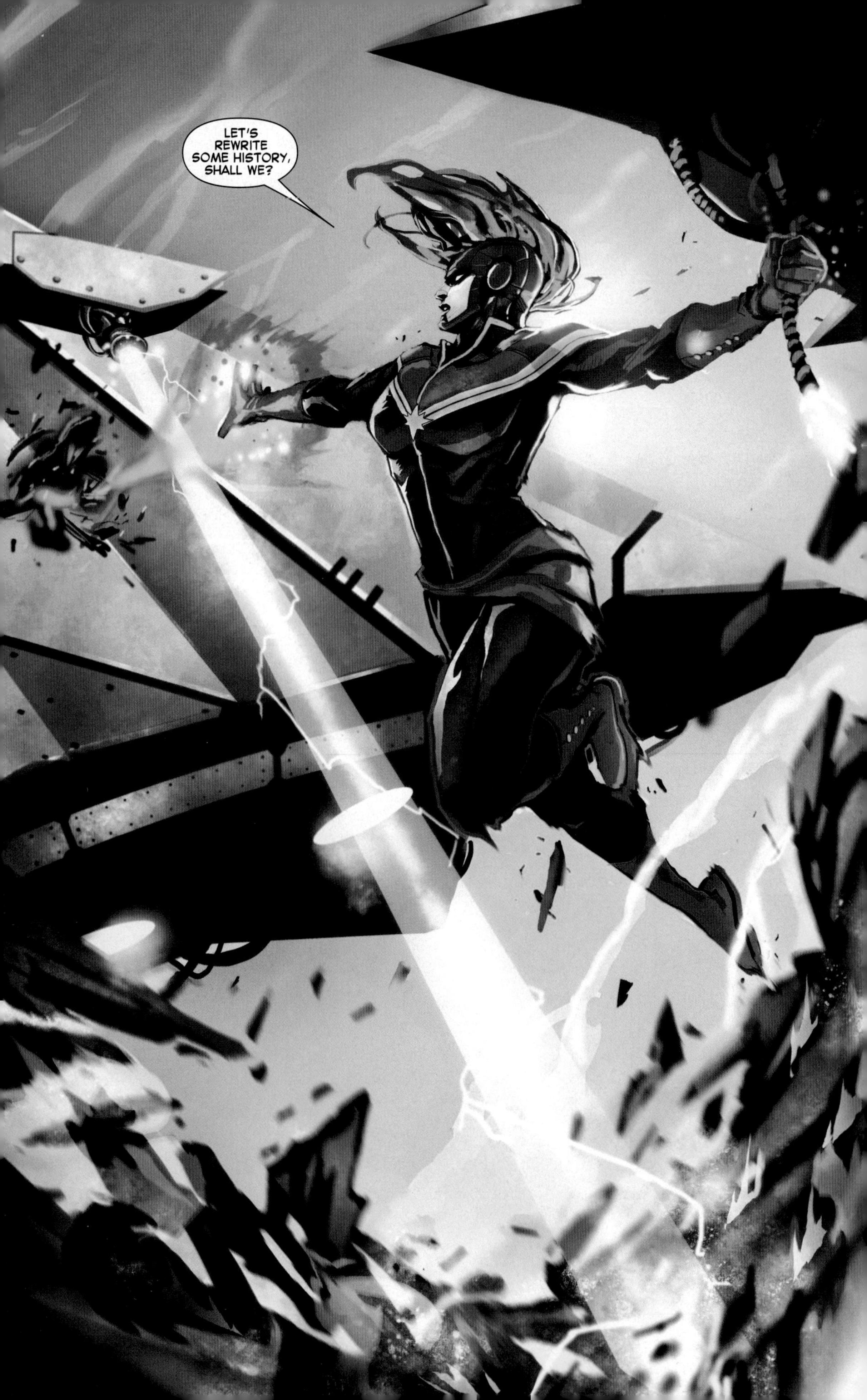
LET'S REWRITE SOME HISTORY, SHALL WE?

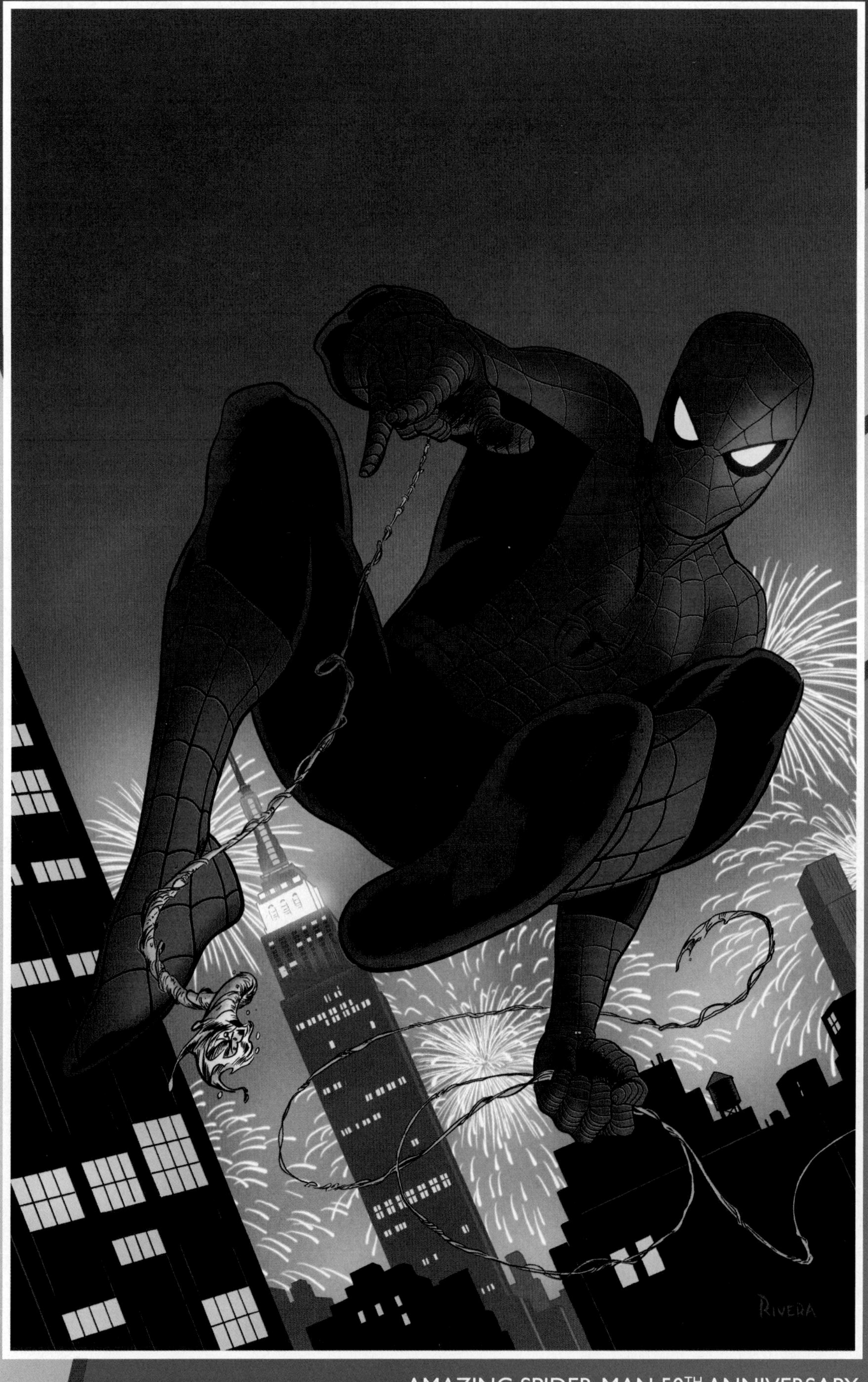
RIVERA

ONE AMAZING SPIDER-MAN 50TH ANNIVERSARY VARIANT BY PAOLO RIVERA

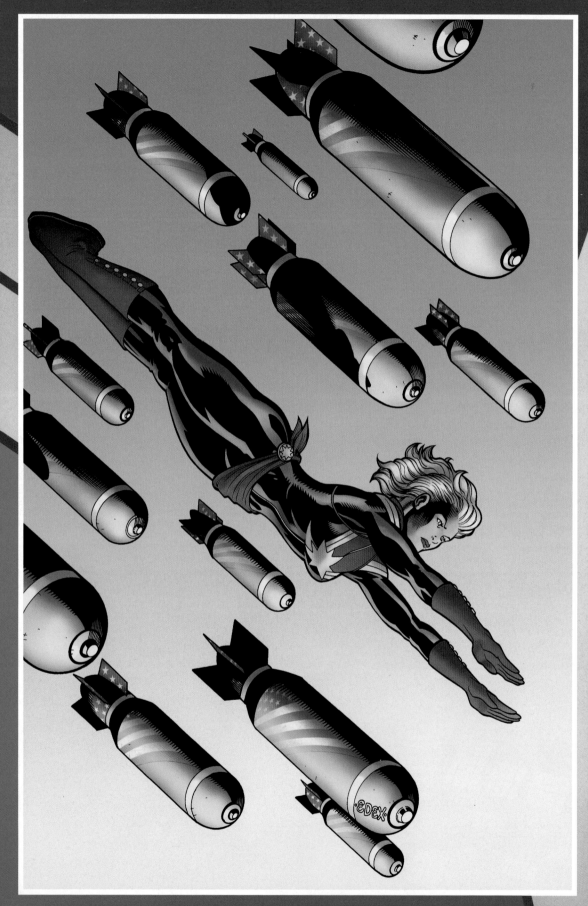

THREE

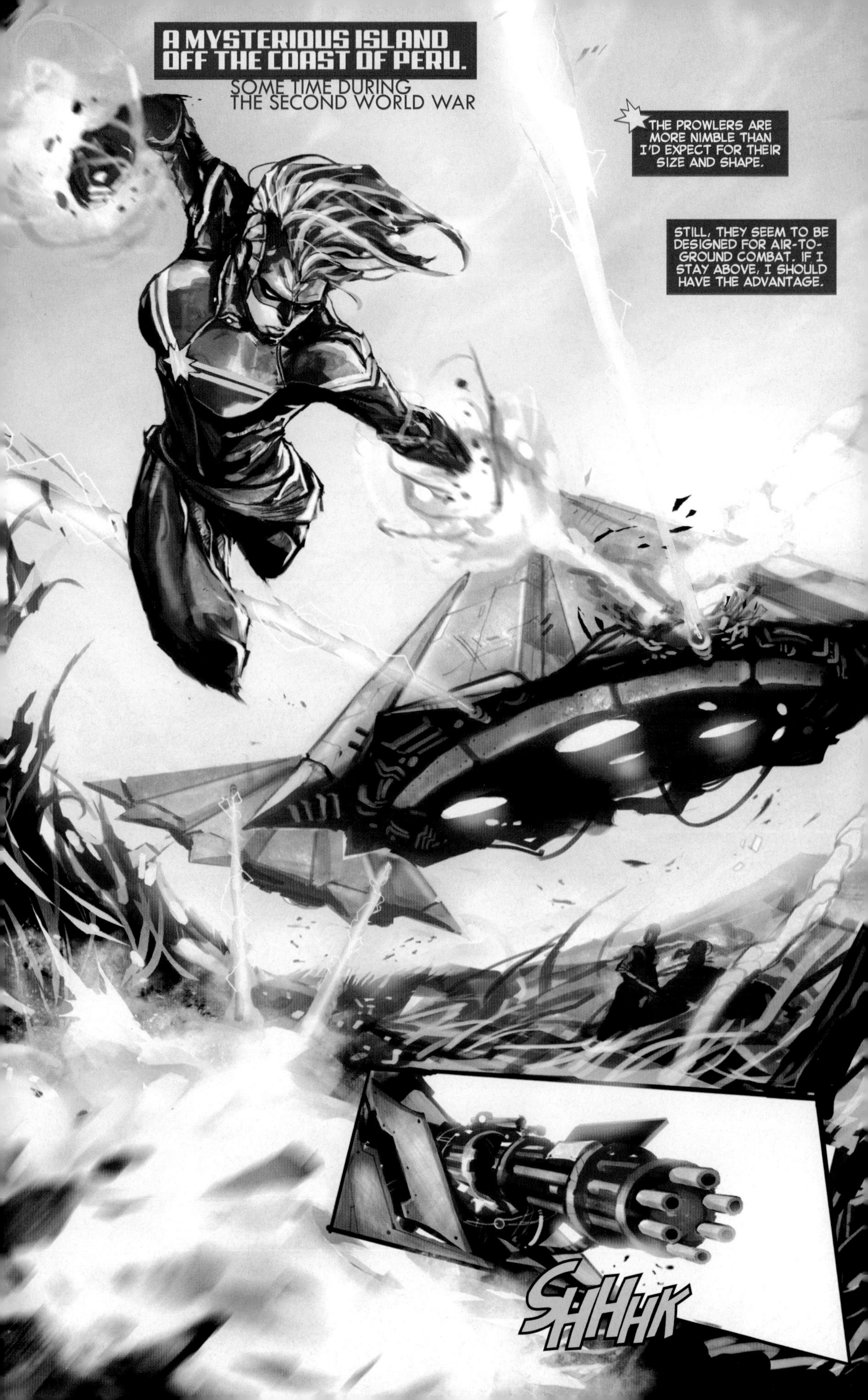
A MYSTERIOUS ISLAND OFF THE COAST OF PERU.
SOME TIME DURING THE SECOND WORLD WAR
THE PROWLERS ARE MORE NIMBLE THAN I'D EXPECT FOR THEIR SIZE AND SHAPE.
STILL, THEY SEEM TO BE DESIGNED FOR AIR-TO-GROUND COMBAT. IF I STAY ABOVE, I SHOULD HAVE THE ADVANTAGE.
SHHHK

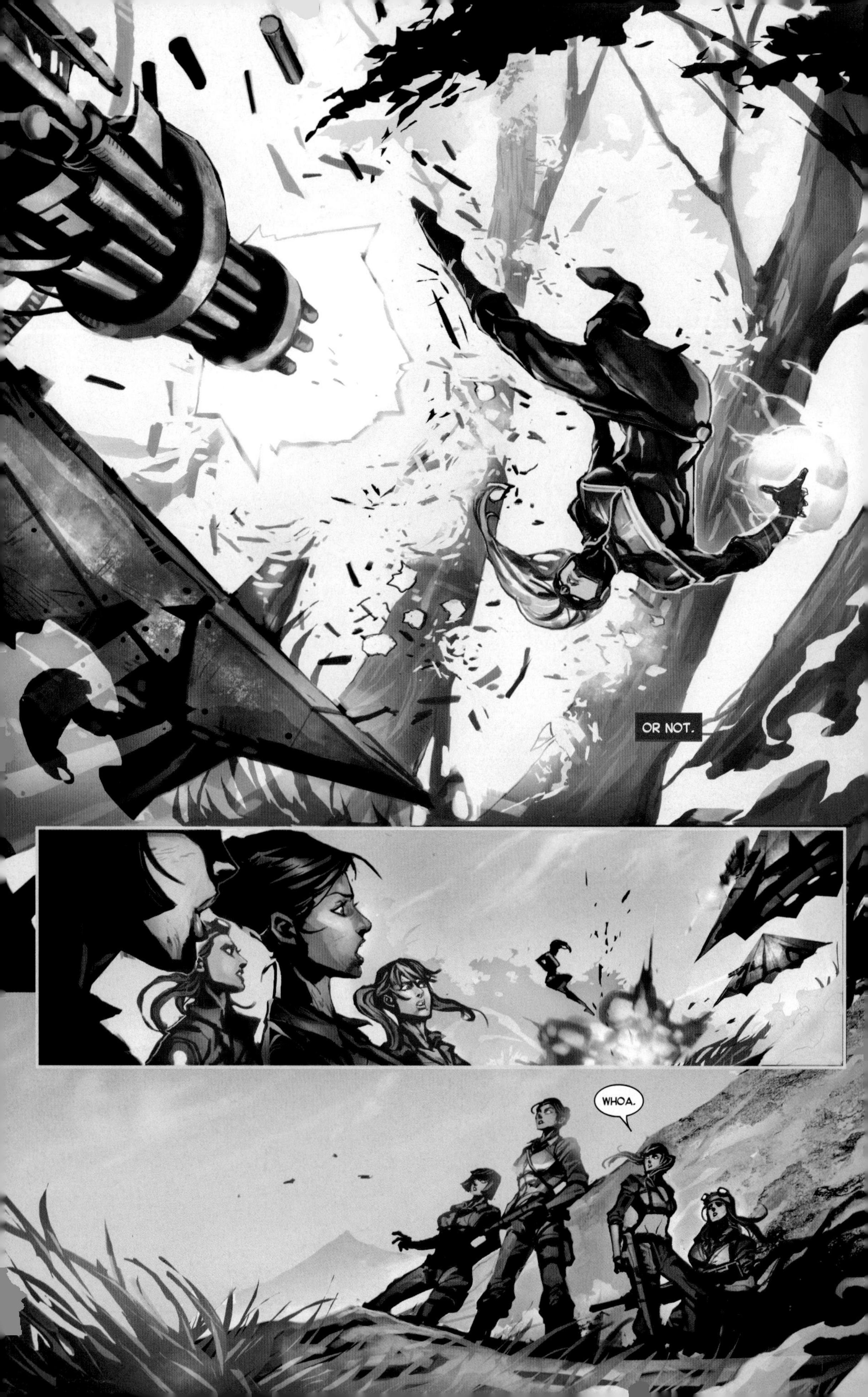
OR NOT.
WHOA.

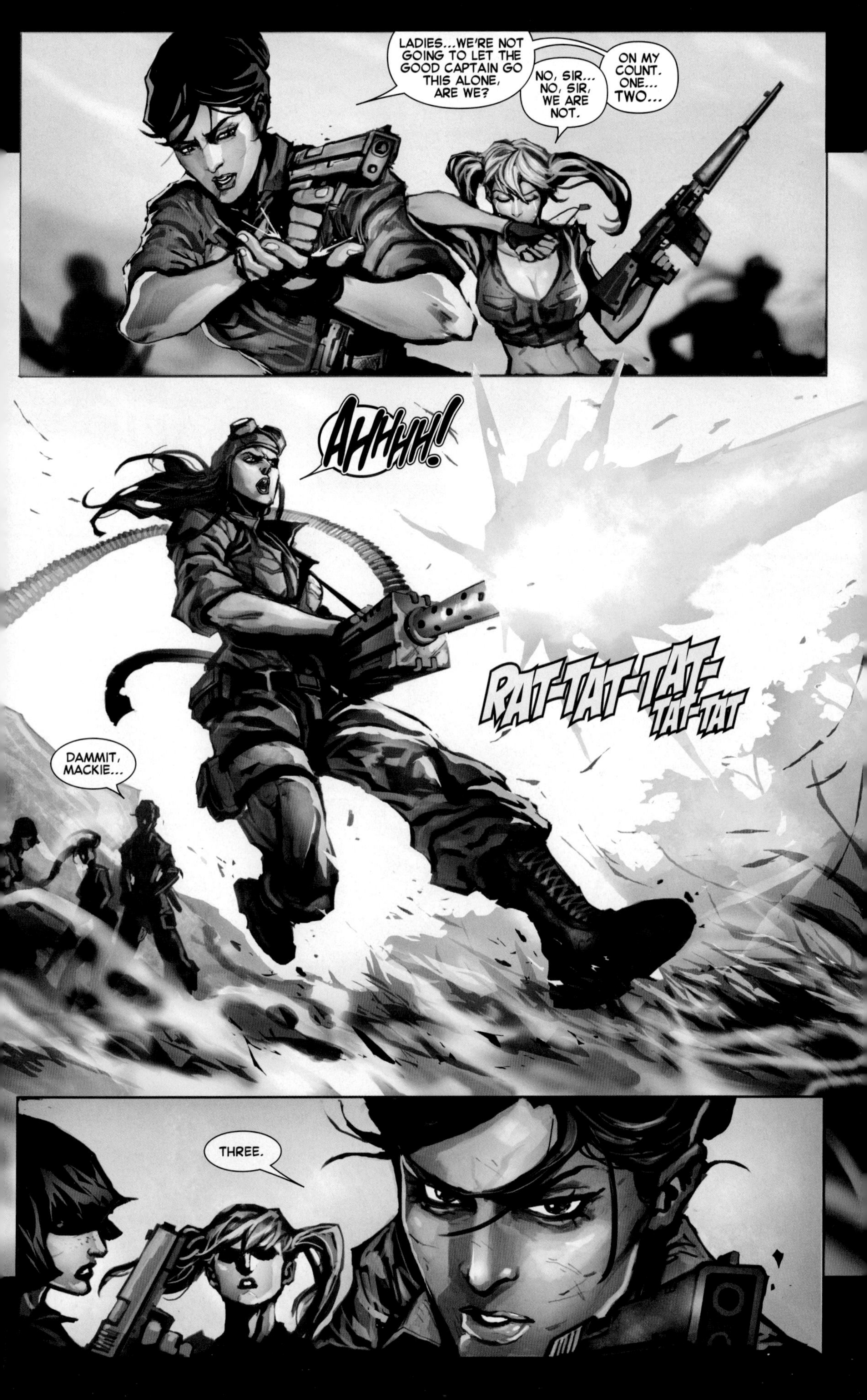
LADIES...WE'RE NOT GOING TO LET THE GOOD CAPTAIN GO THIS ALONE, ARE WE?
NO, SIR... NO, SIR, WE ARE NOT.
ON MY COUNT. ONE... TWO...
AHHHH!
RAT-TAT-TAT-TAT-TAT
DAMMIT, MACKIE...
THREE.

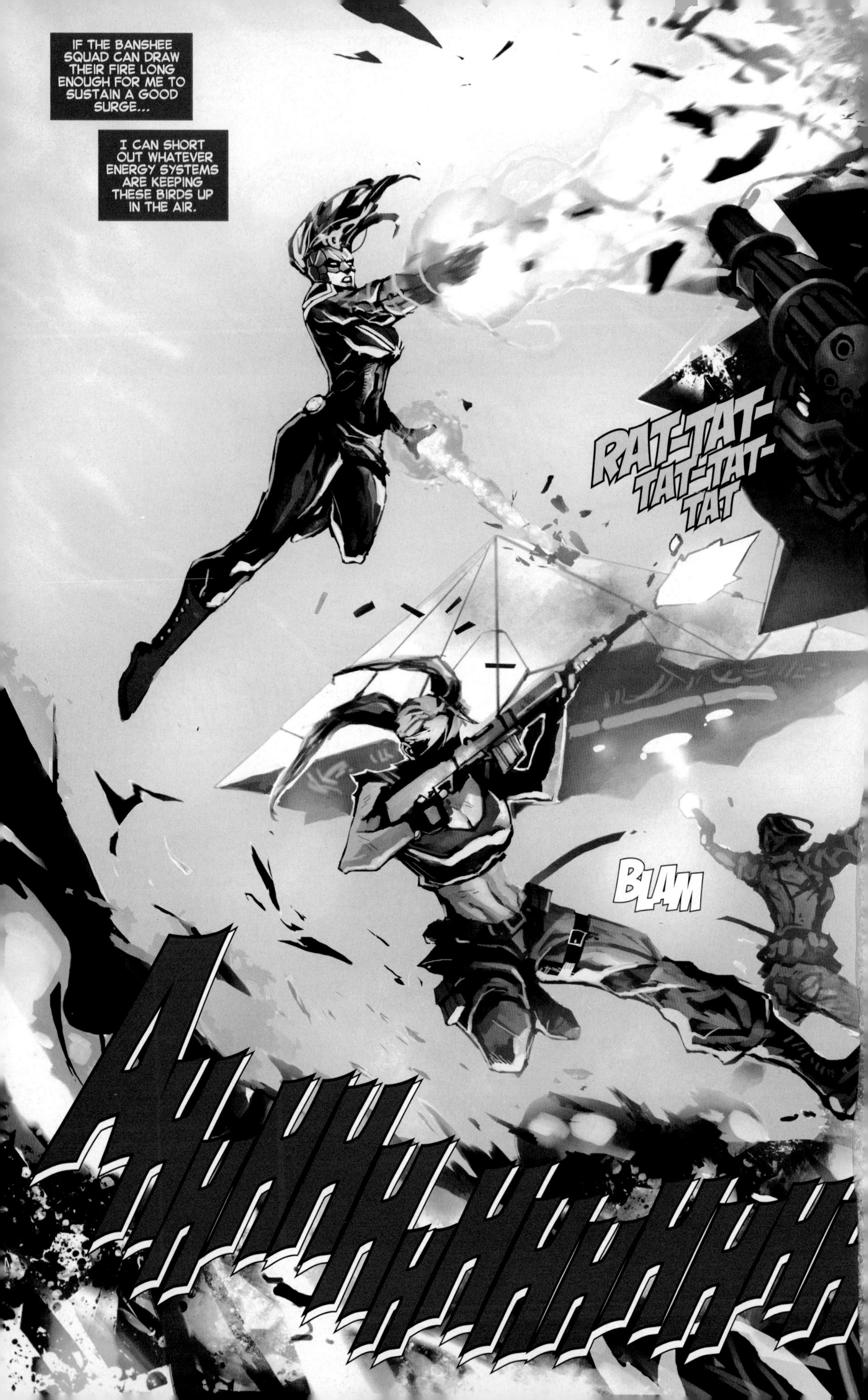
IF THE BANSHEE SQUAD CAN DRAW THEIR FIRE LONG ENOUGH FOR ME TO SUSTAIN A GOOD SURGE...
I CAN SHORT OUT WHATEVER ENERGY SYSTEMS ARE KEEPING THESE BIRDS UP IN THE AIR.
RAT-TAT-TAT-TAT-TAT
BLAM
AHHHHHHHHHHH

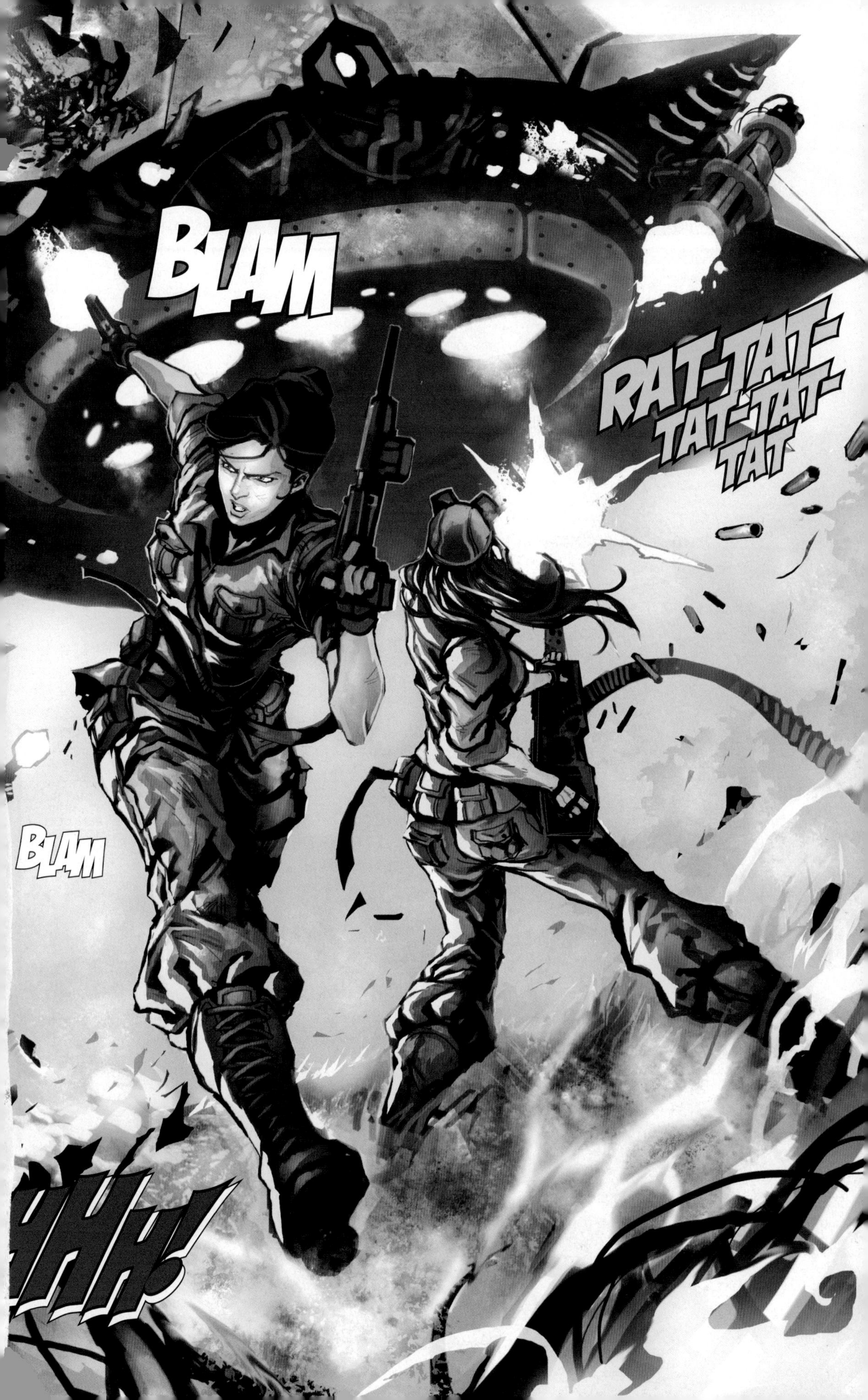
BLAM
RAT-TAT-TAT-TAT-TAT
BLAM
HHH!

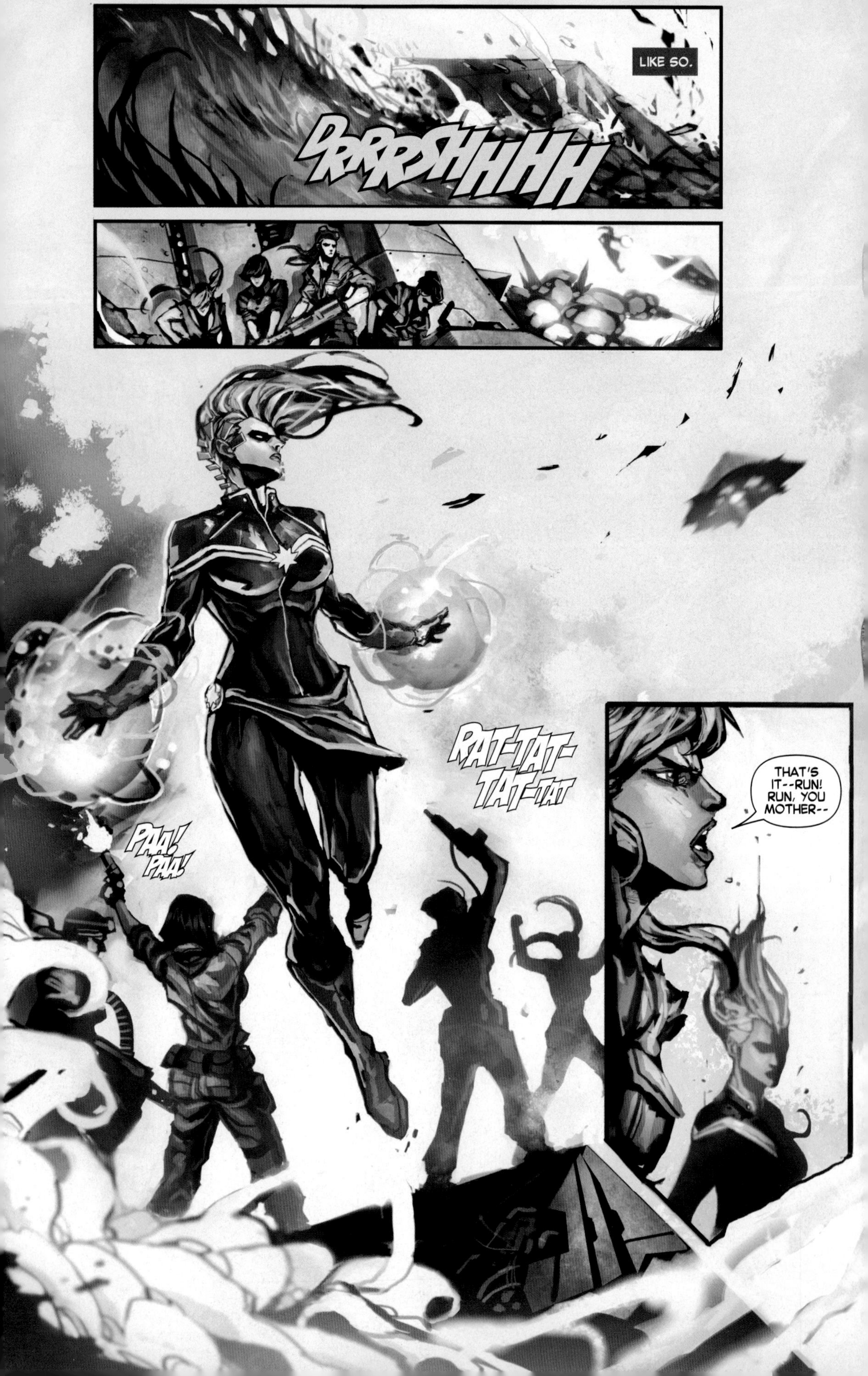
LIKE SO.
DRRRSHHHHH
RAT-TAT-TAT-TAT
PAA! PAA!
THAT'S IT--RUN! RUN, YOU MOTHER--

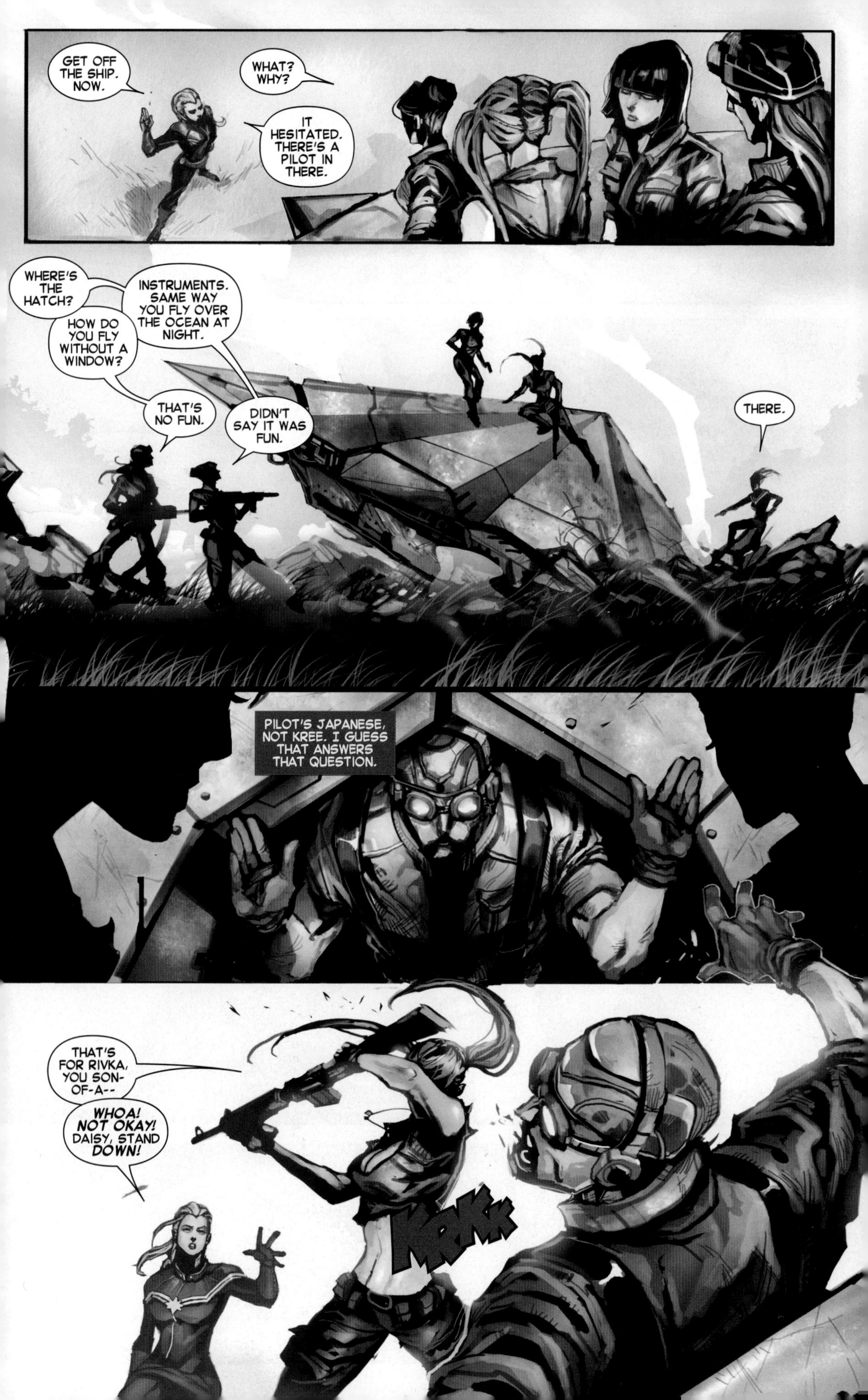
GET OFF THE SHIP. NOW.
WHAT? WHY?
IT HESITATED. THERE'S A PILOT IN THERE.
WHERE'S THE HATCH?
INSTRUMENTS. SAME WAY YOU FLY OVER THE OCEAN AT NIGHT.
HOW DO YOU FLY WITHOUT A WINDOW?
THAT'S NO FUN.
DIDN'T SAY IT WAS FUN.
THERE.
PILOT'S JAPANESE, NOT KREE. I GUESS THAT ANSWERS THAT QUESTION.
THAT'S FOR RIVKA, YOU SON-OF-A--
WHOA! NOT OKAY! DAISY, STAND DOWN!
KRKK

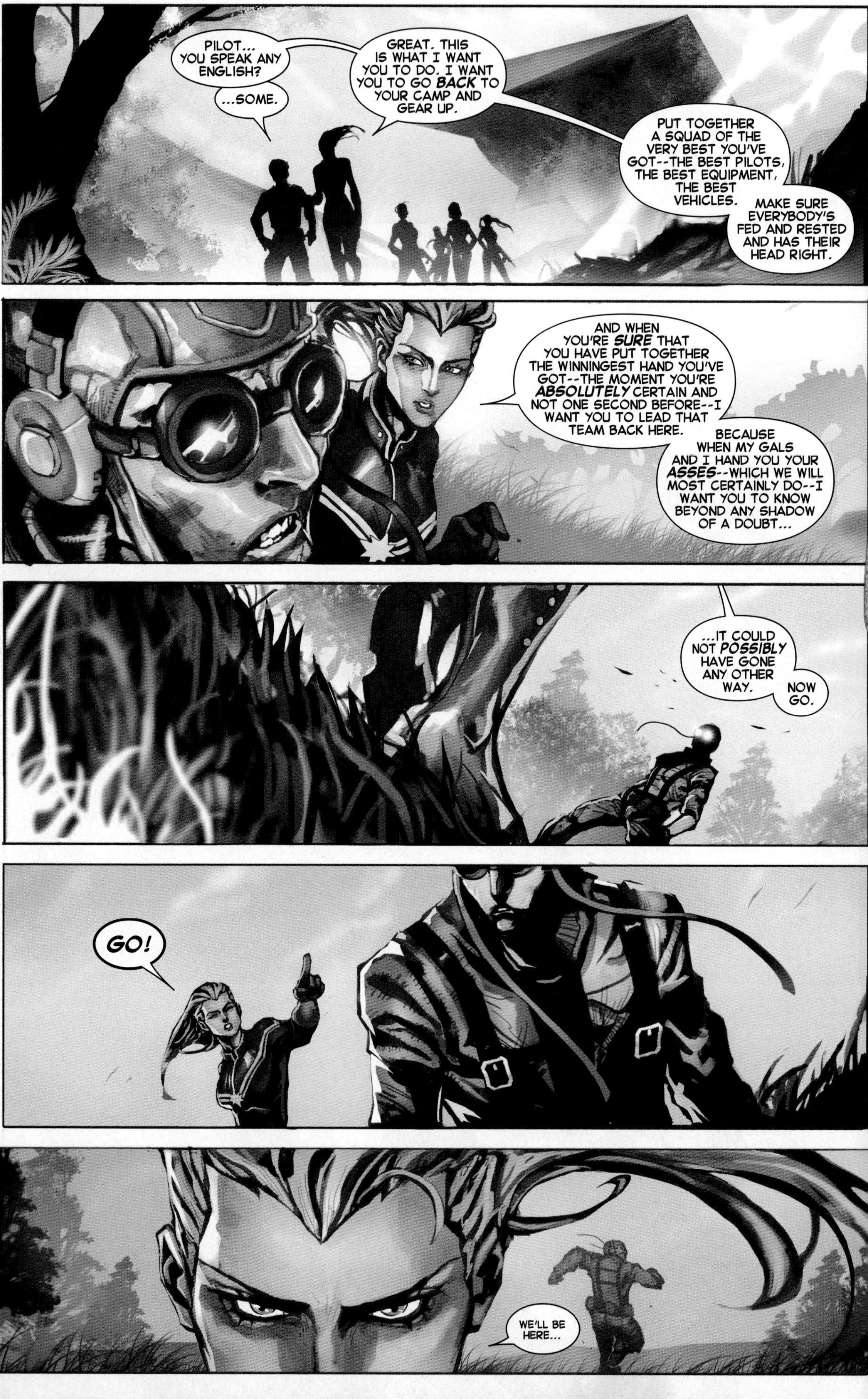
PILOT... YOU SPEAK ANY ENGLISH?
...SOME.
GREAT. THIS IS WHAT I WANT YOU TO DO. I WANT YOU TO GO BACK TO YOUR CAMP AND GEAR UP.
PUT TOGETHER A SQUAD OF THE VERY BEST YOU'VE GOT--THE BEST PILOTS, THE BEST EQUIPMENT, THE BEST VEHICLES.
MAKE SURE EVERYBODY'S FED AND RESTED AND HAS THEIR HEAD RIGHT.
AND WHEN YOU'RE SURE THAT YOU HAVE PUT TOGETHER THE WINNINGEST HAND YOU'VE GOT--THE MOMENT YOU'RE ABSOLUTELY CERTAIN AND NOT ONE SECOND BEFORE--I WANT YOU TO LEAD THAT TEAM BACK HERE.
BECAUSE WHEN MY GALS AND I HAND YOU YOUR ASSES--WHICH WE WILL MOST CERTAINLY DO--I WANT YOU TO KNOW BEYOND ANY SHADOW OF A DOUBT...
...IT COULD NOT POSSIBLY HAVE GONE ANY OTHER WAY.
NOW GO.
GO!
WE'LL BE HERE...

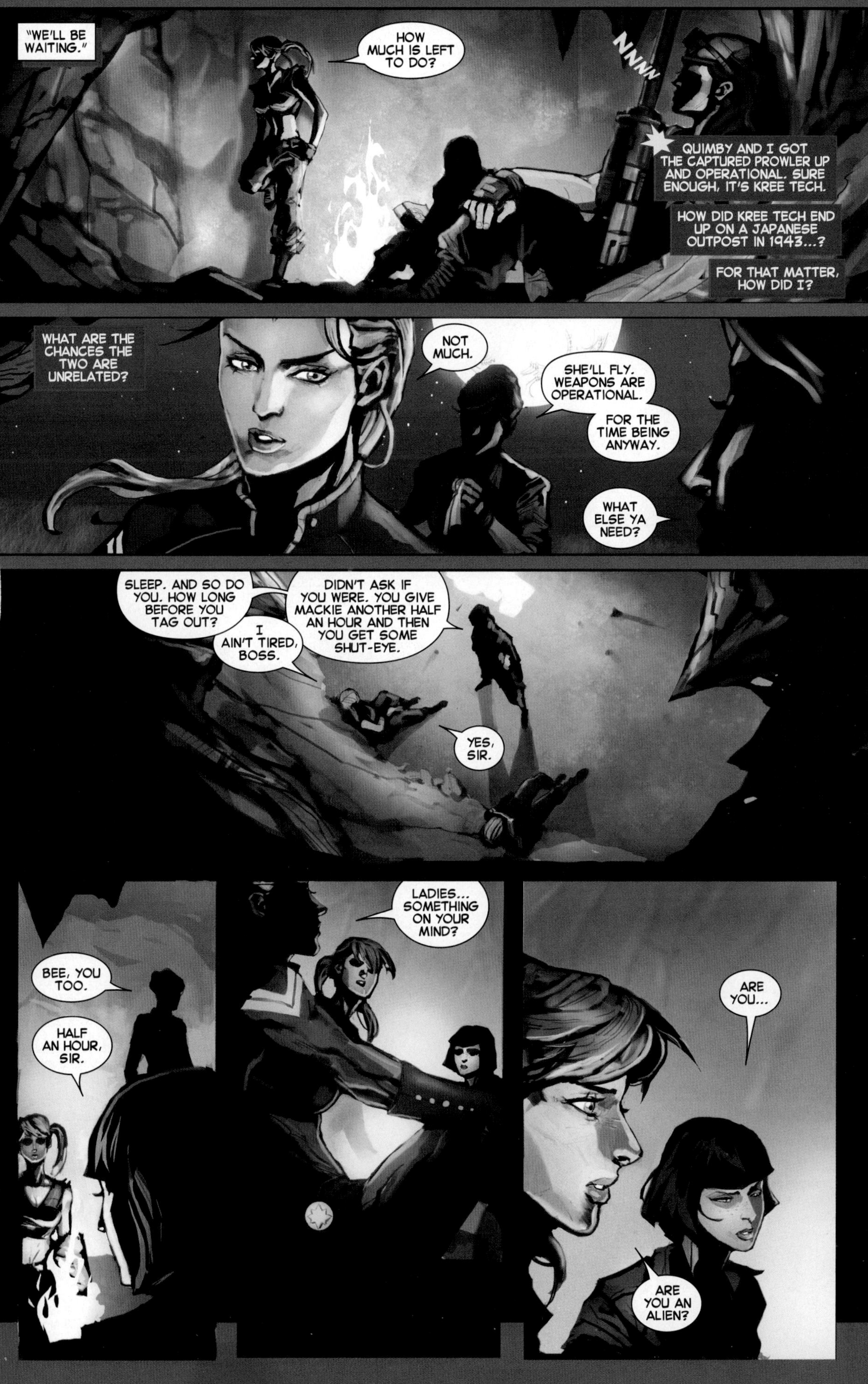
"WE'LL BE WAITING."
HOW MUCH IS LEFT TO DO?
NNNN
QUIMBY AND I GOT THE CAPTURED PROWLER UP AND OPERATIONAL. SURE ENOUGH, IT'S KREE TECH.
HOW DID KREE TECH END UP ON A JAPANESE OUTPOST IN 1943...?
FOR THAT MATTER, HOW DID I?
WHAT ARE THE CHANCES THE TWO ARE UNRELATED?
NOT MUCH.
SHE'LL FLY. WEAPONS ARE OPERATIONAL.
FOR THE TIME BEING ANYWAY.
WHAT ELSE YA NEED?
SLEEP. AND SO DO YOU. HOW LONG BEFORE YOU TAG OUT?
I AIN'T TIRED, BOSS.
DIDN'T ASK IF YOU WERE. YOU GIVE MACKIE ANOTHER HALF AN HOUR AND THEN YOU GET SOME SHUT-EYE.
YES, SIR.
BEE, YOU TOO.
HALF AN HOUR, SIR.
LADIES... SOMETHING ON YOUR MIND?
ARE YOU...
ARE YOU AN ALIEN?

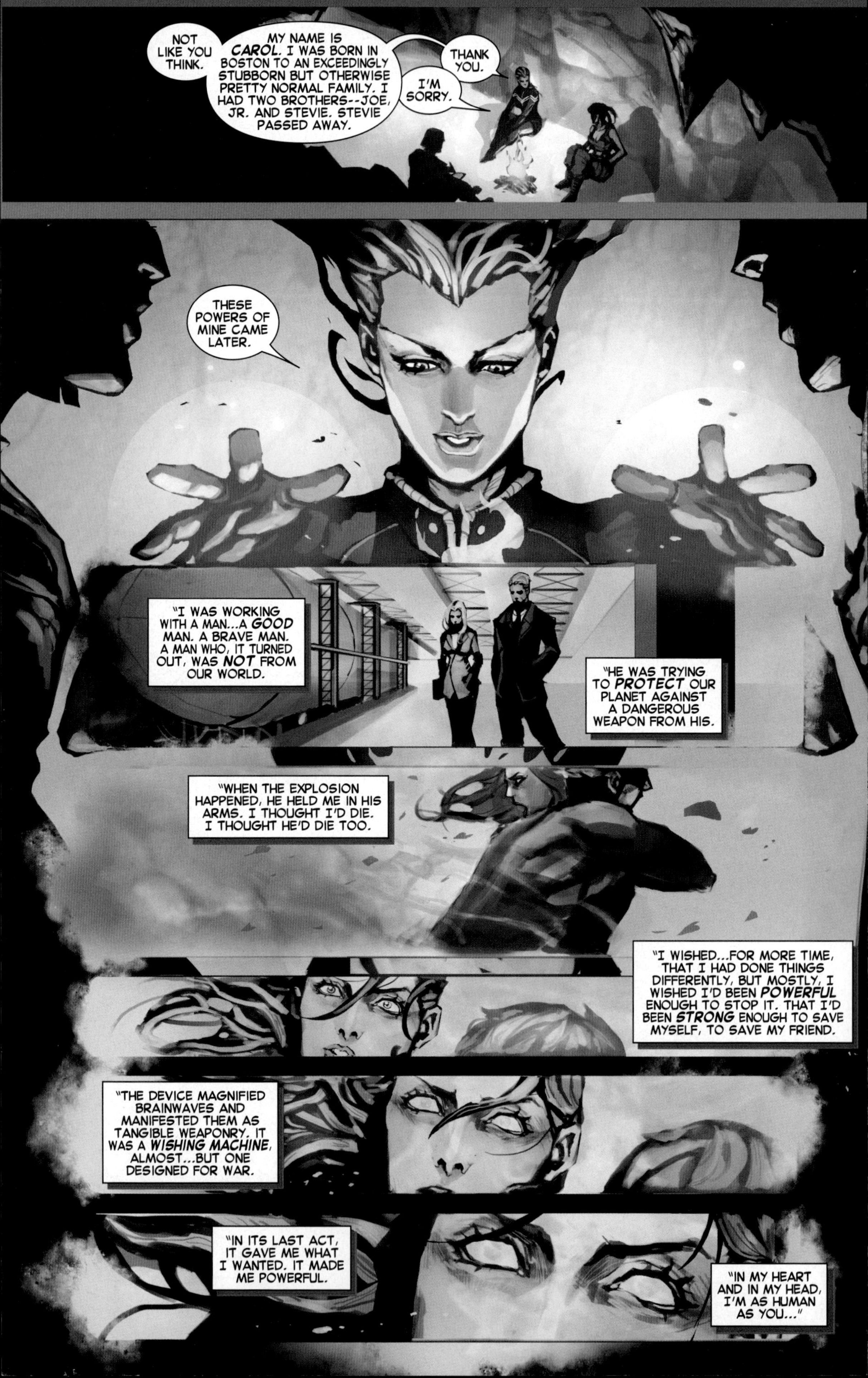
NOT LIKE YOU THINK.
MY NAME IS CAROL. I WAS BORN IN BOSTON TO AN EXCEEDINGLY STUBBORN BUT OTHERWISE PRETTY NORMAL FAMILY. I HAD TWO BROTHERS--JOE, JR. AND STEVIE. STEVIE PASSED AWAY.
THANK YOU.
I'M SORRY.
THESE POWERS OF MINE CAME LATER.
"I WAS WORKING WITH A MAN...A GOOD MAN. A BRAVE MAN. A MAN WHO, IT TURNED OUT, WAS NOT FROM OUR WORLD.
"HE WAS TRYING TO PROTECT OUR PLANET AGAINST A DANGEROUS WEAPON FROM HIS.
"WHEN THE EXPLOSION HAPPENED, HE HELD ME IN HIS ARMS. I THOUGHT I'D DIE. I THOUGHT HE'D DIE TOO.
"I WISHED...FOR MORE TIME, THAT I HAD DONE THINGS DIFFERENTLY, BUT MOSTLY, I WISHED I'D BEEN POWERFUL ENOUGH TO STOP IT. THAT I'D BEEN STRONG ENOUGH TO SAVE MYSELF, TO SAVE MY FRIEND.
"THE DEVICE MAGNIFIED BRAINWAVES AND MANIFESTED THEM AS TANGIBLE WEAPONRY. IT WAS A WISHING MACHINE, ALMOST...BUT ONE DESIGNED FOR WAR.
"IN ITS LAST ACT, IT GAVE ME WHAT I WANTED. IT MADE ME POWERFUL.
"IN MY HEART AND IN MY HEAD, I'M AS HUMAN AS YOU..."

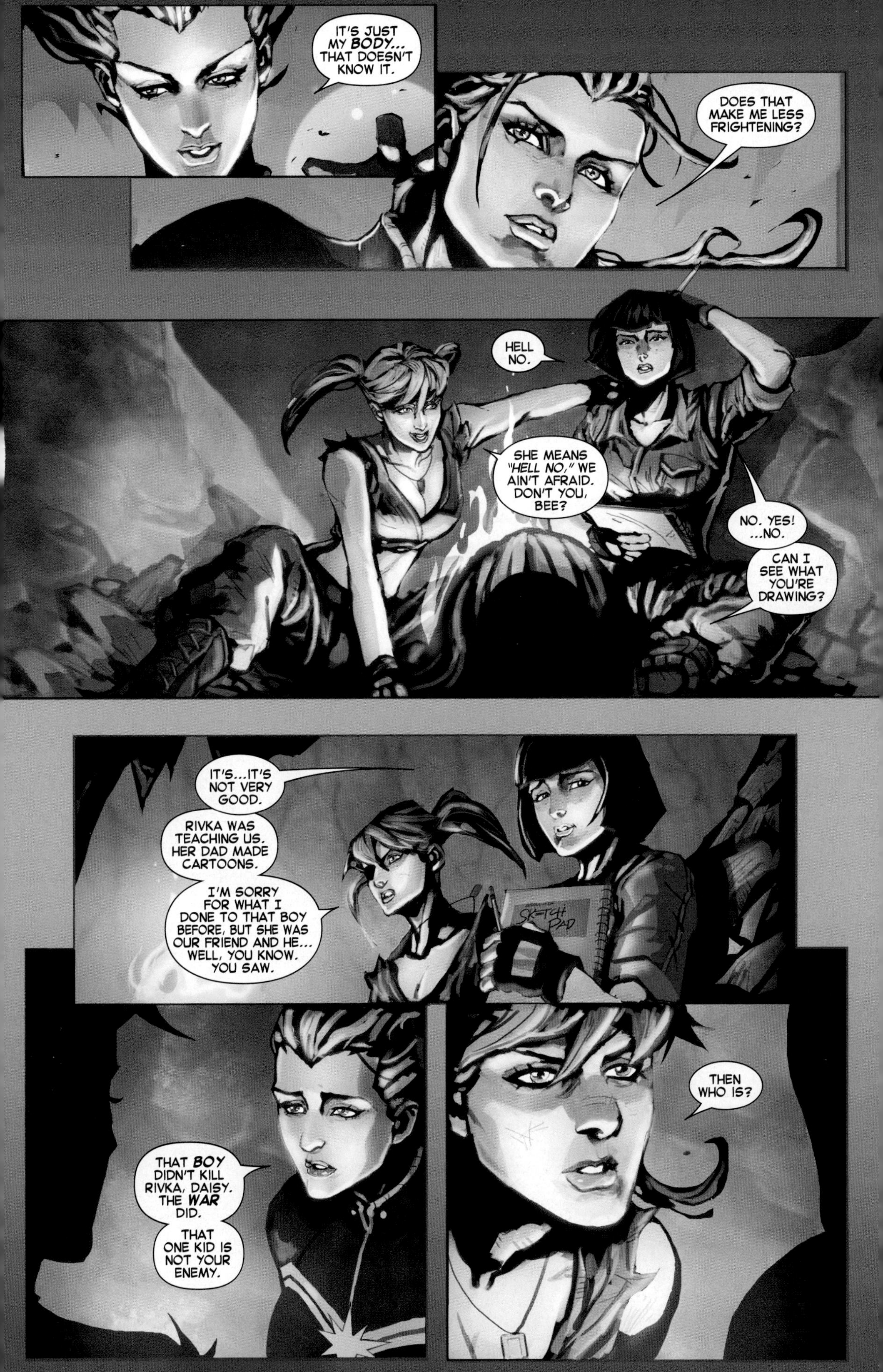
IT'S JUST MY BODY... THAT DOESN'T KNOW IT.
DOES THAT MAKE ME LESS FRIGHTENING?
HELL NO.
SHE MEANS "HELL NO," WE AIN'T AFRAID. DON'T YOU, BEE?
NO. YES! ...NO.
CAN I SEE WHAT YOU'RE DRAWING?
IT'S...IT'S NOT VERY GOOD.
RIVKA WAS TEACHING US. HER DAD MADE CARTOONS.
I'M SORRY FOR WHAT I DONE TO THAT BOY BEFORE, BUT SHE WAS OUR FRIEND AND HE... WELL, YOU KNOW. YOU SAW.
SKETCH PAD
THAT BOY DIDN'T KILL RIVKA, DAISY. THE WAR DID.
THAT ONE KID IS NOT YOUR ENEMY.
THEN WHO IS?

THE PROWLERS COME FROM THE SAME WORLD AS MY POWERS. THEY'RE *"KREE."*

WE'RE FIGHTIN' ALIENS?!

OR ALIEN TECH. I DUNNO YET.

I DON'T EVEN KNOW IF ANY OF THIS IS REALLY HERE.

CAPTAIN, I WAS BORN IN BOSTON, TOO. MY MOM IS *FRENCH* AND MY DAD'S *JAPANESE* AND THAT'S HOW I ENDED UP WITH A *CRAZY* NAME LIKE BIJOUX KAWASAKI. I'M *HERE.* DAISY'S *HERE.* AND RIVKA...

RIVKA WAS *HERE,* TOO.

I'LL TAKE WATCH. YOU TWO GO GET SOME SLEEP.

"THAT KID IS NOT YOUR ENEMY."

"THEN WHO IS?"

"DUNNO YET..."

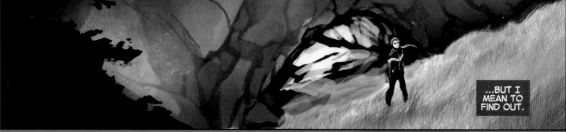

...BUT I MEAN TO FIND OUT.

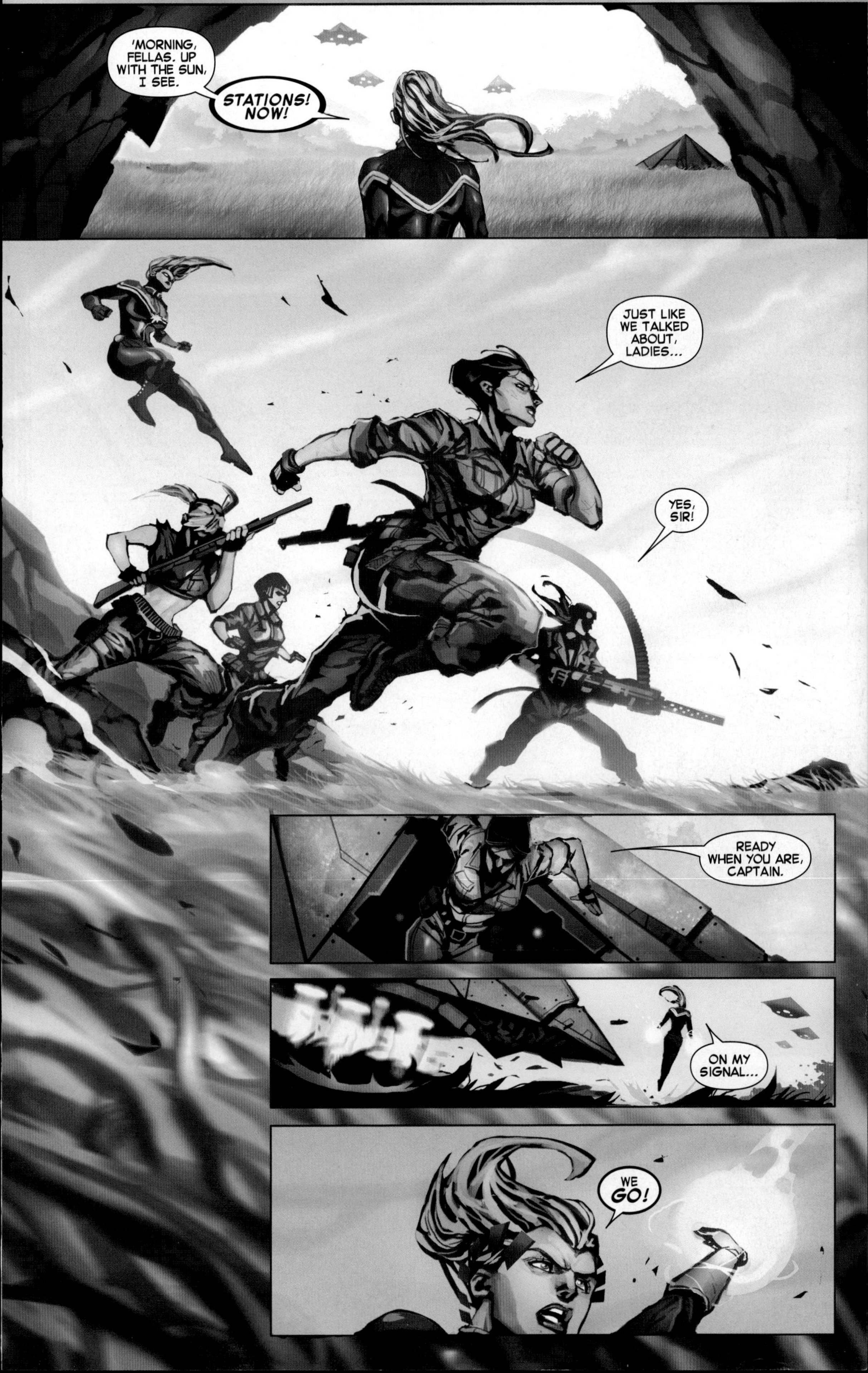
'MORNING, FELLAS. UP WITH THE SUN, I SEE.
STATIONS! NOW!
JUST LIKE WE TALKED ABOUT, LADIES...
YES, SIR!
READY WHEN YOU ARE, CAPTAIN.
ON MY SIGNAL...
WE GO!

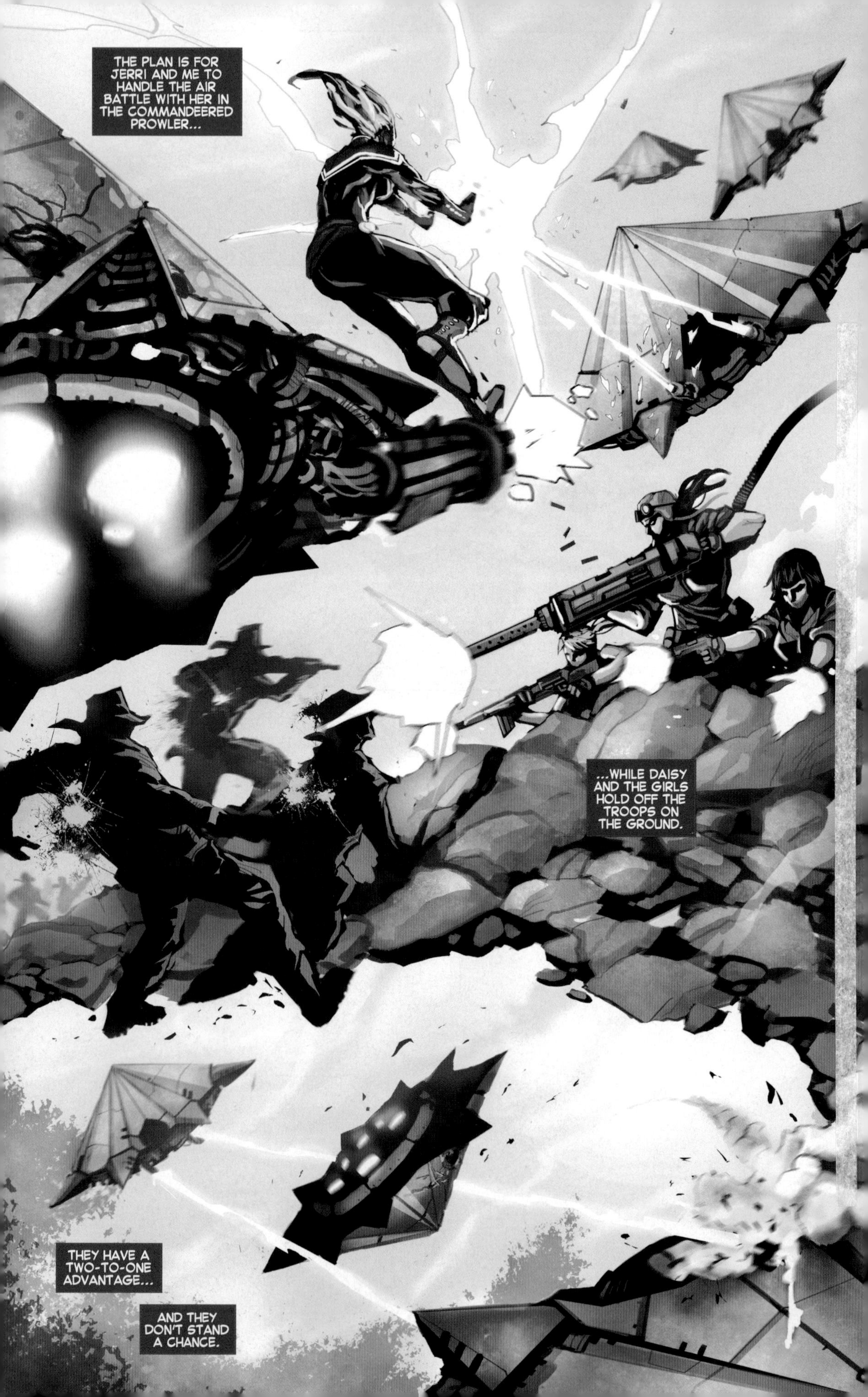
THE PLAN IS FOR JERRI AND ME TO HANDLE THE AIR BATTLE WITH HER IN THE COMMANDEERED PROWLER...
...WHILE DAISY AND THE GIRLS HOLD OFF THE TROOPS ON THE GROUND.
THEY HAVE A TWO-TO-ONE ADVANTAGE...
AND THEY DON'T STAND A CHANCE.

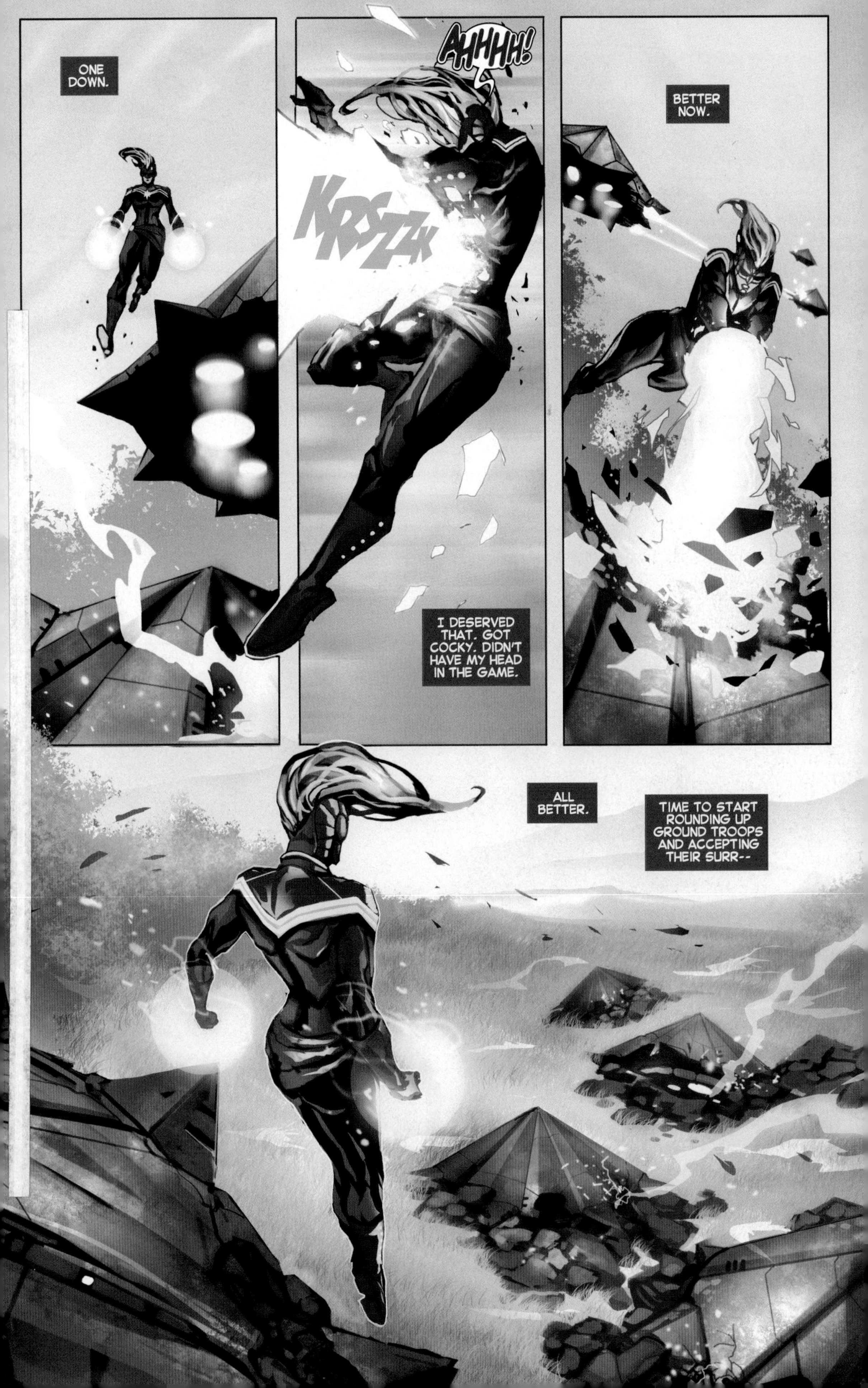
ONE DOWN.
AHHHH!
KRSZZK
I DESERVED THAT. GOT COCKY. DIDN'T HAVE MY HEAD IN THE GAME.
BETTER NOW.
ALL BETTER.
TIME TO START ROUNDING UP GROUND TROOPS AND ACCEPTING THEIR SURR--

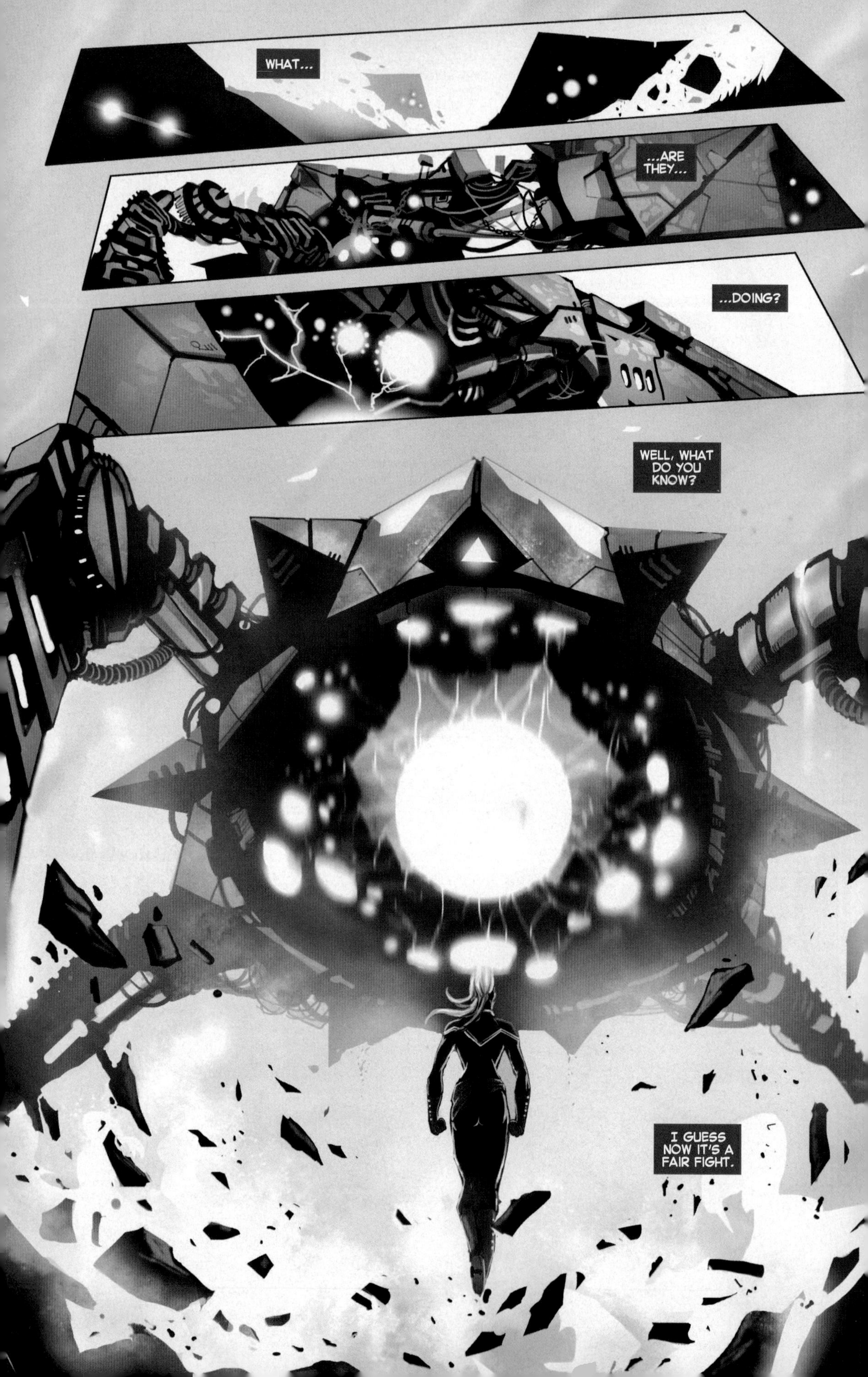
WHAT...
...ARE THEY...
...DOING?
WELL, WHAT DO YOU KNOW?
I GUESS NOW IT'S A FAIR FIGHT.

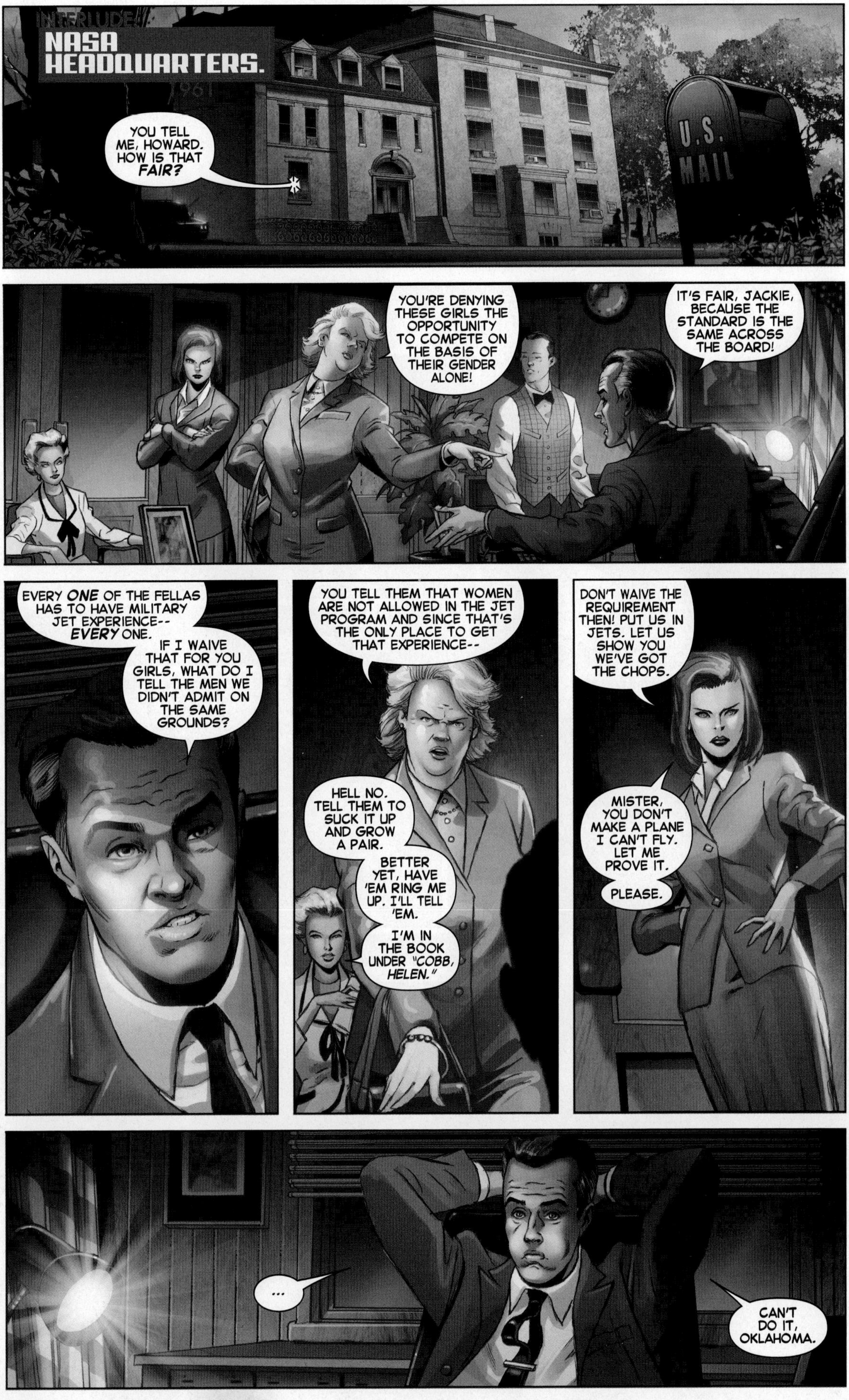
INTERLUDE:
NASA HEADQUARTERS.
1961
YOU TELL ME, HOWARD. HOW IS THAT FAIR?
U.S. MAIL
YOU'RE DENYING THESE GIRLS THE OPPORTUNITY TO COMPETE ON THE BASIS OF THEIR GENDER ALONE!
IT'S FAIR, JACKIE, BECAUSE THE STANDARD IS THE SAME ACROSS THE BOARD!
EVERY ONE OF THE FELLAS HAS TO HAVE MILITARY JET EXPERIENCE-- EVERY ONE.
IF I WAIVE THAT FOR YOU GIRLS, WHAT DO I TELL THE MEN WE DIDN'T ADMIT ON THE SAME GROUNDS?
YOU TELL THEM THAT WOMEN ARE NOT ALLOWED IN THE JET PROGRAM AND SINCE THAT'S THE ONLY PLACE TO GET THAT EXPERIENCE--
HELL NO. TELL THEM TO SUCK IT UP AND GROW A PAIR.
BETTER YET, HAVE 'EM RING ME UP. I'LL TELL 'EM.
I'M IN THE BOOK UNDER "COBB, HELEN."
DON'T WAIVE THE REQUIREMENT THEN! PUT US IN JETS. LET US SHOW YOU WE'VE GOT THE CHOPS.
MISTER, YOU DON'T MAKE A PLANE I CAN'T FLY. LET ME PROVE IT.
PLEASE.
...
CAN'T DO IT, OKLAHOMA.

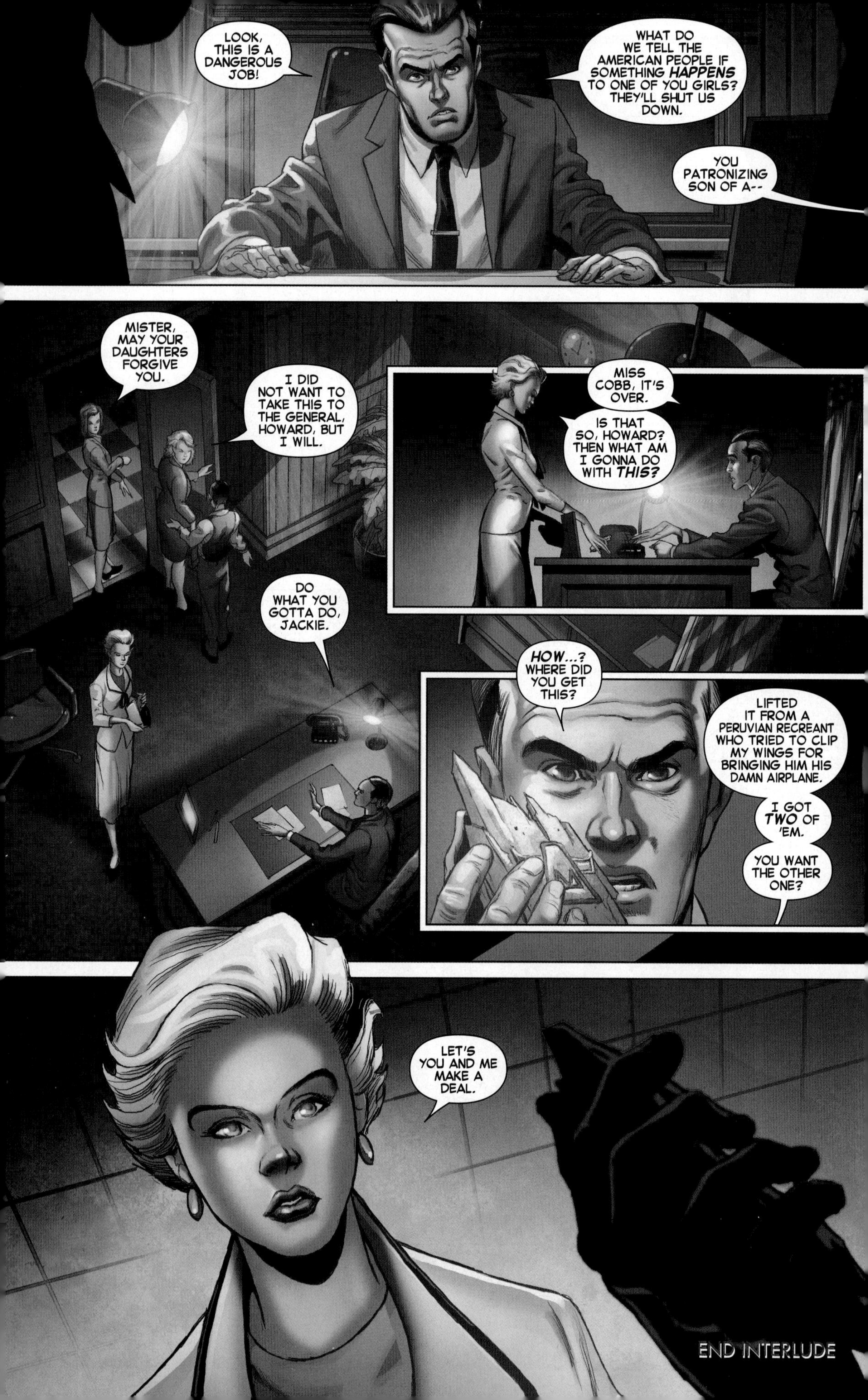
LOOK, THIS IS A DANGEROUS JOB!
WHAT DO WE TELL THE AMERICAN PEOPLE IF SOMETHING HAPPENS TO ONE OF YOU GIRLS? THEY'LL SHUT US DOWN.
YOU PATRONIZING SON OF A--
MISTER, MAY YOUR DAUGHTERS FORGIVE YOU.
I DID NOT WANT TO TAKE THIS TO THE GENERAL, HOWARD, BUT I WILL.
DO WHAT YOU GOTTA DO, JACKIE.
MISS COBB, IT'S OVER.
IS THAT SO, HOWARD? THEN WHAT AM I GONNA DO WITH THIS?
HOW...? WHERE DID YOU GET THIS?
LIFTED IT FROM A PERUVIAN RECREANT WHO TRIED TO CLIP MY WINGS FOR BRINGING HIM HIS DAMN AIRPLANE.
I GOT TWO OF 'EM.
YOU WANT THE OTHER ONE?
LET'S YOU AND ME MAKE A DEAL.
END INTERLUDE

ARCHIVE
#MAR1970-58

The DAILY BUGLE Sunday Color Supplement

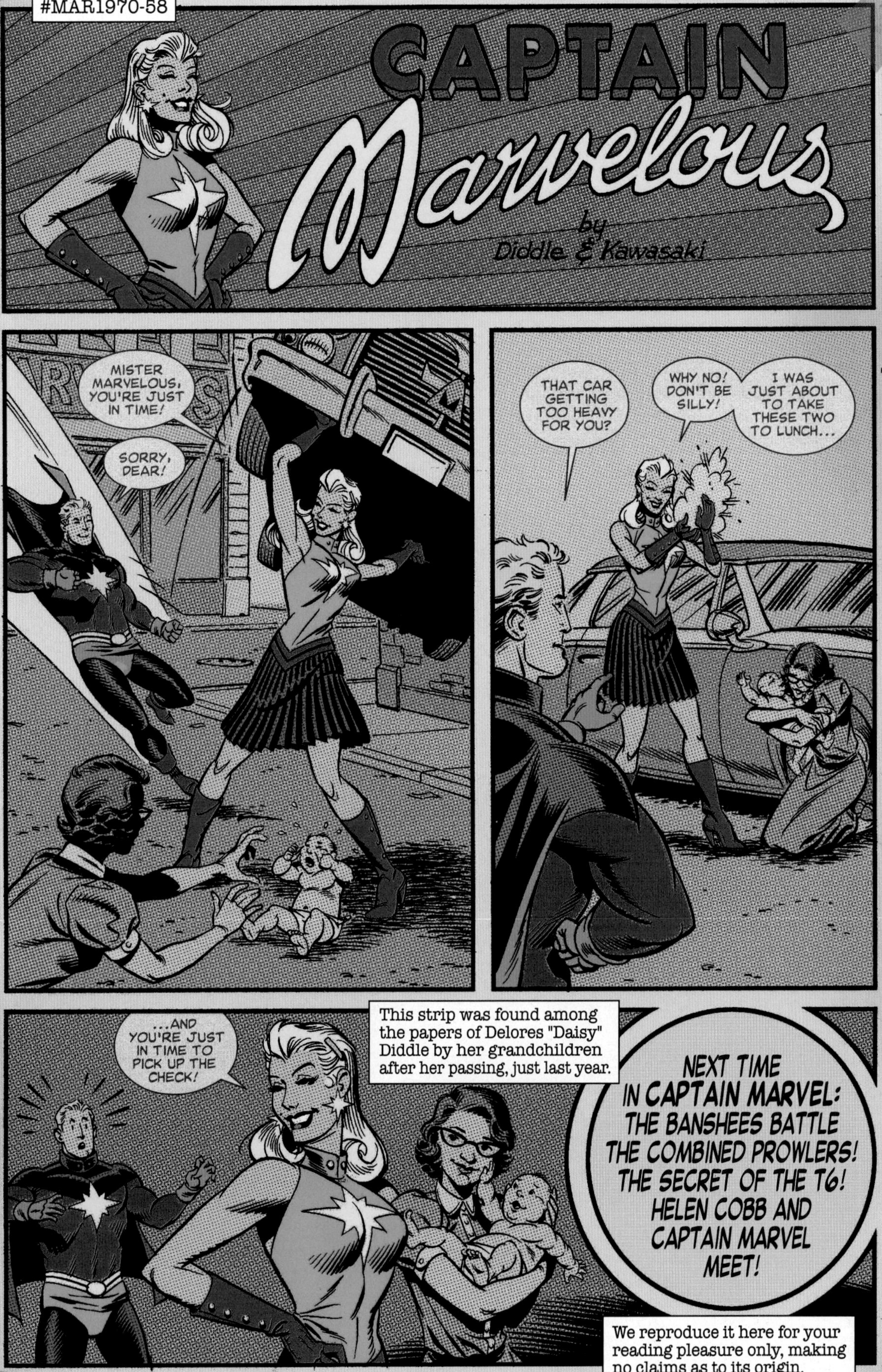
CAPTAIN Marvelous
by Diddle & Kawasaki
MISTER MARVELOUS, YOU'RE JUST IN TIME!
SORRY, DEAR!
THAT CAR GETTING TOO HEAVY FOR YOU?
WHY NO! DON'T BE SILLY!
I WAS JUST ABOUT TO TAKE THESE TWO TO LUNCH...
...AND YOU'RE JUST IN TIME TO PICK UP THE CHECK!
This strip was found among the papers of Delores "Daisy" Diddle by her grandchildren after her passing, just last year.
NEXT TIME IN CAPTAIN MARVEL: THE BANSHEES BATTLE THE COMBINED PROWLERS! THE SECRET OF THE T6! HELEN COBB AND CAPTAIN MARVEL MEET!
We reproduce it here for your reading pleasure only, making no claims as to its origin.

Tomorrow's Color Feature—"WAVES in War," by Richard M. Fletcher

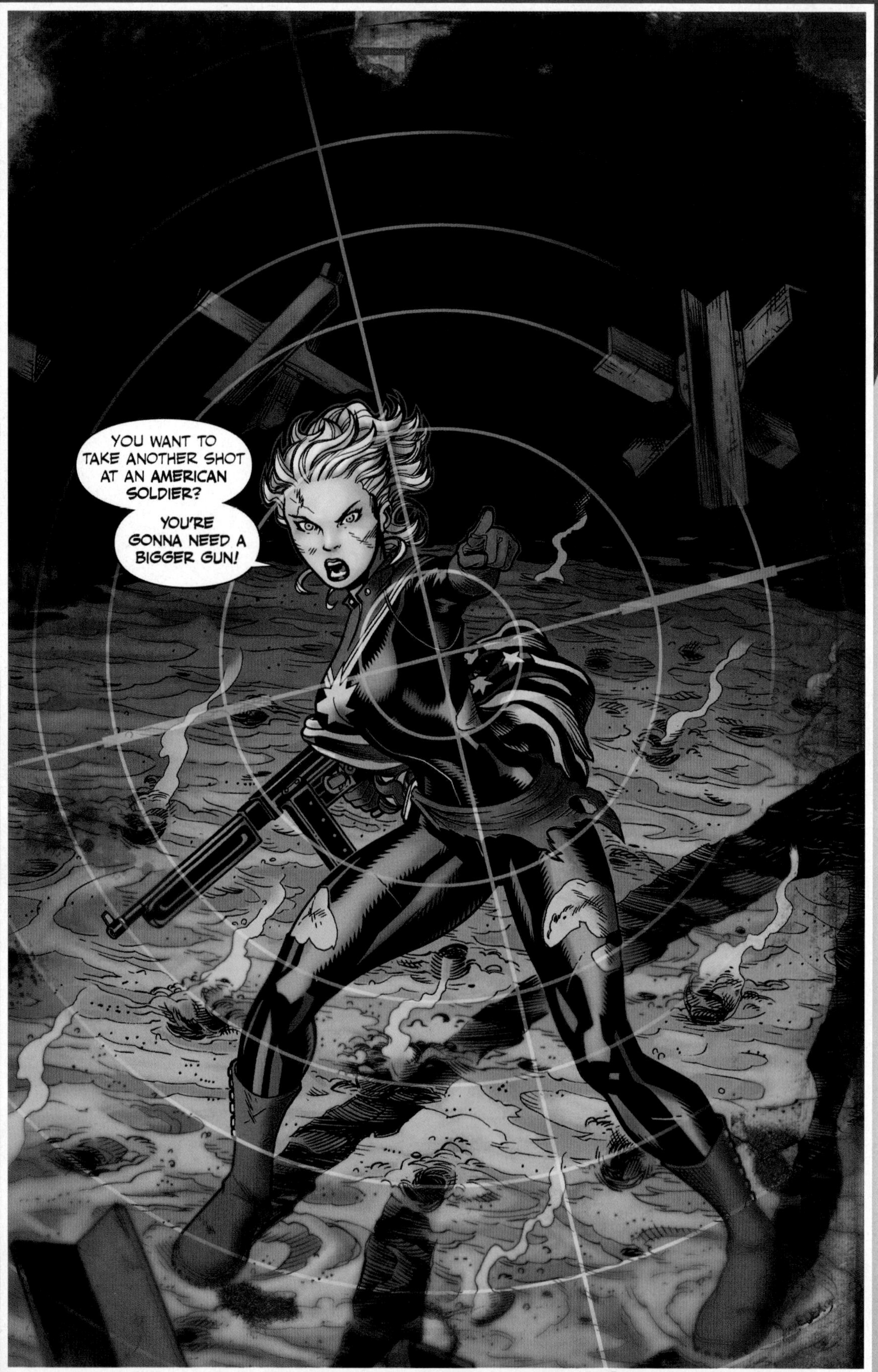
YOU WANT TO TAKE ANOTHER SHOT AT AN AMERICAN SOLDIER?
YOU'RE GONNA NEED A BIGGER GUN!

FOUR

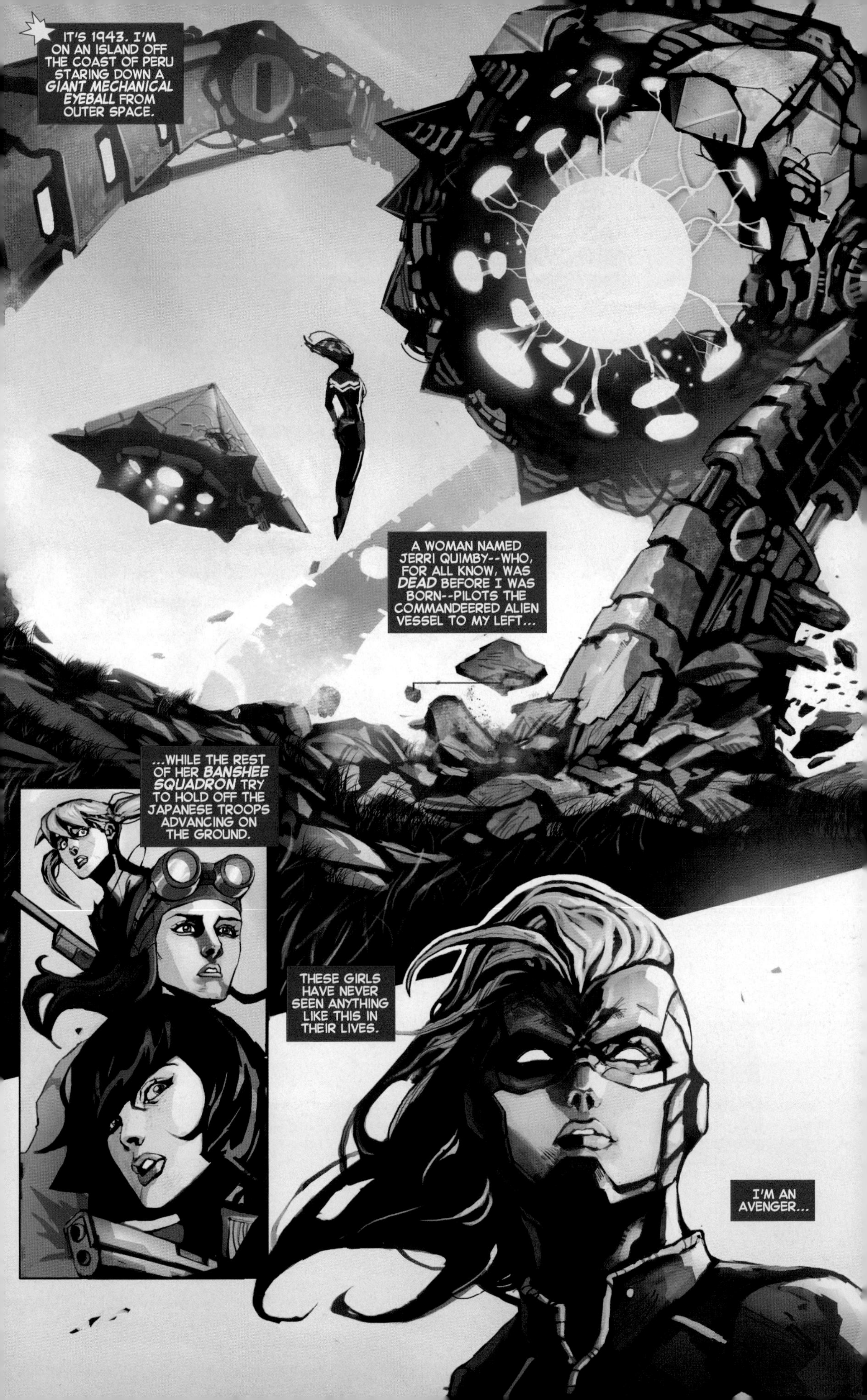
IT'S 1943. I'M ON AN ISLAND OFF THE COAST OF PERU STARING DOWN A GIANT MECHANICAL EYEBALL FROM OUTER SPACE.
A WOMAN NAMED JERRI QUIMBY--WHO, FOR ALL KNOW, WAS DEAD BEFORE I WAS BORN--PILOTS THE COMMANDEERED ALIEN VESSEL TO MY LEFT...
...WHILE THE REST OF HER BANSHEE SQUADRON TRY TO HOLD OFF THE JAPANESE TROOPS ADVANCING ON THE GROUND.
THESE GIRLS HAVE NEVER SEEN ANYTHING LIKE THIS IN THEIR LIVES.
I'M AN AVENGER...

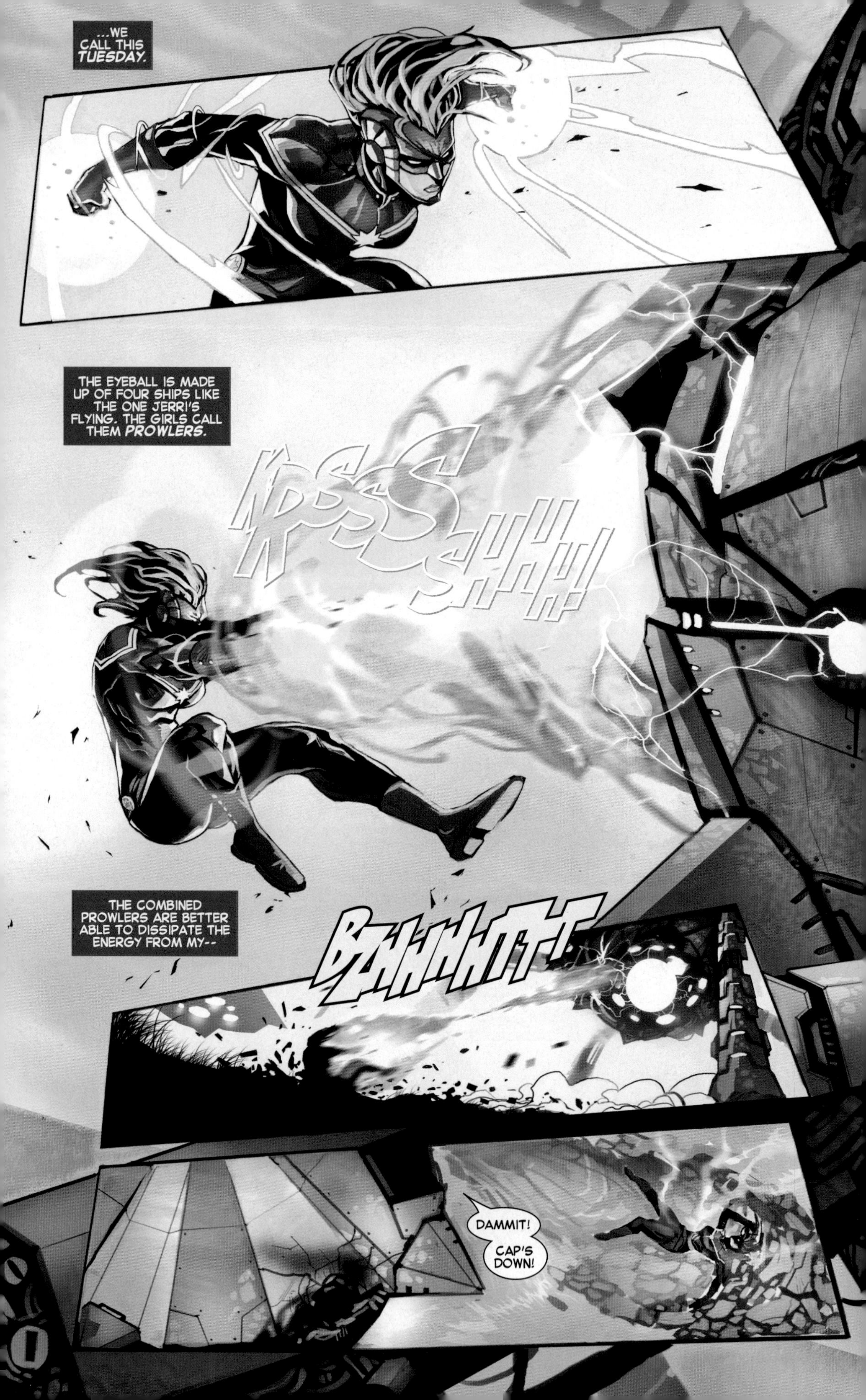
...WE CALL THIS *TUESDAY.*
THE EYEBALL IS MADE UP OF FOUR SHIPS LIKE THE ONE JERRI'S FLYING. THE GIRLS CALL THEM *PROWLERS.*
KRSSSSHHHH!
THE COMBINED PROWLERS ARE BETTER ABLE TO DISSIPATE THE ENERGY FROM MY--
BZHHHHTTT
DAMMIT!
CAP'S DOWN!

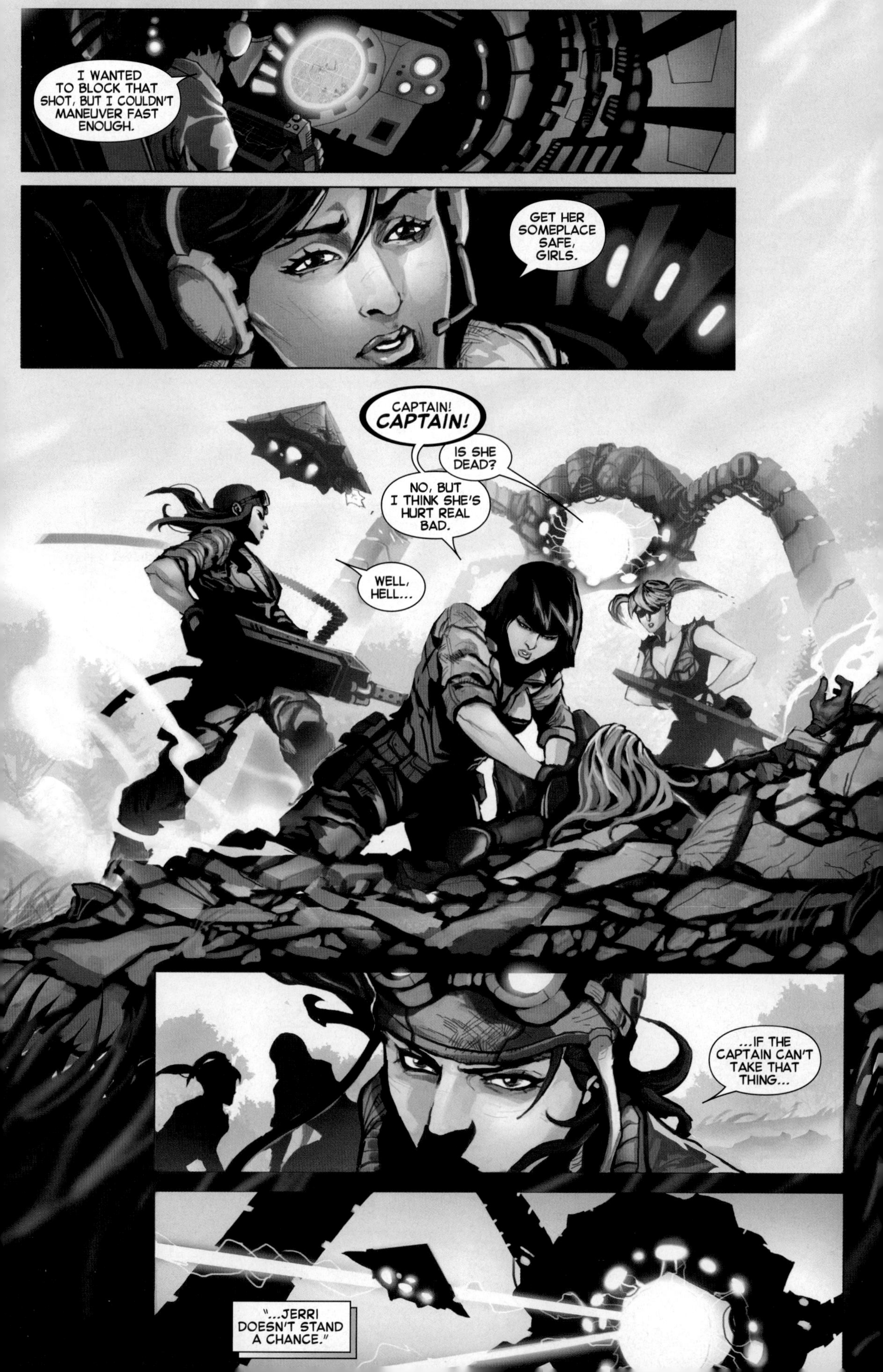
I WANTED TO BLOCK THAT SHOT, BUT I COULDN'T MANEUVER FAST ENOUGH.
GET HER SOMEPLACE SAFE, GIRLS.
CAPTAIN! CAPTAIN!
IS SHE DEAD?
NO, BUT I THINK SHE'S HURT REAL BAD.
WELL, HELL...
...IF THE CAPTAIN CAN'T TAKE THAT THING...
"...JERRI DOESN'T STAND A CHANCE."

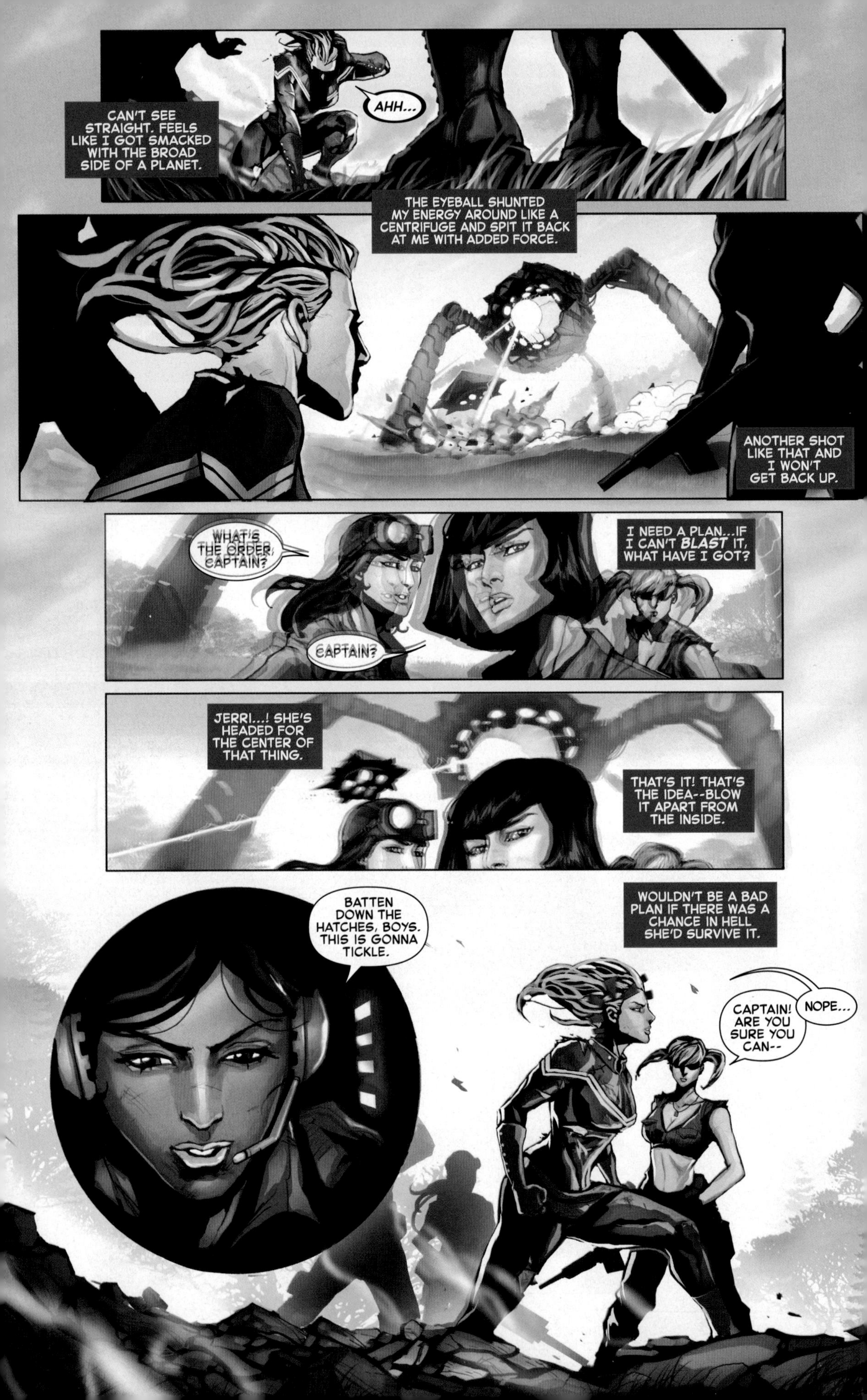

CAN'T SEE STRAIGHT. FEELS LIKE I GOT SMACKED WITH THE BROAD SIDE OF A PLANET.
AHH...
THE EYEBALL SHUNTED MY ENERGY AROUND LIKE A CENTRIFUGE AND SPIT IT BACK AT ME WITH ADDED FORCE.
ANOTHER SHOT LIKE THAT AND I WON'T GET BACK UP.
WHAT'S THE ORDER, CAPTAIN?
CAPTAIN?
I NEED A PLAN...IF I CAN'T BLAST IT, WHAT HAVE I GOT?
JERRI...! SHE'S HEADED FOR THE CENTER OF THAT THING.
THAT'S IT! THAT'S THE IDEA--BLOW IT APART FROM THE INSIDE.
BATTEN DOWN THE HATCHES, BOYS. THIS IS GONNA TICKLE.
WOULDN'T BE A BAD PLAN IF THERE WAS A CHANCE IN HELL SHE'D SURVIVE IT.
CAPTAIN! ARE YOU SURE YOU CAN--
NOPE...

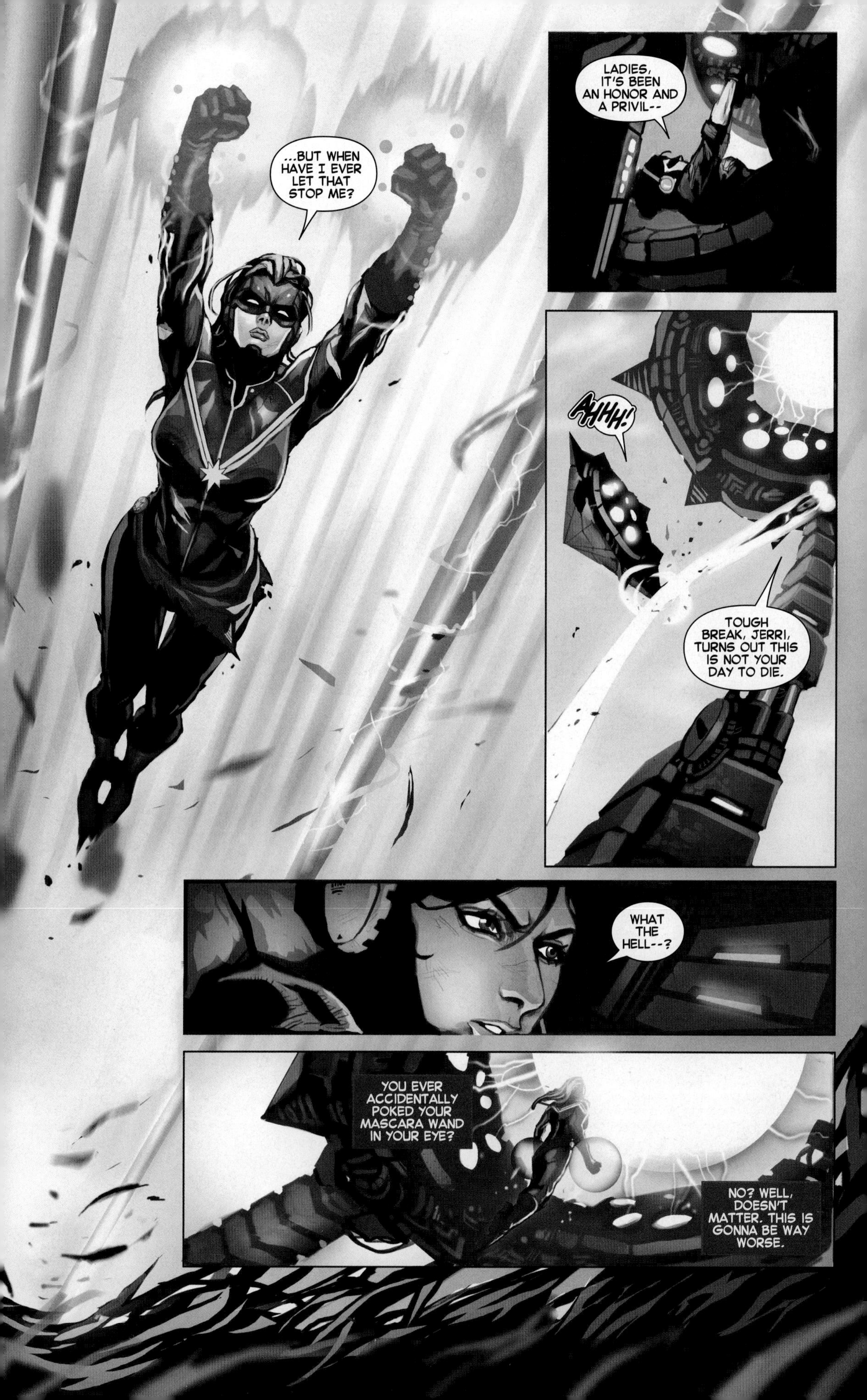
...BUT WHEN HAVE I EVER LET THAT STOP ME?
LADIES, IT'S BEEN AN HONOR AND A PRIVIL--
AHHH!
TOUGH BREAK, JERRI, TURNS OUT THIS IS NOT YOUR DAY TO DIE.
WHAT THE HELL--?
YOU EVER ACCIDENTALLY POKED YOUR MASCARA WAND IN YOUR EYE?
NO? WELL, DOESN'T MATTER. THIS IS GONNA BE WAY WORSE.

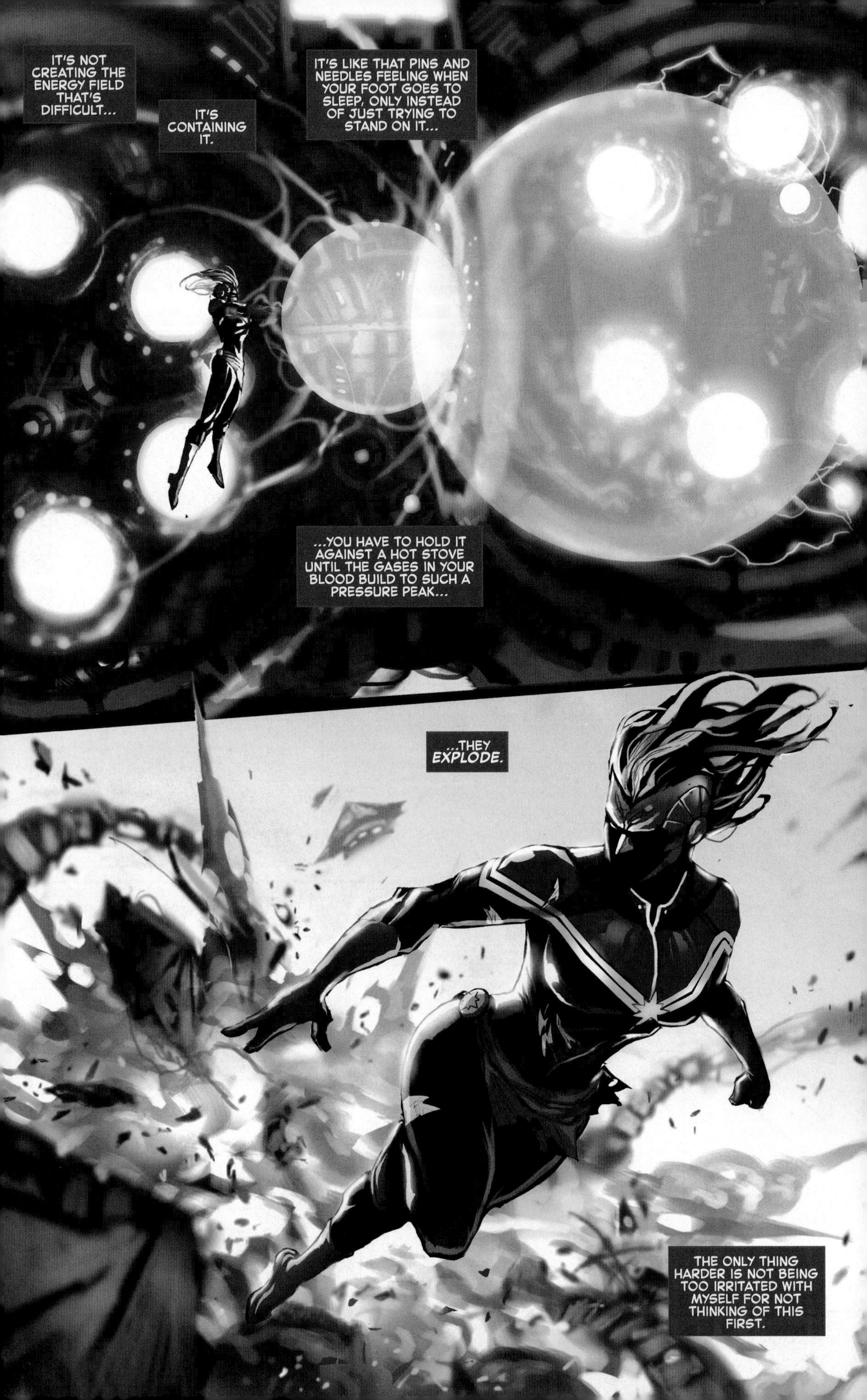
IT'S NOT CREATING THE ENERGY FIELD THAT'S DIFFICULT...
IT'S CONTAINING IT.
IT'S LIKE THAT PINS AND NEEDLES FEELING WHEN YOUR FOOT GOES TO SLEEP, ONLY INSTEAD OF JUST TRYING TO STAND ON IT...
...YOU HAVE TO HOLD IT AGAINST A HOT STOVE UNTIL THE GASES IN YOUR BLOOD BUILD TO SUCH A PRESSURE PEAK...
...THEY *EXPLODE.*
THE ONLY THING HARDER IS NOT BEING TOO IRRITATED WITH MYSELF FOR NOT THINKING OF THIS FIRST.

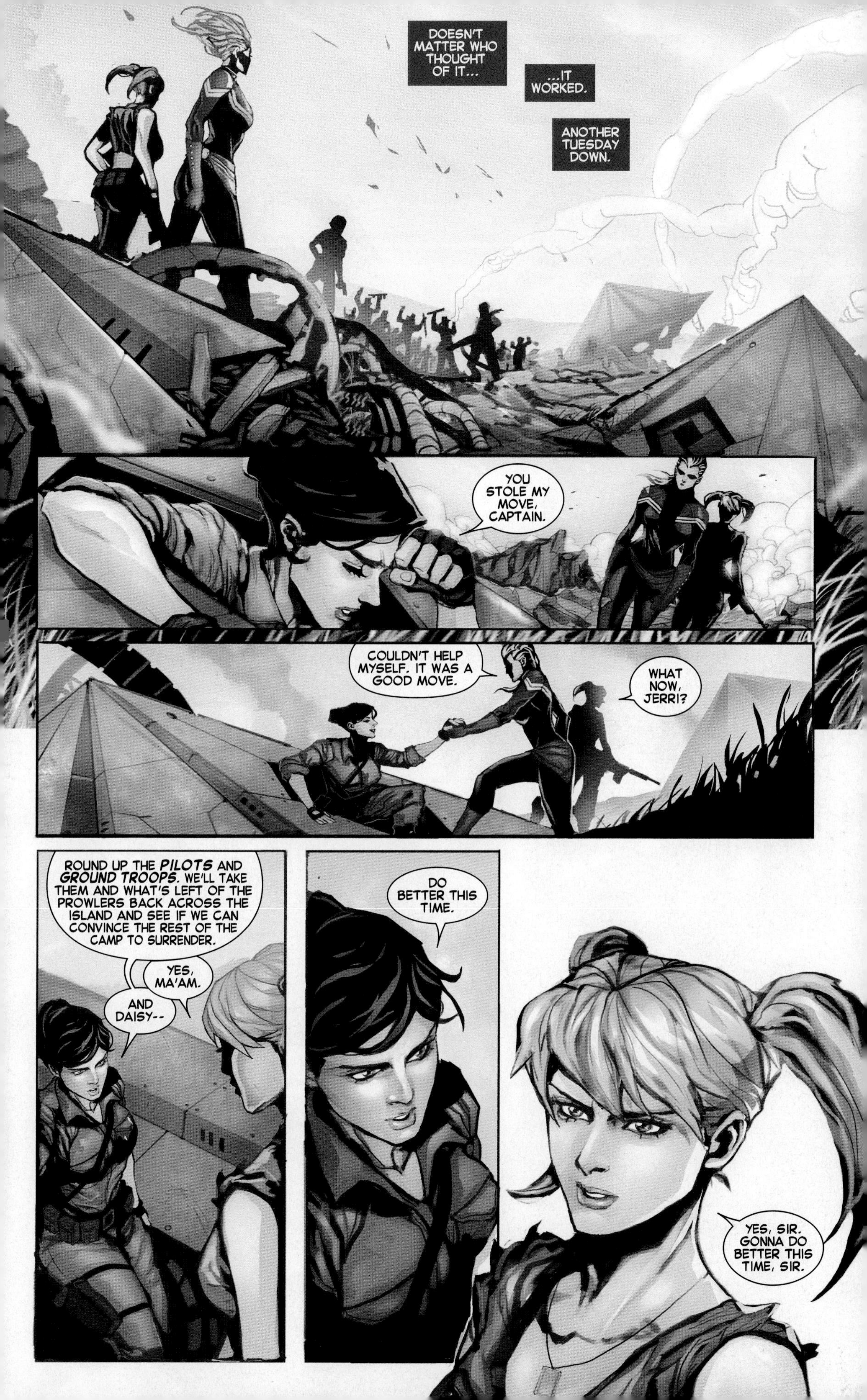
DOESN'T MATTER WHO THOUGHT OF IT...
...IT WORKED.
ANOTHER TUESDAY DOWN.
YOU STOLE MY MOVE, CAPTAIN.
COULDN'T HELP MYSELF. IT WAS A GOOD MOVE.
WHAT NOW, JERRI?
ROUND UP THE *PILOTS* AND *GROUND TROOPS.* WE'LL TAKE THEM AND WHAT'S LEFT OF THE PROWLERS BACK ACROSS THE ISLAND AND SEE IF WE CAN CONVINCE THE REST OF THE CAMP TO SURRENDER.
YES, MA'AM.
AND DAISY--
DO BETTER THIS TIME.
YES, SIR. GONNA DO BETTER THIS TIME, SIR.

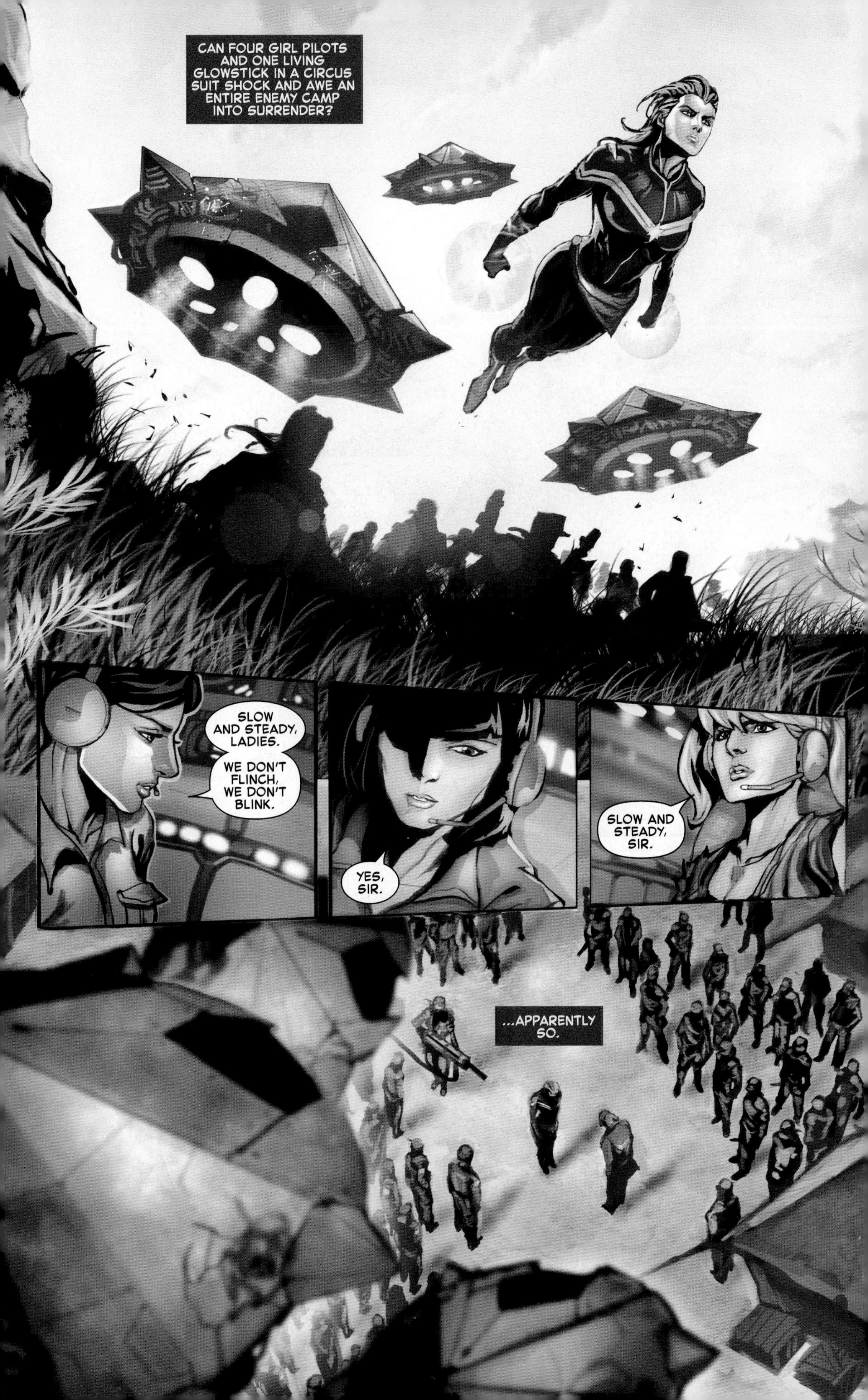
CAN FOUR GIRL PILOTS AND ONE LIVING GLOWSTICK IN A CIRCUS SUIT SHOCK AND AWE AN ENTIRE ENEMY CAMP INTO SURRENDER?
SLOW AND STEADY, LADIES.
WE DON'T FLINCH, WE DON'T BLINK.
YES, SIR.
SLOW AND STEADY, SIR.
...APPARENTLY SO.

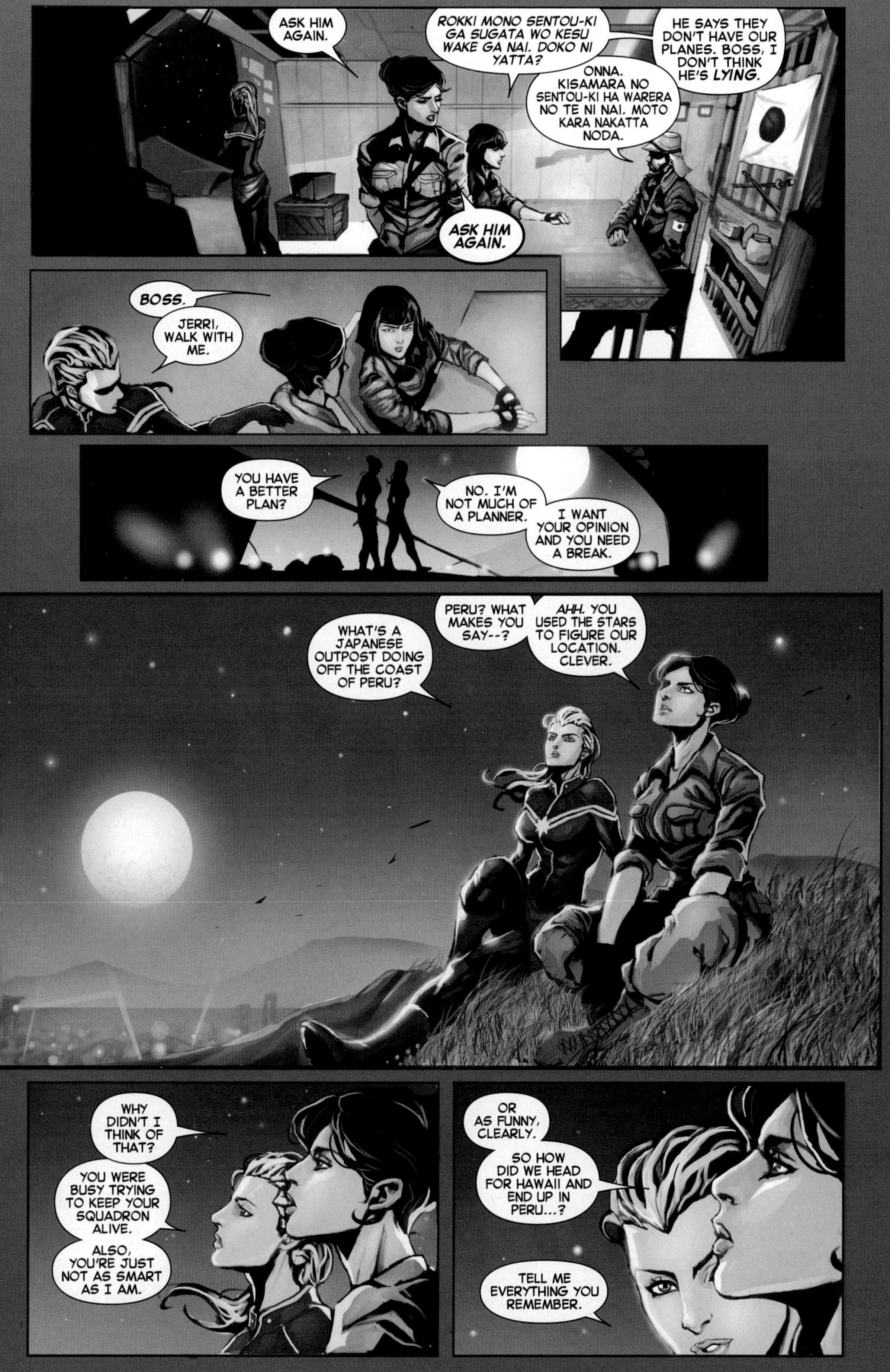
ASK HIM AGAIN.
ROKKI MONO SENTOU-KI GA SUGATA WO KESU WAKE GA NAI. DOKO NI YATTA?
HE SAYS THEY DON'T HAVE OUR PLANES. BOSS, I DON'T THINK HE'S LYING.
ONNA. KISAMARA NO SENTOU-KI HA WARERA NO TE NI NAI. MOTO KARA NAKATTA NODA.
ASK HIM AGAIN.
BOSS.
JERRI, WALK WITH ME.
YOU HAVE A BETTER PLAN?
NO. I'M NOT MUCH OF A PLANNER.
I WANT YOUR OPINION AND YOU NEED A BREAK.
WHAT'S A JAPANESE OUTPOST DOING OFF THE COAST OF PERU?
PERU? WHAT MAKES YOU SAY--?
AHH. YOU USED THE STARS TO FIGURE OUR LOCATION. CLEVER.
WHY DIDN'T I THINK OF THAT?
YOU WERE BUSY TRYING TO KEEP YOUR SQUADRON ALIVE.
ALSO, YOU'RE JUST NOT AS SMART AS I AM.
OR AS FUNNY, CLEARLY.
SO HOW DID WE HEAD FOR HAWAII AND END UP IN PERU...?
TELL ME EVERYTHING YOU REMEMBER.

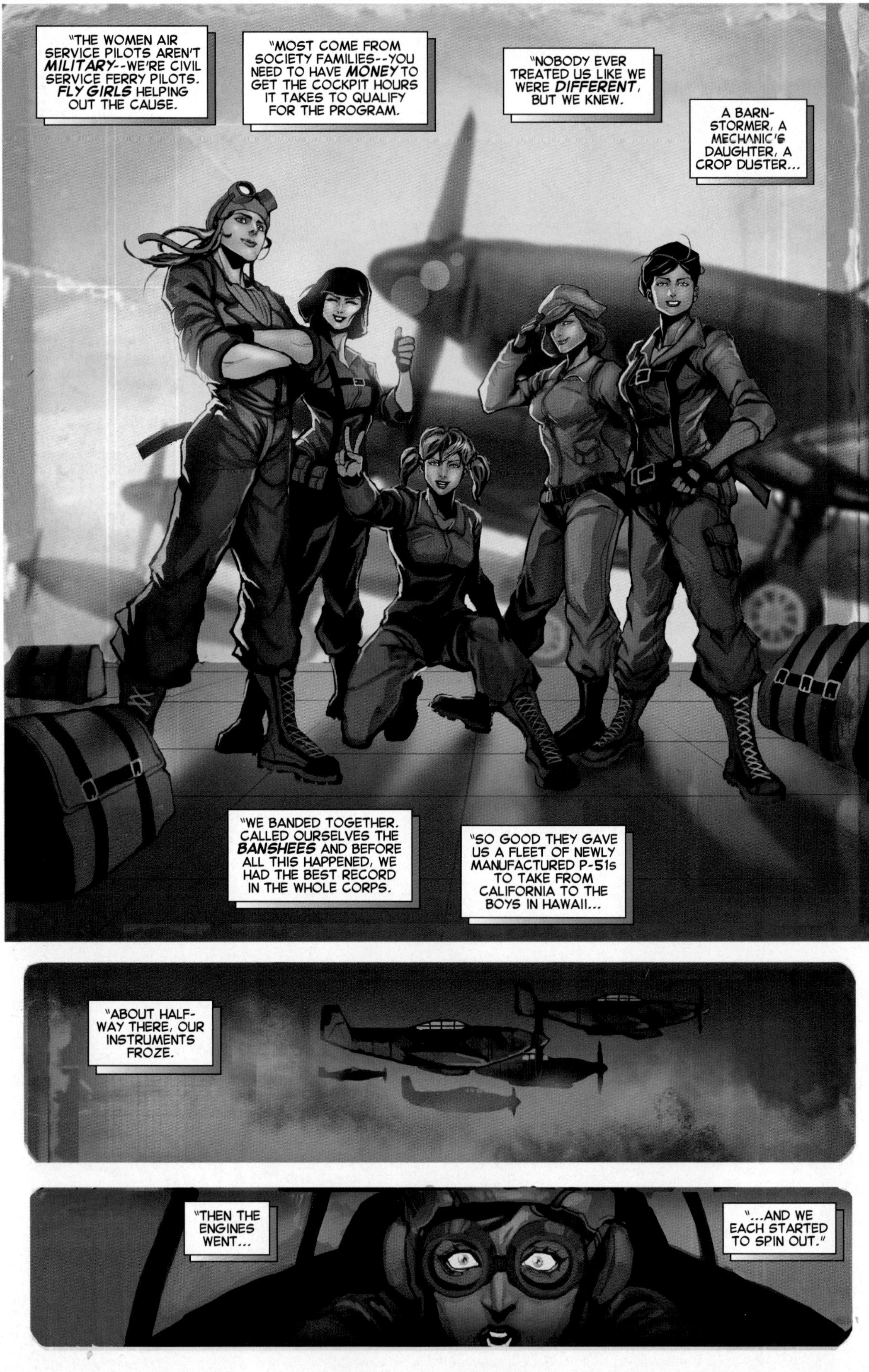
"THE WOMEN AIR SERVICE PILOTS AREN'T MILITARY--WE'RE CIVIL SERVICE FERRY PILOTS. FLY GIRLS HELPING OUT THE CAUSE.
"MOST COME FROM SOCIETY FAMILIES--YOU NEED TO HAVE MONEY TO GET THE COCKPIT HOURS IT TAKES TO QUALIFY FOR THE PROGRAM.
"NOBODY EVER TREATED US LIKE WE WERE DIFFERENT, BUT WE KNEW.
A BARN-STORMER, A MECHANIC'S DAUGHTER, A CROP DUSTER...
"WE BANDED TOGETHER. CALLED OURSELVES THE BANSHEES AND BEFORE ALL THIS HAPPENED, WE HAD THE BEST RECORD IN THE WHOLE CORPS.
"SO GOOD THEY GAVE US A FLEET OF NEWLY MANUFACTURED P-51s TO TAKE FROM CALIFORNIA TO THE BOYS IN HAWAII...
"ABOUT HALF-WAY THERE, OUR INSTRUMENTS FROZE.
"THEN THE ENGINES WENT...
"...AND WE EACH STARTED TO SPIN OUT."

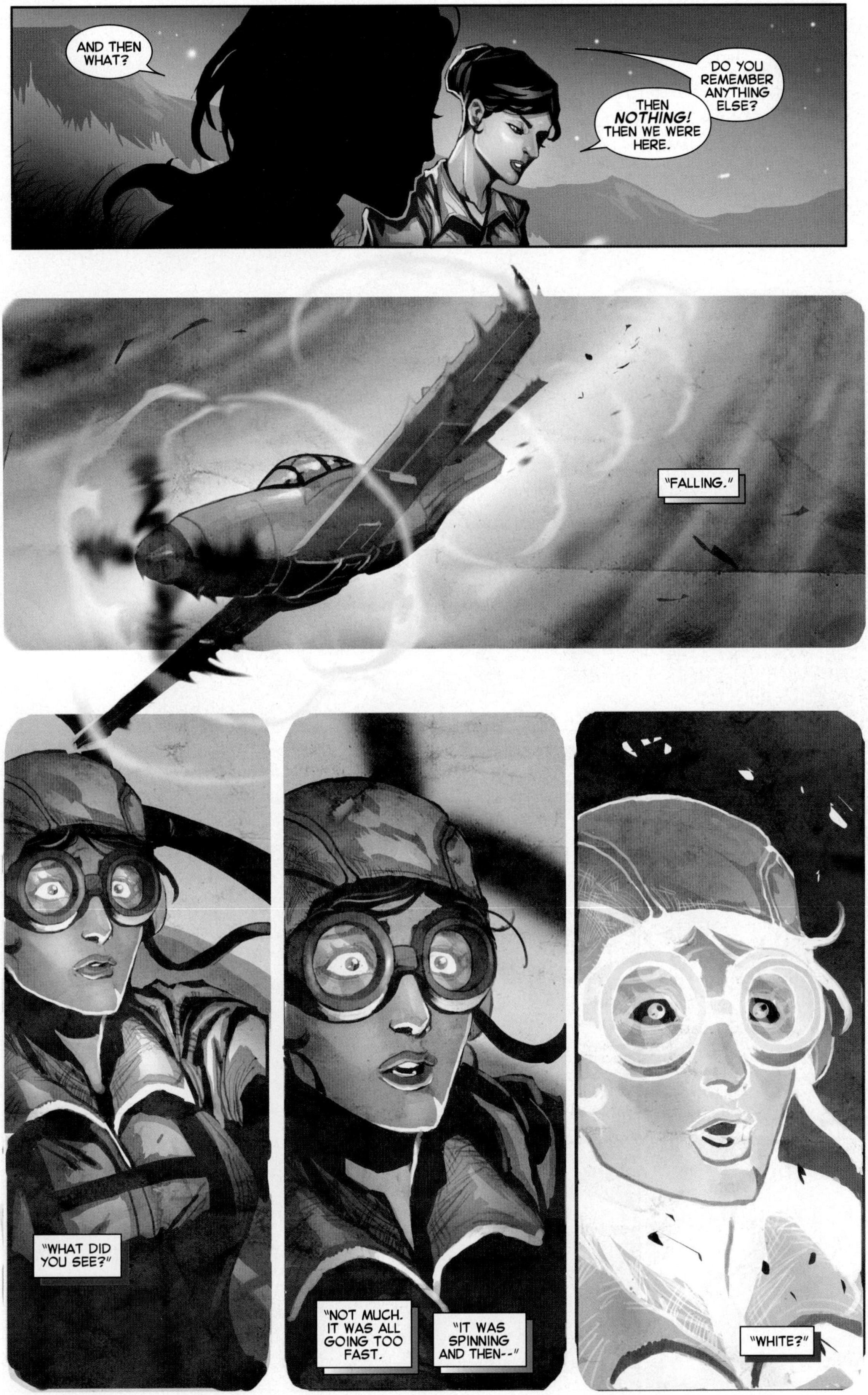
AND THEN WHAT?
DO YOU REMEMBER ANYTHING ELSE?
THEN *NOTHING!* THEN WE WERE HERE.
"FALLING."
"WHAT DID YOU SEE?"
"NOT MUCH. IT WAS ALL GOING TOO FAST.
"IT WAS SPINNING AND THEN--"
"WHITE?"

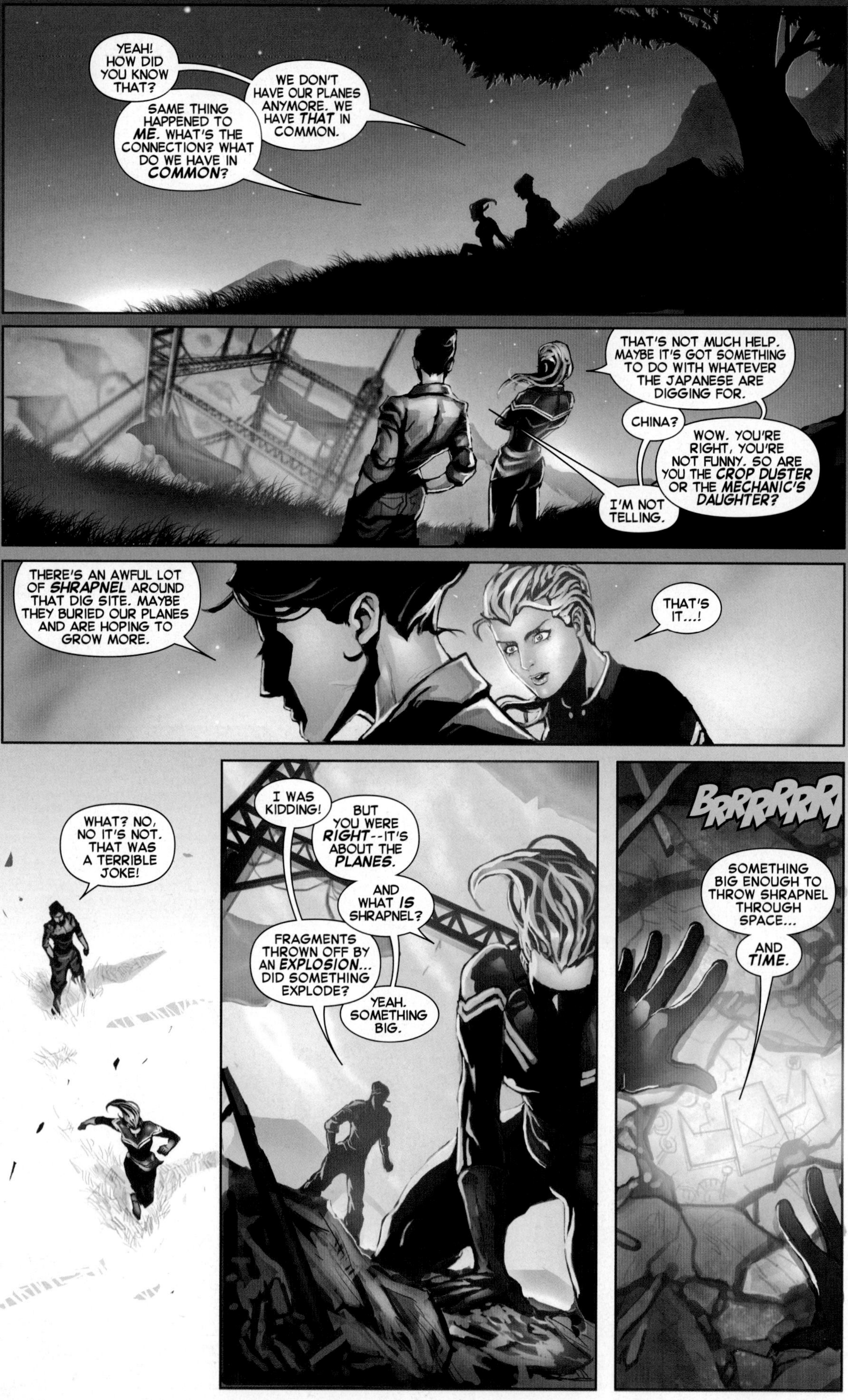
YEAH! HOW DID YOU KNOW THAT?
SAME THING HAPPENED TO ME. WHAT'S THE CONNECTION? WHAT DO WE HAVE IN COMMON?
WE DON'T HAVE OUR PLANES ANYMORE. WE HAVE THAT IN COMMON.
THAT'S NOT MUCH HELP. MAYBE IT'S GOT SOMETHING TO DO WITH WHATEVER THE JAPANESE ARE DIGGING FOR.
CHINA?
WOW. YOU'RE RIGHT, YOU'RE NOT FUNNY. SO ARE YOU THE CROP DUSTER OR THE MECHANIC'S DAUGHTER?
I'M NOT TELLING.
THERE'S AN AWFUL LOT OF SHRAPNEL AROUND THAT DIG SITE. MAYBE THEY BURIED OUR PLANES AND ARE HOPING TO GROW MORE.
THAT'S IT...!
WHAT? NO, NO IT'S NOT. THAT WAS A TERRIBLE JOKE!
I WAS KIDDING!
BUT YOU WERE RIGHT--IT'S ABOUT THE PLANES.
AND WHAT IS SHRAPNEL?
FRAGMENTS THROWN OFF BY AN EXPLOSION... DID SOMETHING EXPLODE?
YEAH. SOMETHING BIG.
BRRRRRRR
SOMETHING BIG ENOUGH TO THROW SHRAPNEL THROUGH SPACE...
AND TIME.

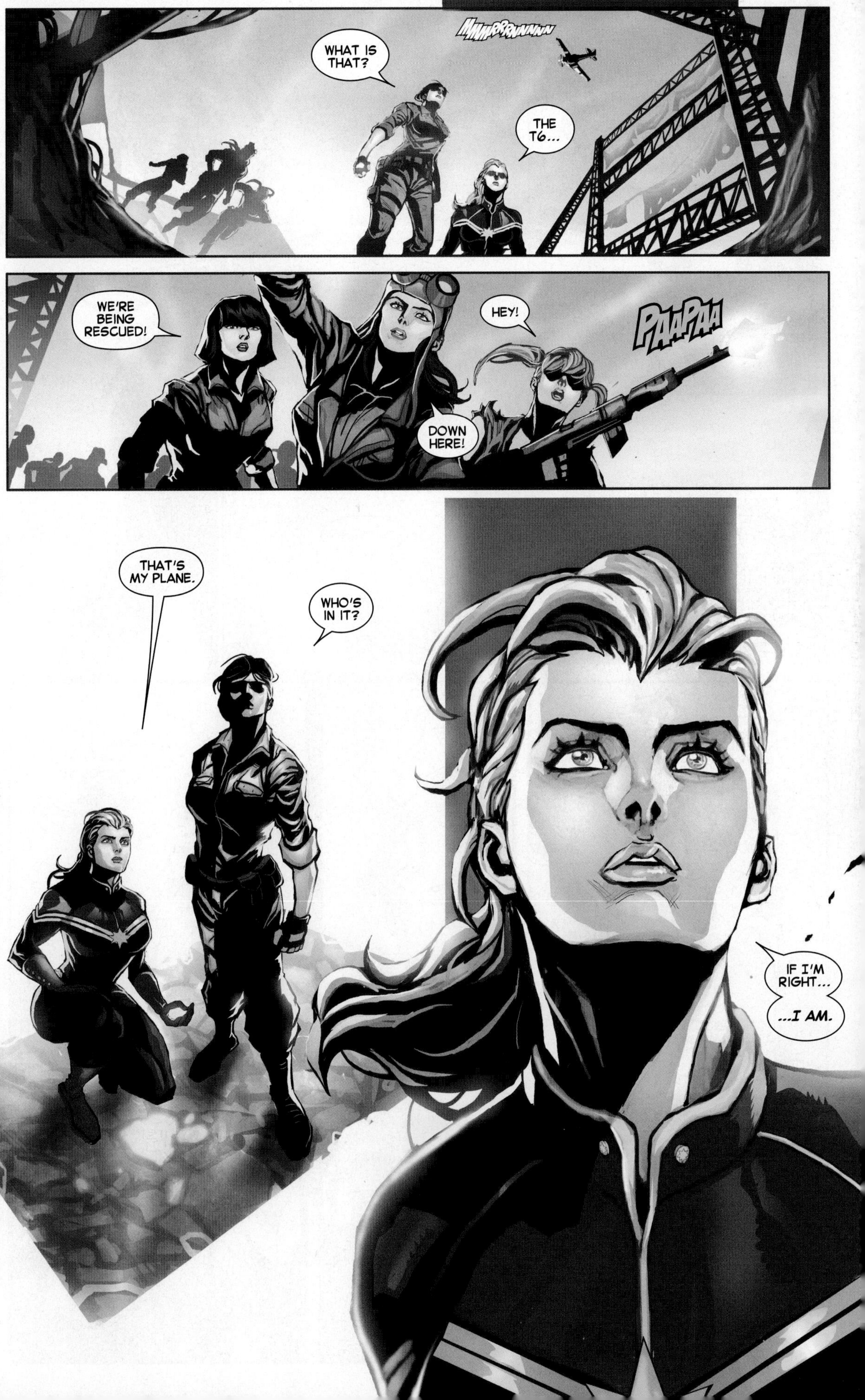
MMMRRRNNNNN
WHAT IS THAT?
THE T6...
WE'RE BEING RESCUED!
HEY!
PAAPAA
DOWN HERE!
THAT'S MY PLANE.
WHO'S IN IT?
IF I'M RIGHT...
...I AM.

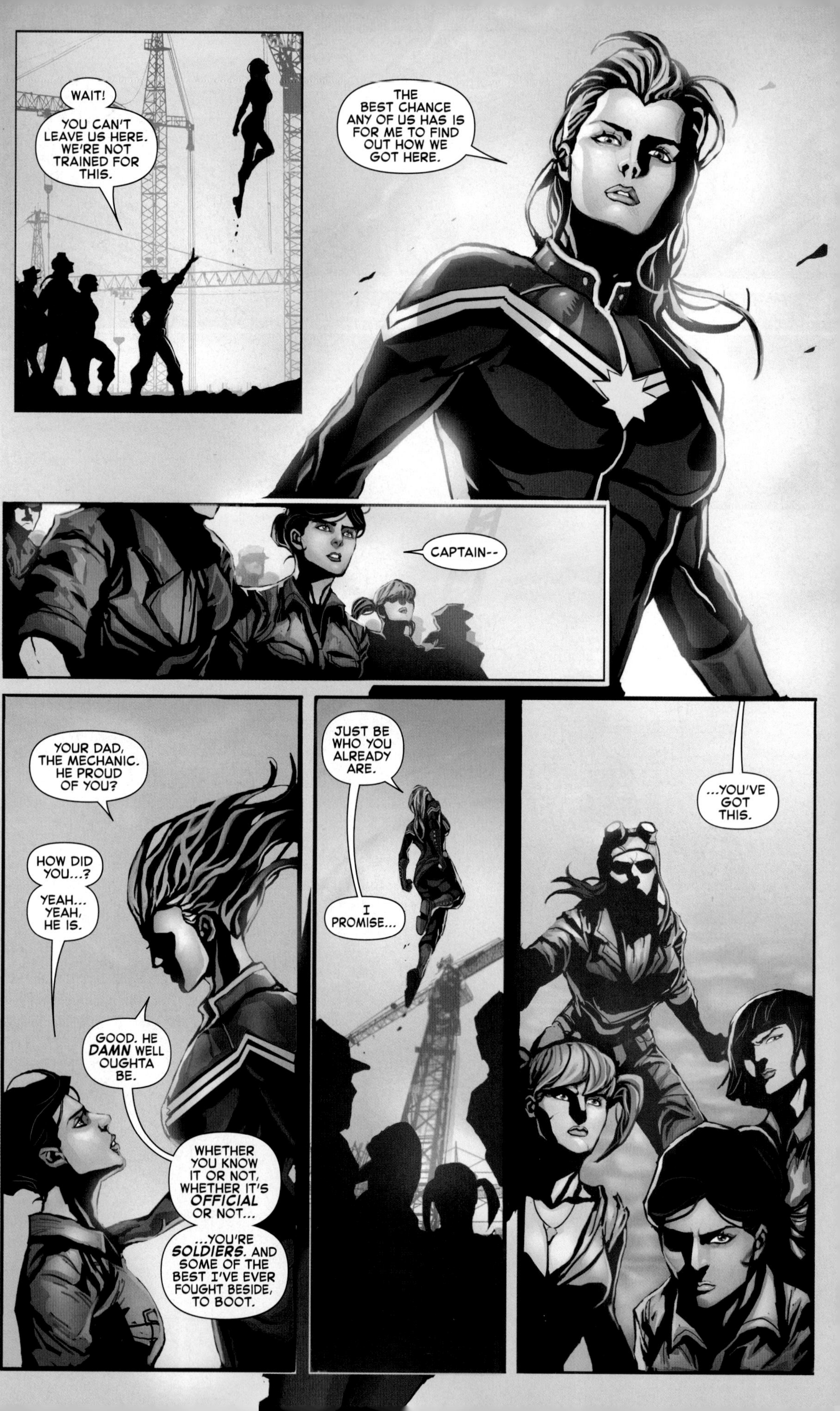
WAIT!
YOU CAN'T LEAVE US HERE. WE'RE NOT TRAINED FOR THIS.
THE BEST CHANCE ANY OF US HAS IS FOR ME TO FIND OUT HOW WE GOT HERE.
CAPTAIN--
YOUR DAD, THE MECHANIC. HE PROUD OF YOU?
HOW DID YOU...?
YEAH... YEAH, HE IS.
GOOD. HE DAMN WELL OUGHTA BE.
WHETHER YOU KNOW IT OR NOT, WHETHER IT'S OFFICIAL OR NOT...
...YOU'RE SOLDIERS. AND SOME OF THE BEST I'VE EVER FOUGHT BESIDE, TO BOOT.
JUST BE WHO YOU ALREADY ARE.
I PROMISE...
...YOU'VE GOT THIS.

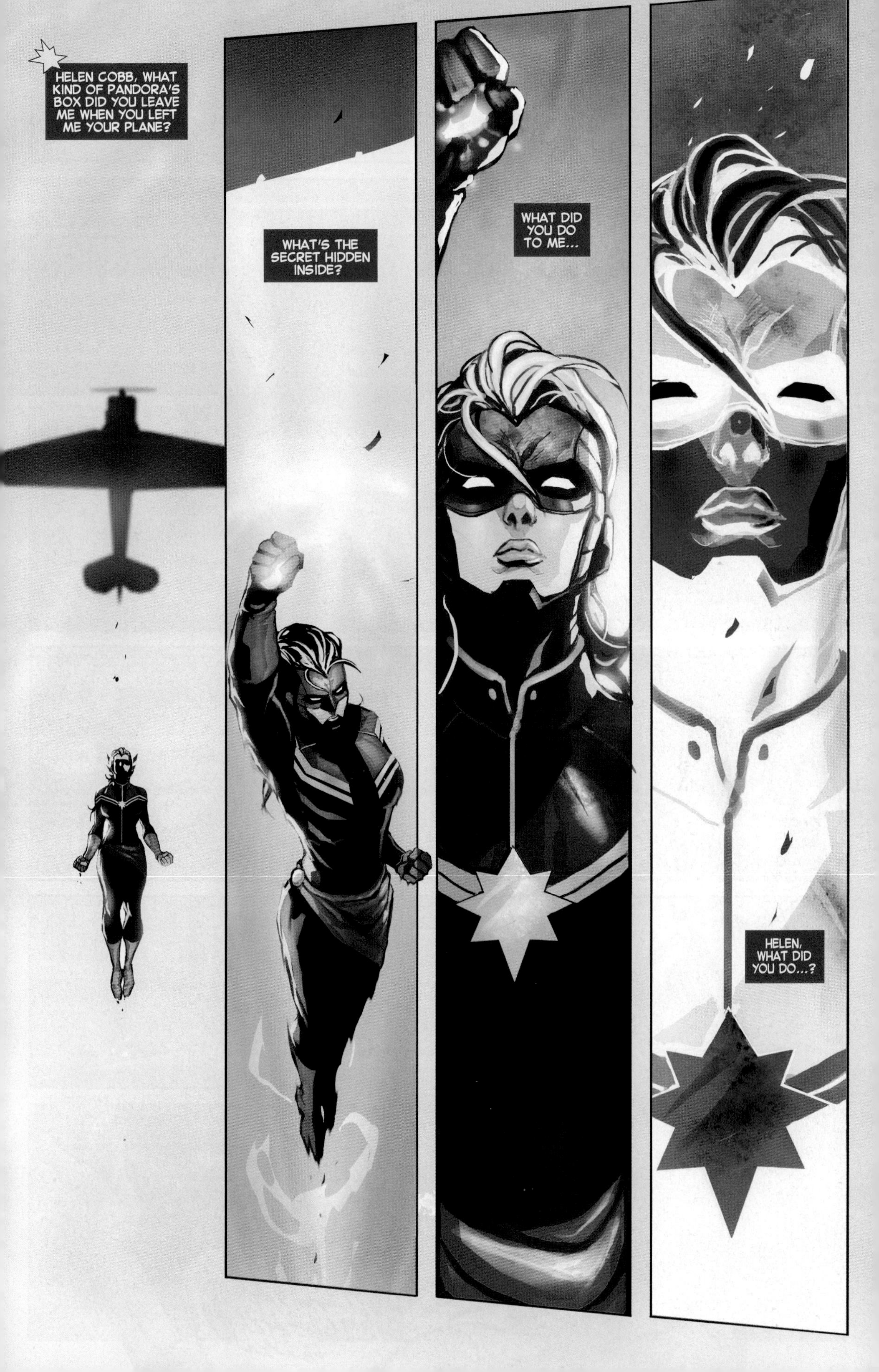
HELEN COBB, WHAT KIND OF PANDORA'S BOX DID YOU LEAVE ME WHEN YOU LEFT ME YOUR PLANE?
WHAT'S THE SECRET HIDDEN INSIDE?
WHAT DID YOU DO TO ME...
HELEN, WHAT DID YOU DO...?

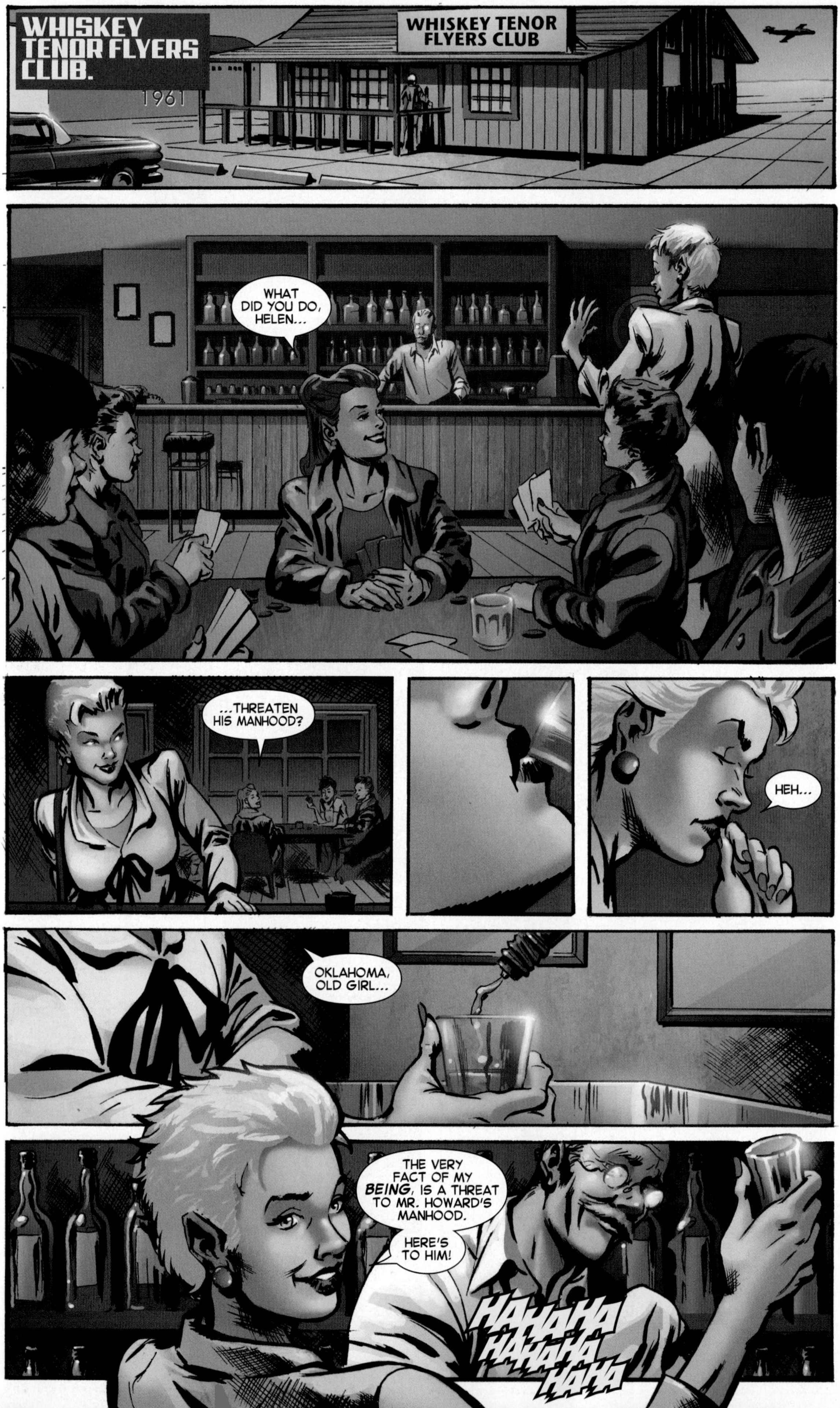
WHISKEY TENOR FLYERS CLUB.
1961
WHISKEY TENOR FLYERS CLUB
WHAT DID YOU DO, HELEN...
...THREATEN HIS MANHOOD?
HEH...
OKLAHOMA, OLD GIRL...
THE VERY FACT OF MY *BEING*, IS A THREAT TO MR. HOWARD'S MANHOOD.
HERE'S TO HIM!
HAHAHA HAHAHA HAHA

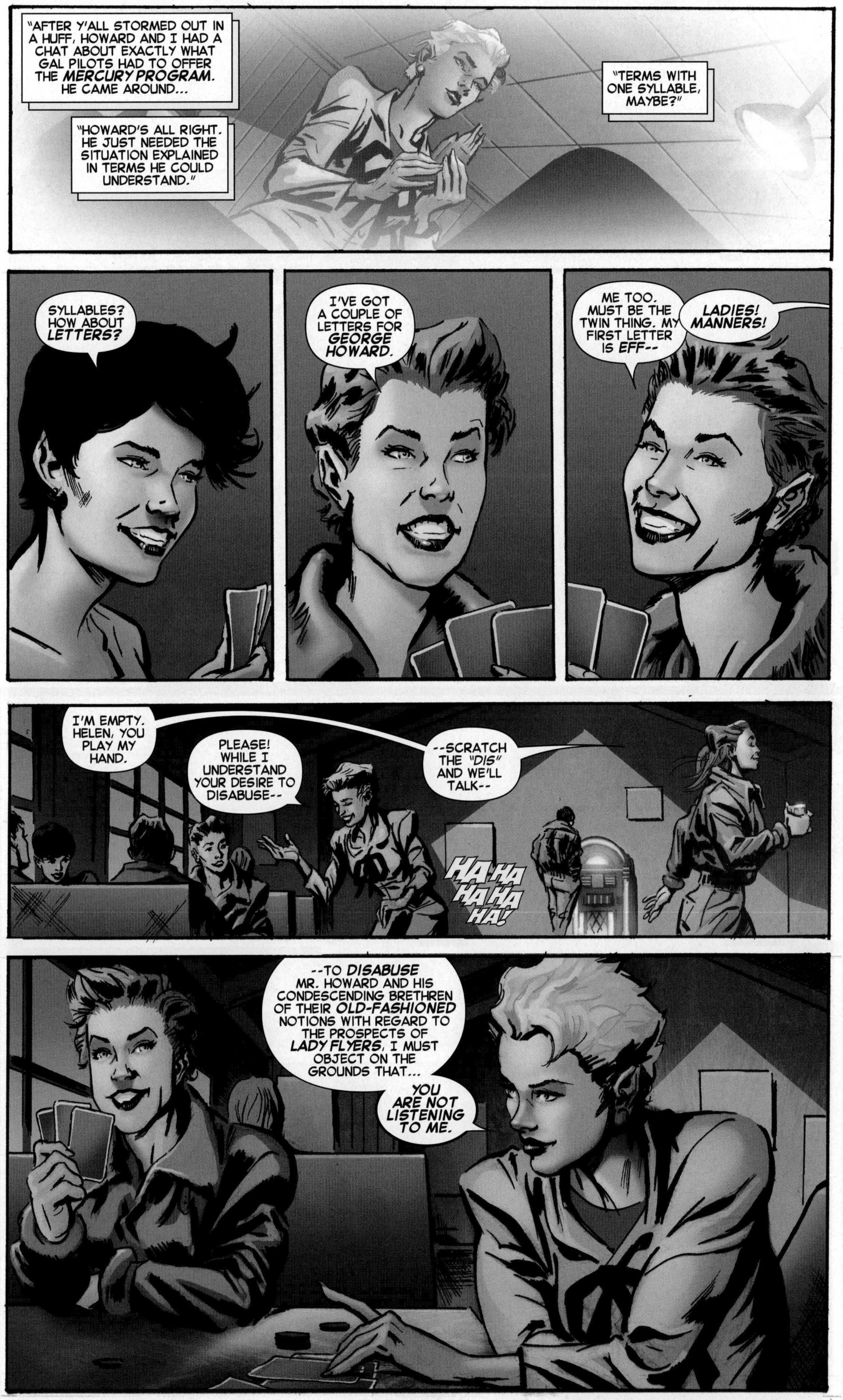
"AFTER Y'ALL STORMED OUT IN A HUFF, HOWARD AND I HAD A CHAT ABOUT EXACTLY WHAT GAL PILOTS HAD TO OFFER THE MERCURY PROGRAM. HE CAME AROUND...
"HOWARD'S ALL RIGHT. HE JUST NEEDED THE SITUATION EXPLAINED IN TERMS HE COULD UNDERSTAND."
"TERMS WITH ONE SYLLABLE, MAYBE?"
SYLLABLES? HOW ABOUT LETTERS?
I'VE GOT A COUPLE OF LETTERS FOR GEORGE HOWARD.
ME TOO. MUST BE THE TWIN THING. MY FIRST LETTER IS EFF--
LADIES! MANNERS!
I'M EMPTY. HELEN, YOU PLAY MY HAND.
PLEASE! WHILE I UNDERSTAND YOUR DESIRE TO DISABUSE--
--SCRATCH THE "DIS" AND WE'LL TALK--
HA HA HA HA HA!
--TO DISABUSE MR. HOWARD AND HIS CONDESCENDING BRETHREN OF THEIR OLD-FASHIONED NOTIONS WITH REGARD TO THE PROSPECTS OF LADY FLYERS, I MUST OBJECT ON THE GROUNDS THAT...
YOU ARE NOT LISTENING TO ME.

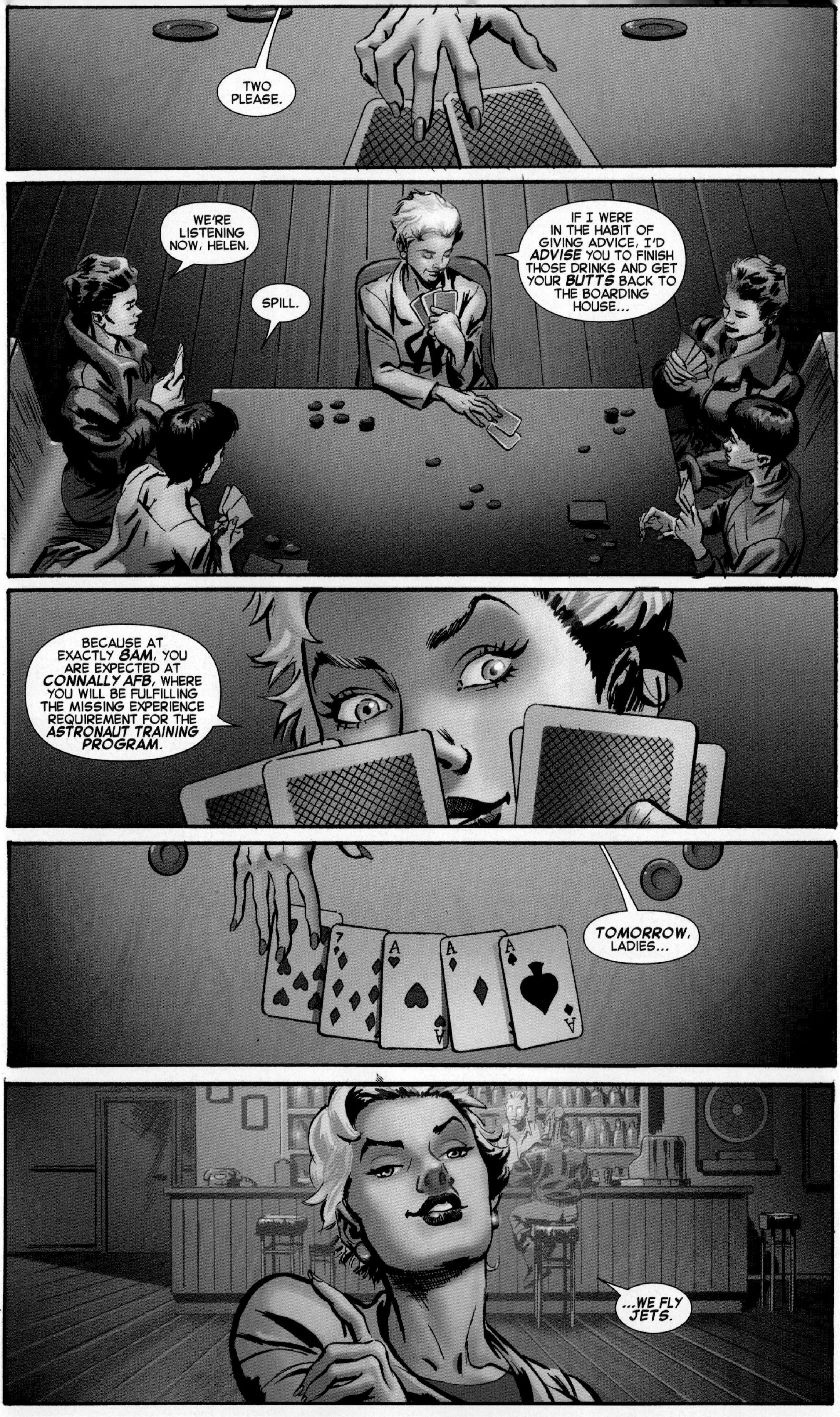
TWO PLEASE.
WE'RE LISTENING NOW, HELEN.
SPILL.
IF I WERE IN THE HABIT OF GIVING ADVICE, I'D ADVISE YOU TO FINISH THOSE DRINKS AND GET YOUR BUTTS BACK TO THE BOARDING HOUSE...
BECAUSE AT EXACTLY 8AM, YOU ARE EXPECTED AT CONNALLY AFB, WHERE YOU WILL BE FULFILLING THE MISSING EXPERIENCE REQUIREMENT FOR THE ASTRONAUT TRAINING PROGRAM.
TOMORROW, LADIES...
...WE FLY JETS.

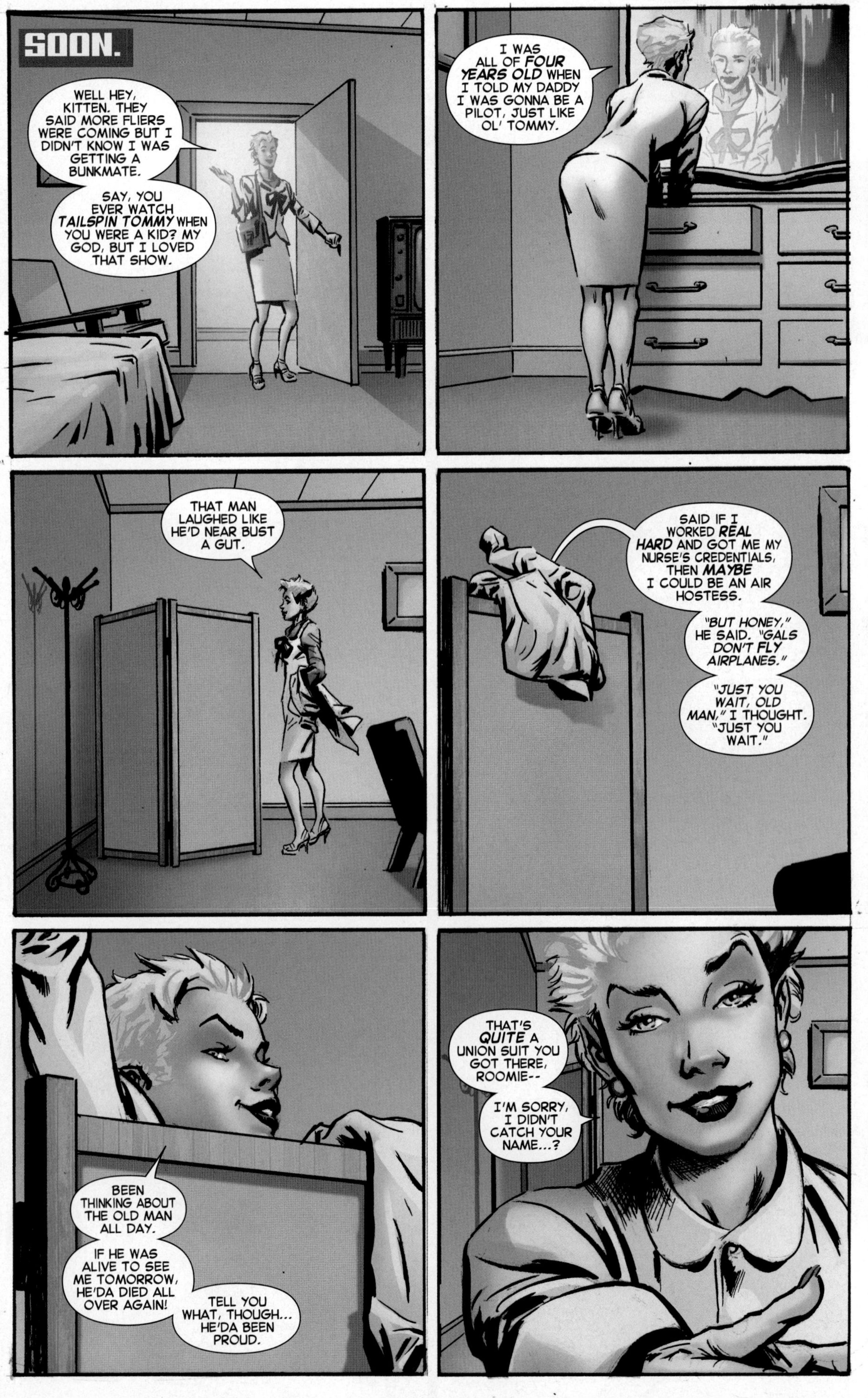
SOON.
WELL HEY, KITTEN. THEY SAID MORE FLIERS WERE COMING BUT I DIDN'T KNOW I WAS GETTING A BUNKMATE.
SAY, YOU EVER WATCH TAILSPIN TOMMY WHEN YOU WERE A KID? MY GOD, BUT I LOVED THAT SHOW.
I WAS ALL OF FOUR YEARS OLD WHEN I TOLD MY DADDY I WAS GONNA BE A PILOT, JUST LIKE OL' TOMMY.
THAT MAN LAUGHED LIKE HE'D NEAR BUST A GUT.
SAID IF I WORKED REAL HARD AND GOT ME MY NURSE'S CREDENTIALS, THEN MAYBE I COULD BE AN AIR HOSTESS.
"BUT HONEY," HE SAID. "GALS DON'T FLY AIRPLANES."
"JUST YOU WAIT, OLD MAN," I THOUGHT. "JUST YOU WAIT."
BEEN THINKING ABOUT THE OLD MAN ALL DAY.
IF HE WAS ALIVE TO SEE ME TOMORROW, HE'DA DIED ALL OVER AGAIN!
TELL YOU WHAT, THOUGH... HE'DA BEEN PROUD.
THAT'S QUITE A UNION SUIT YOU GOT THERE, ROOMIE--
I'M SORRY, I DIDN'T CATCH YOUR NAME...?

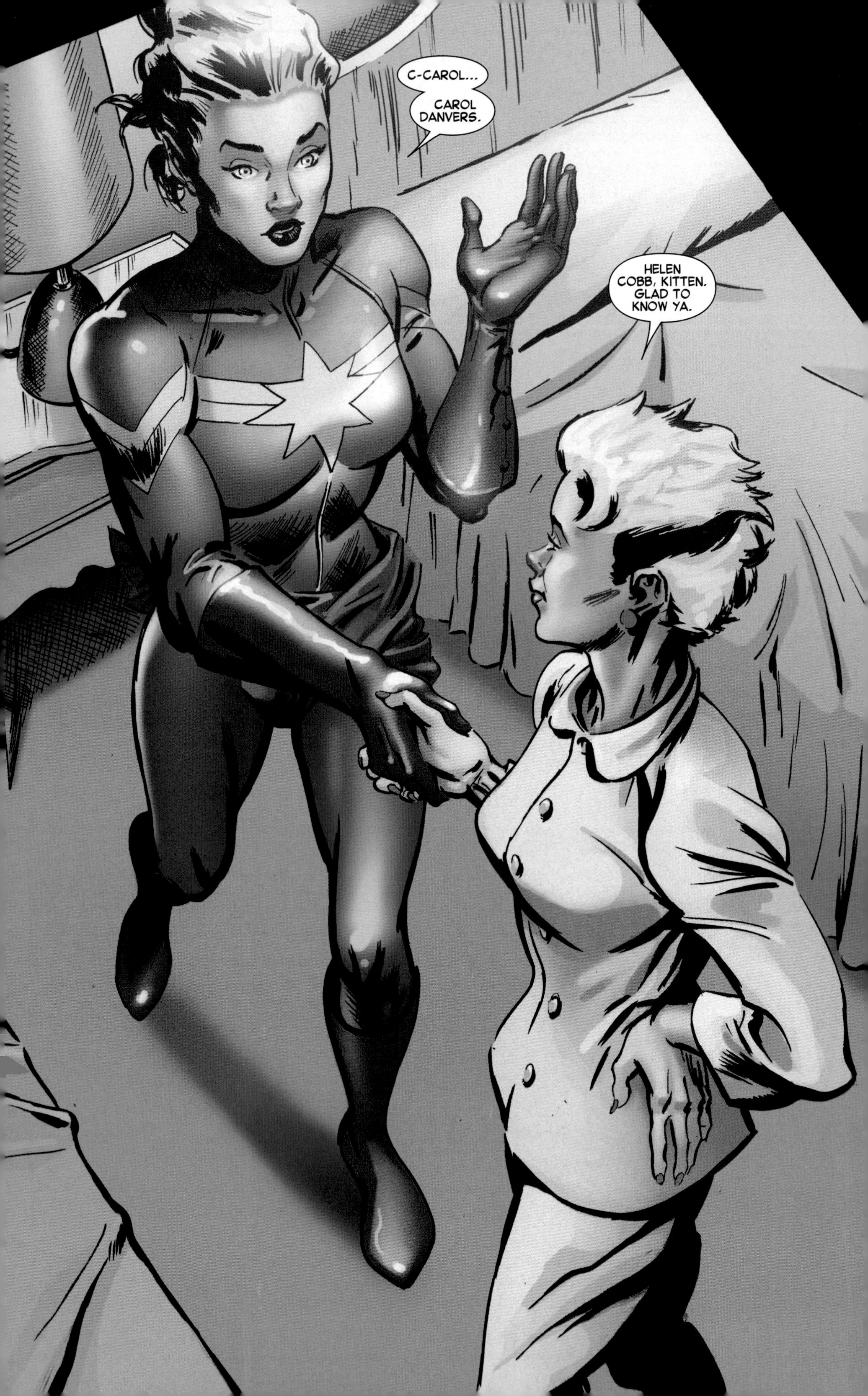
C-CAROL...
CAROL DANVERS.
HELEN COBB, KITTEN. GLAD TO KNOW YA.

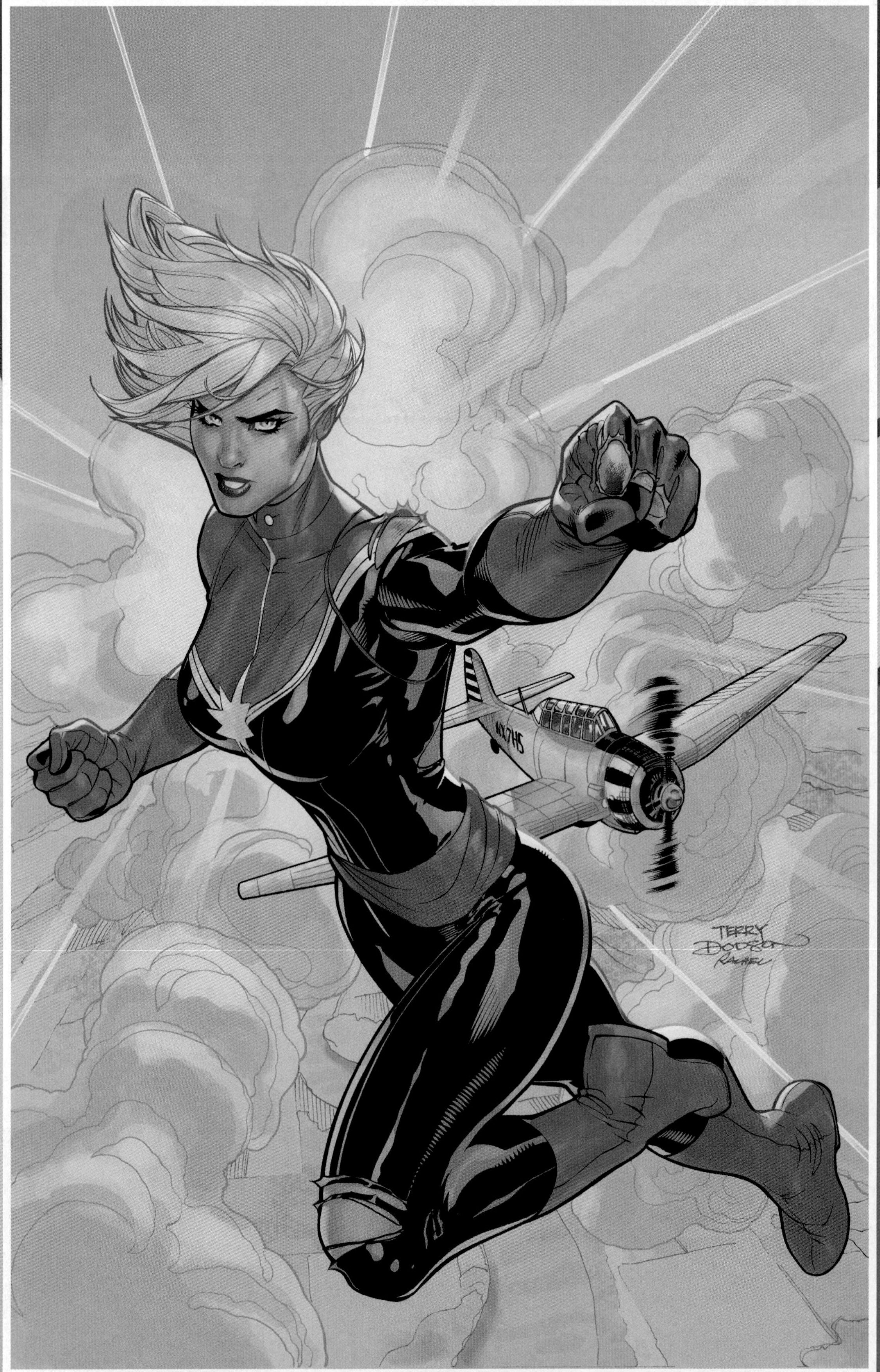
TERRY
DODSON
RACHEL

FIVE

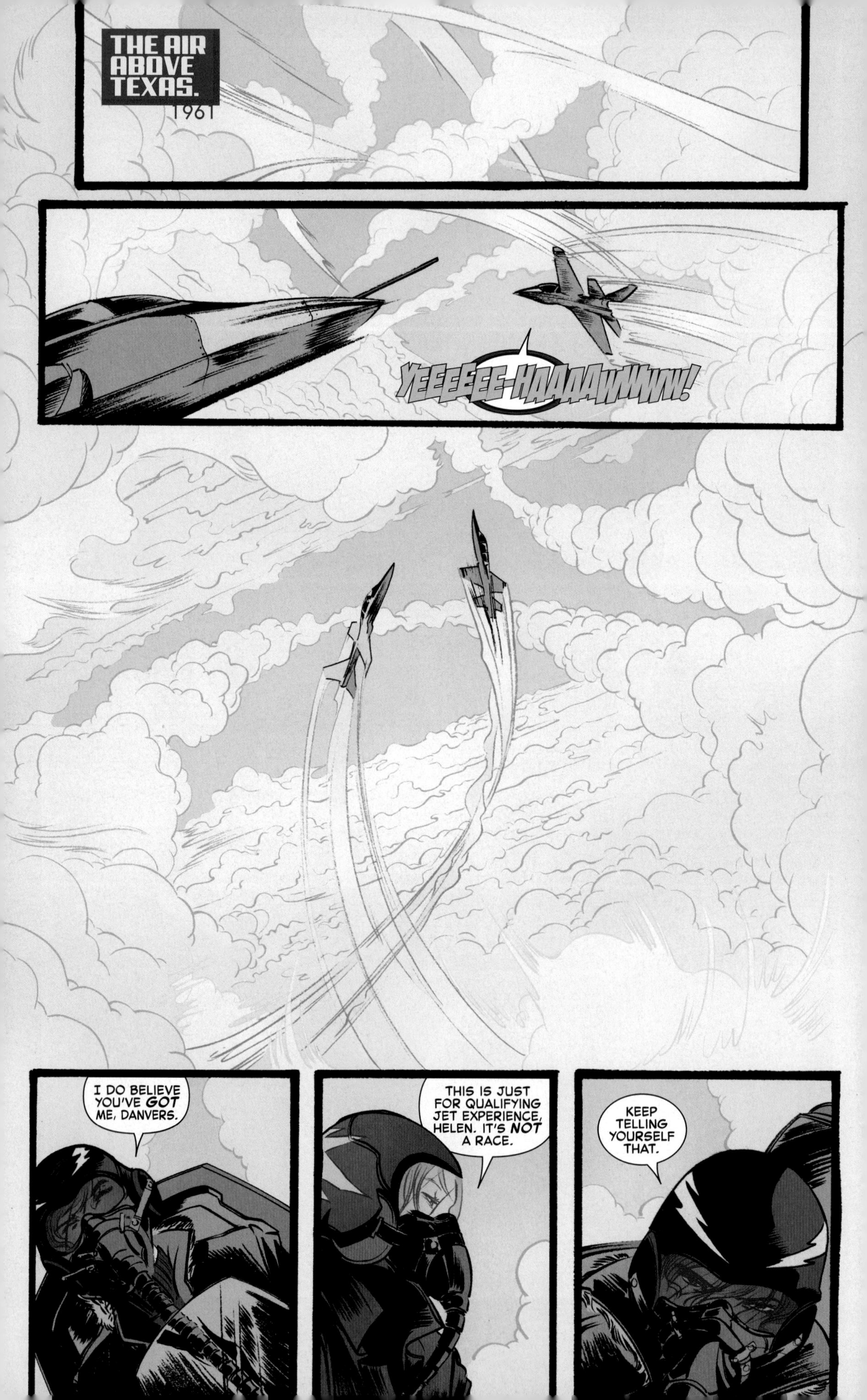
THE AIR ABOVE TEXAS.
1961
YEEEEEE-HAAAAWWWW!
I DO BELIEVE YOU'VE GOT ME, DANVERS.
THIS IS JUST FOR QUALIFYING JET EXPERIENCE, HELEN. IT'S NOT A RACE.
KEEP TELLING YOURSELF THAT.

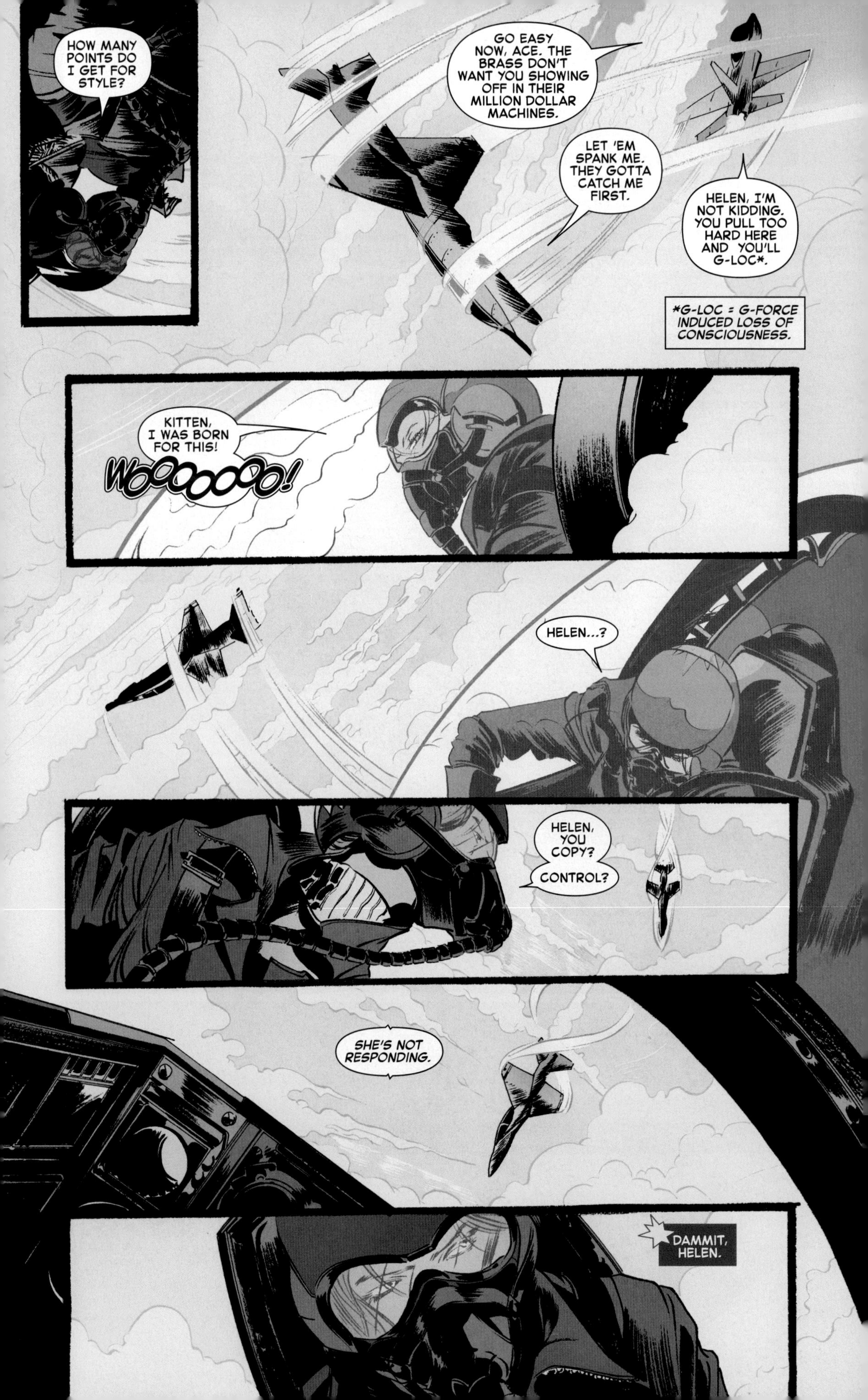
HOW MANY POINTS DO I GET FOR STYLE?
GO EASY NOW, ACE. THE BRASS DON'T WANT YOU SHOWING OFF IN THEIR MILLION DOLLAR MACHINES.
LET 'EM SPANK ME. THEY GOTTA CATCH ME FIRST.
HELEN, I'M NOT KIDDING. YOU PULL TOO HARD HERE AND YOU'LL G-LOC*.
*G-LOC = G-FORCE INDUCED LOSS OF CONSCIOUSNESS.
KITTEN, I WAS BORN FOR THIS!
WOOOOOOOO!
HELEN...?
HELEN, YOU COPY?
CONTROL?
SHE'S NOT RESPONDING.
DAMMIT, HELEN.

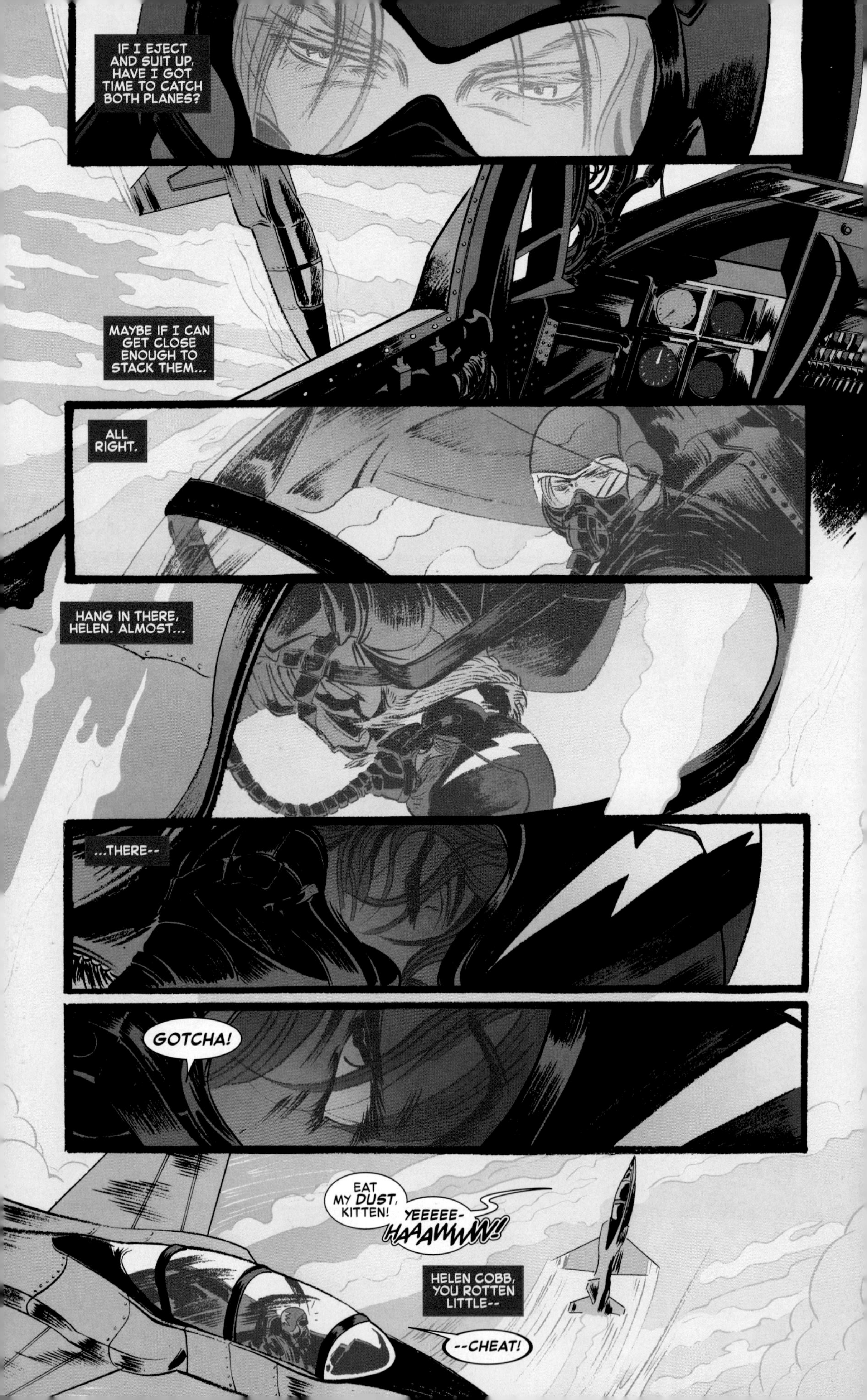
IF I EJECT AND SUIT UP, HAVE I GOT TIME TO CATCH BOTH PLANES?
MAYBE IF I CAN GET CLOSE ENOUGH TO STACK THEM...
ALL RIGHT.
HANG IN THERE, HELEN. ALMOST...
...THERE--
GOTCHA!
EAT MY DUST, KITTEN!
YEEEEE-HAAAWWW!
HELEN COBB, YOU ROTTEN LITTLE--
--CHEAT!

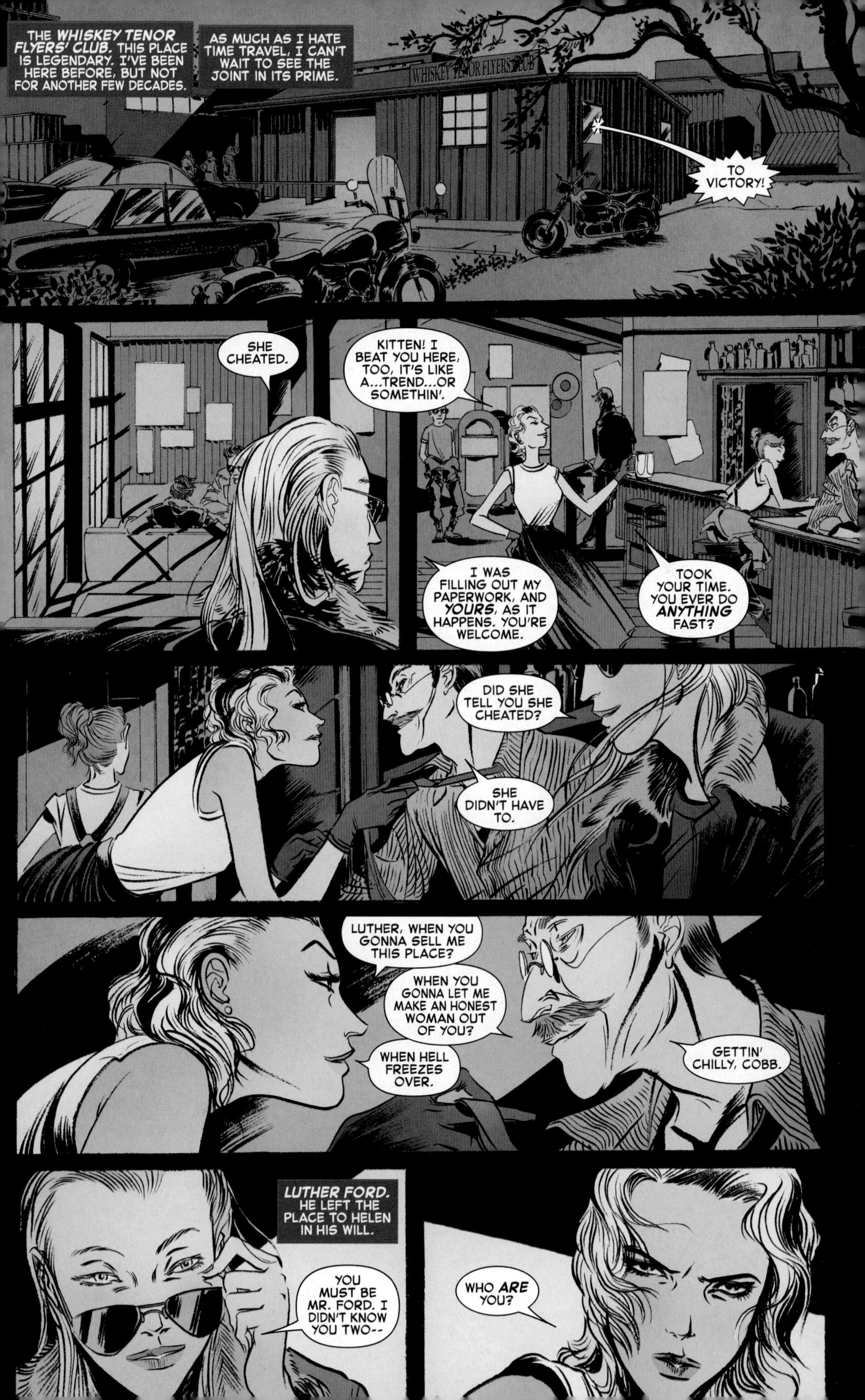
THE *WHISKEY TENOR FLYERS' CLUB.* THIS PLACE IS LEGENDARY. I'VE BEEN HERE BEFORE, BUT NOT FOR ANOTHER FEW DECADES.
AS MUCH AS I HATE TIME TRAVEL, I CAN'T WAIT TO SEE THE JOINT IN ITS PRIME.
WHISKEY TENOR FLYERS CLUB
TO VICTORY!
SHE CHEATED.
KITTEN! I BEAT YOU HERE, TOO, IT'S LIKE A...TREND...OR SOMETHIN'.
I WAS FILLING OUT MY PAPERWORK, AND *YOURS*, AS IT HAPPENS. YOU'RE WELCOME.
TOOK YOUR TIME. YOU EVER DO *ANYTHING* FAST?
DID SHE TELL YOU SHE CHEATED?
SHE DIDN'T HAVE TO.
LUTHER, WHEN YOU GONNA SELL ME THIS PLACE?
WHEN YOU GONNA LET ME MAKE AN HONEST WOMAN OUT OF YOU?
WHEN HELL FREEZES OVER.
GETTIN' CHILLY, COBB.
LUTHER FORD. HE LEFT THE PLACE TO HELEN IN HIS WILL.
YOU MUST BE MR. FORD. I DIDN'T KNOW YOU TWO--
WHO *ARE* YOU?

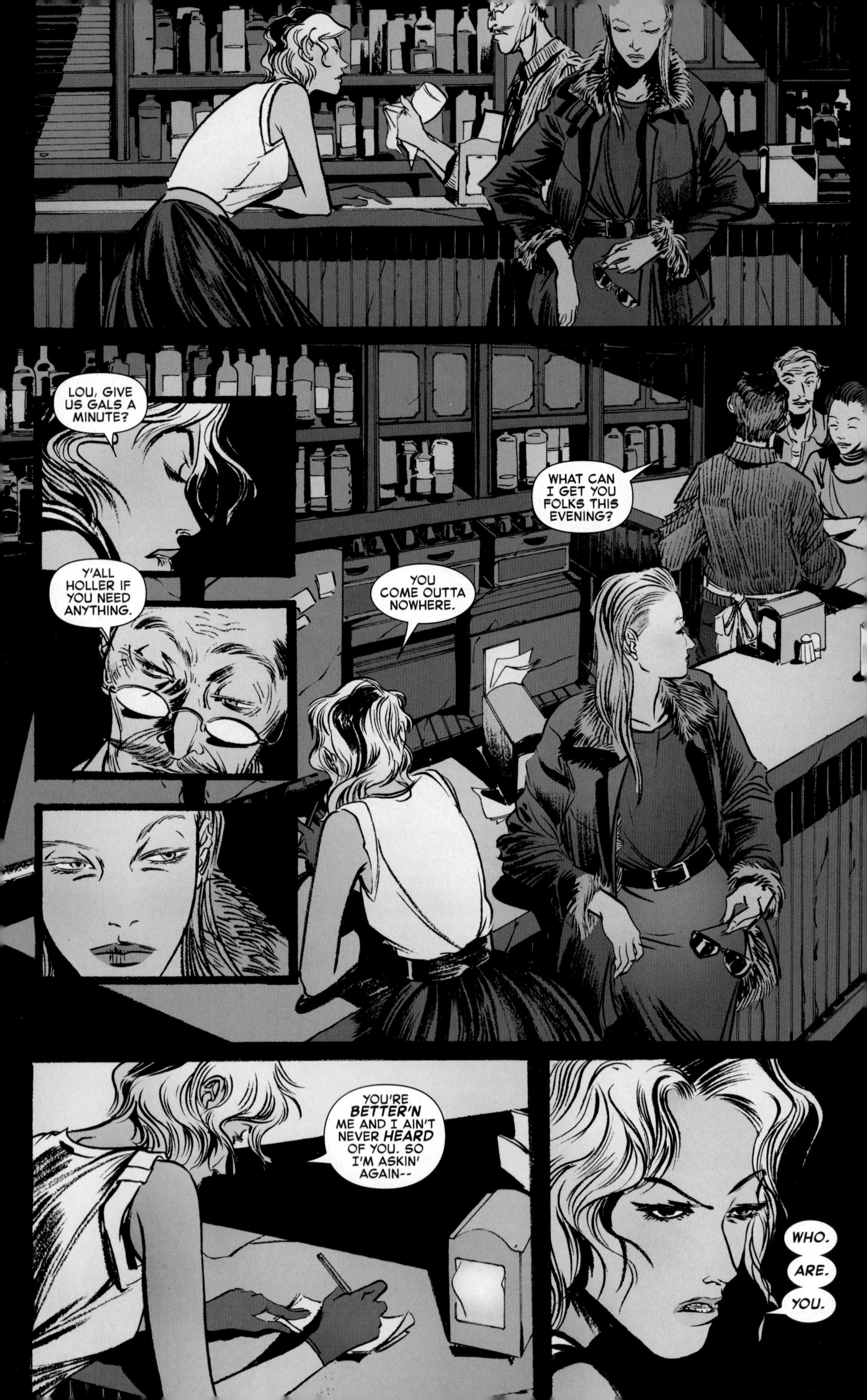
LOU, GIVE US GALS A MINUTE?
Y'ALL HOLLER IF YOU NEED ANYTHING.
YOU COME OUTTA NOWHERE.
WHAT CAN I GET YOU FOLKS THIS EVENING?
YOU'RE BETTER'N ME AND I AIN'T NEVER HEARD OF YOU. SO I'M ASKIN' AGAIN--
WHO.
ARE.
YOU.

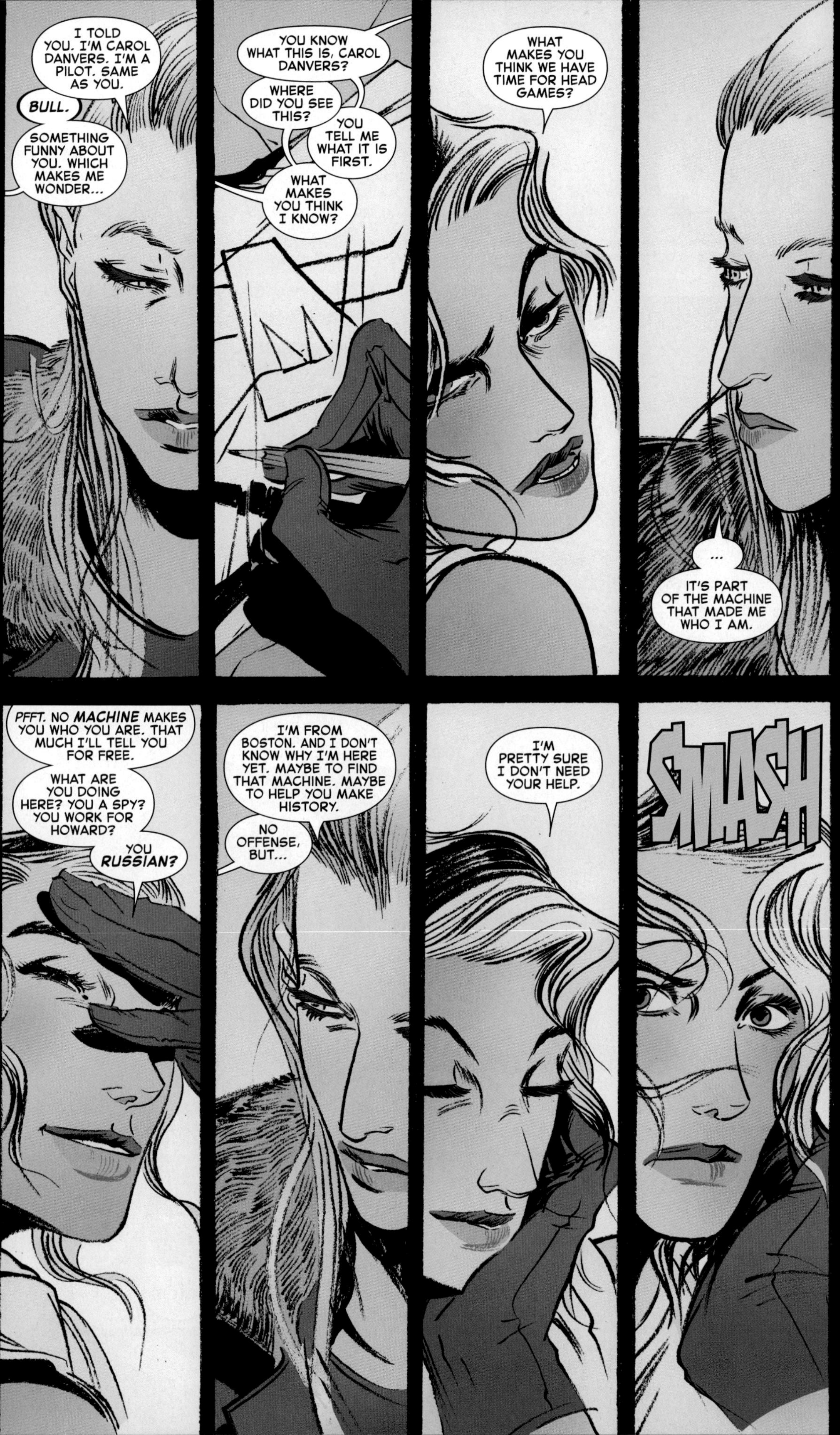
I TOLD YOU. I'M CAROL DANVERS. I'M A PILOT. SAME AS YOU.
BULL.
SOMETHING FUNNY ABOUT YOU. WHICH MAKES ME WONDER...
YOU KNOW WHAT THIS IS, CAROL DANVERS?
WHERE DID YOU SEE THIS?
YOU TELL ME WHAT IT IS FIRST.
WHAT MAKES YOU THINK I KNOW?
WHAT MAKES YOU THINK WE HAVE TIME FOR HEAD GAMES?
...
IT'S PART OF THE MACHINE THAT MADE ME WHO I AM.
PFFT. NO MACHINE MAKES YOU WHO YOU ARE. THAT MUCH I'LL TELL YOU FOR FREE.
WHAT ARE YOU DOING HERE? YOU A SPY? YOU WORK FOR HOWARD?
YOU RUSSIAN?
I'M FROM BOSTON. AND I DON'T KNOW WHY I'M HERE YET. MAYBE TO FIND THAT MACHINE. MAYBE TO HELP YOU MAKE HISTORY.
NO OFFENSE, BUT...
I'M PRETTY SURE I DON'T NEED YOUR HELP.
SMASH

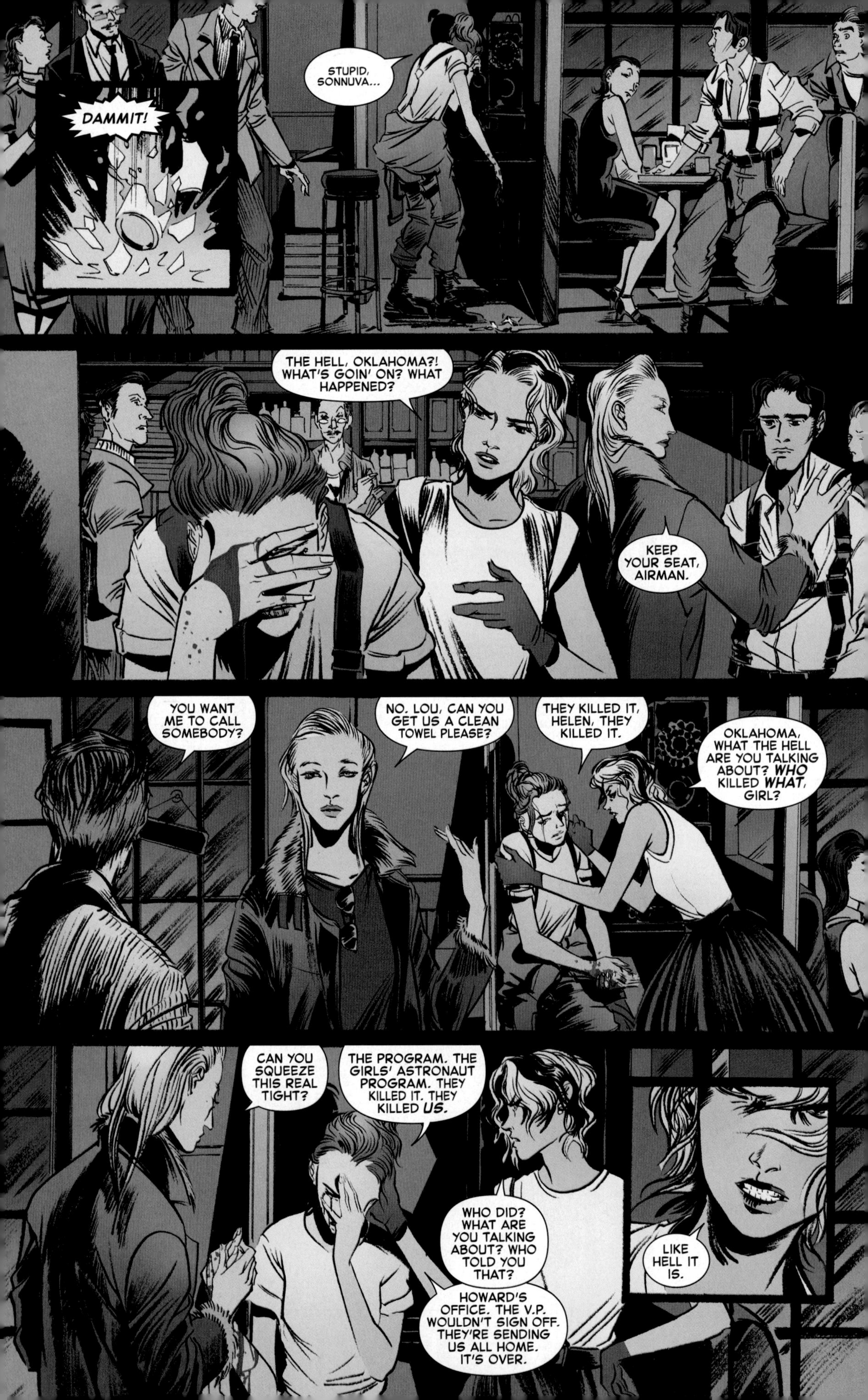
DAMMIT!
STUPID, SONNUVA...
THE HELL, OKLAHOMA?! WHAT'S GOIN' ON? WHAT HAPPENED?
KEEP YOUR SEAT, AIRMAN.
YOU WANT ME TO CALL SOMEBODY?
NO. LOU, CAN YOU GET US A CLEAN TOWEL PLEASE?
THEY KILLED IT, HELEN, THEY KILLED IT.
OKLAHOMA, WHAT THE HELL ARE YOU TALKING ABOUT? WHO KILLED WHAT, GIRL?
CAN YOU SQUEEZE THIS REAL TIGHT?
THE PROGRAM. THE GIRLS' ASTRONAUT PROGRAM. THEY KILLED IT. THEY KILLED US.
WHO DID? WHAT ARE YOU TALKING ABOUT? WHO TOLD YOU THAT?
HOWARD'S OFFICE. THE V.P. WOULDN'T SIGN OFF. THEY'RE SENDING US ALL HOME. IT'S OVER.
LIKE HELL IT IS.

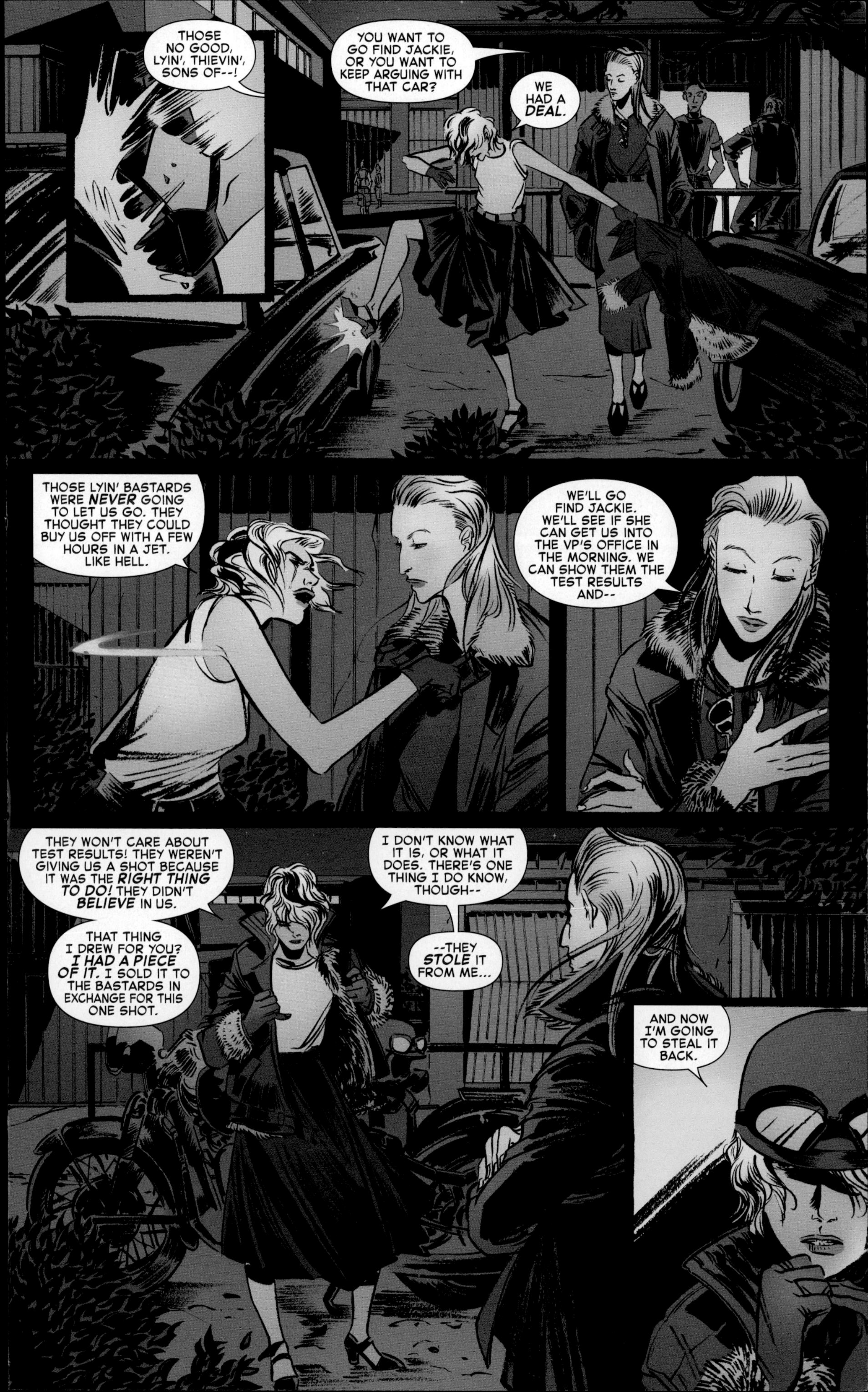
THOSE NO GOOD, LYIN', THIEVIN', SONS OF--!
YOU WANT TO GO FIND JACKIE, OR YOU WANT TO KEEP ARGUING WITH THAT CAR?
WE HAD A DEAL.
THOSE LYIN' BASTARDS WERE NEVER GOING TO LET US GO. THEY THOUGHT THEY COULD BUY US OFF WITH A FEW HOURS IN A JET. LIKE HELL.
WE'LL GO FIND JACKIE. WE'LL SEE IF SHE CAN GET US INTO THE VP'S OFFICE IN THE MORNING. WE CAN SHOW THEM THE TEST RESULTS AND--
THEY WON'T CARE ABOUT TEST RESULTS! THEY WEREN'T GIVING US A SHOT BECAUSE IT WAS THE RIGHT THING TO DO! THEY DIDN'T BELIEVE IN US.
THAT THING I DREW FOR YOU? I HAD A PIECE OF IT. I SOLD IT TO THE BASTARDS IN EXCHANGE FOR THIS ONE SHOT.
I DON'T KNOW WHAT IT IS, OR WHAT IT DOES. THERE'S ONE THING I DO KNOW, THOUGH--
--THEY STOLE IT FROM ME...
AND NOW I'M GOING TO STEAL IT BACK.

THERE'S AN EXTRA HELMET IN THE SADDLEBAG IF YOU WANT IT.

THINK FAST.

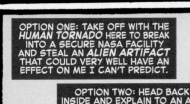

OPTION ONE: TAKE OFF WITH THE *HUMAN TORNADO* HERE TO BREAK INTO A SECURE NASA FACILITY AND STEAL AN *ALIEN ARTIFACT* THAT COULD VERY WELL HAVE AN EFFECT ON ME I CAN'T PREDICT.

OPTION TWO: HEAD BACK INSIDE AND EXPLAIN TO AN ACE GIRL PILOT FROM OKLAHOMA THAT THROUGH *NO FAULT* OF HER OWN, HER DREAMS WERE JUST *TOO BIG.*

NO CONTEST.

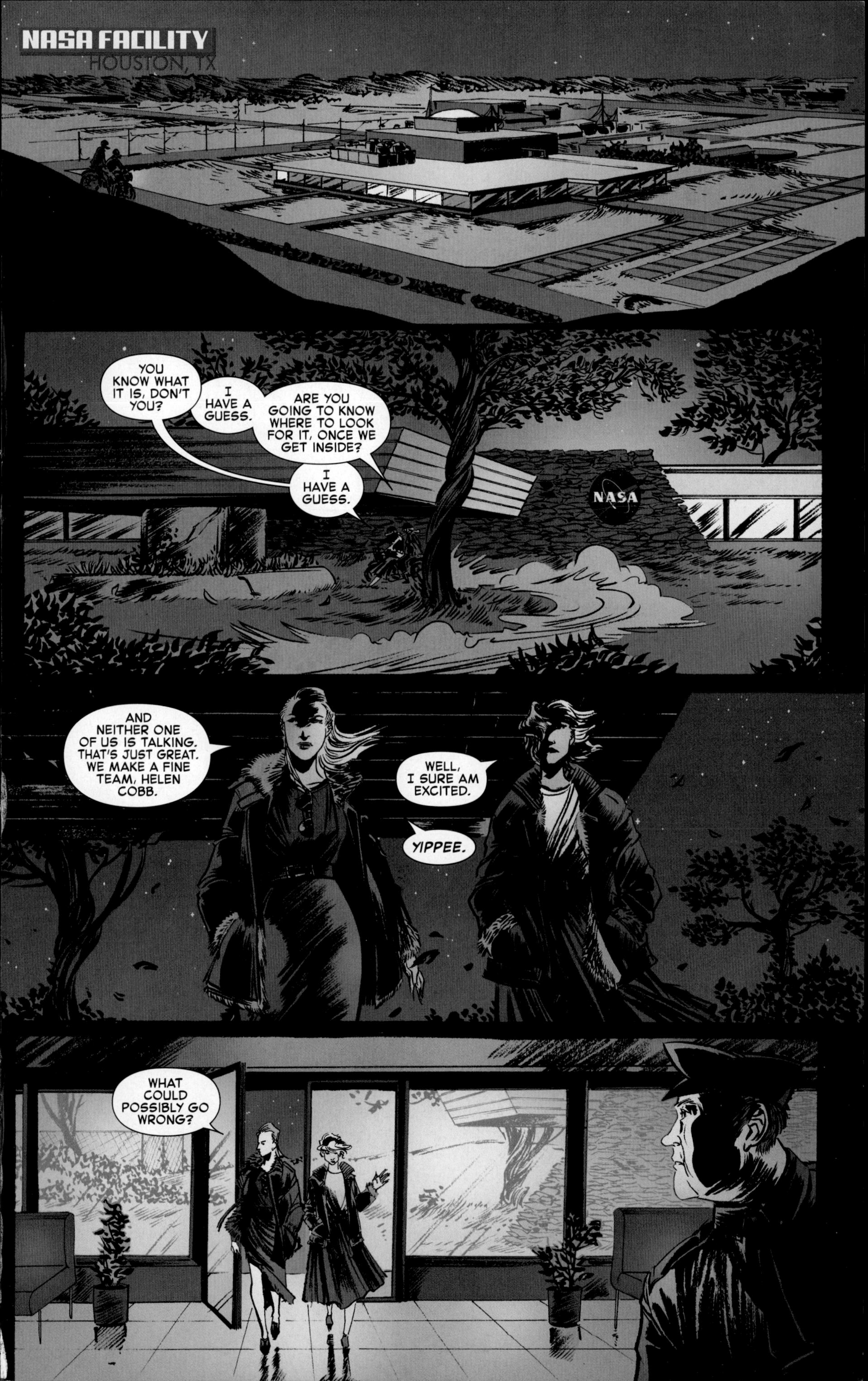
NASA FACILITY
HOUSTON, TX
YOU KNOW WHAT IT IS, DON'T YOU?
I HAVE A GUESS.
ARE YOU GOING TO KNOW WHERE TO LOOK FOR IT, ONCE WE GET INSIDE?
I HAVE A GUESS.
NASA
AND NEITHER ONE OF US IS TALKING. THAT'S JUST GREAT. WE MAKE A FINE TEAM, HELEN COBB.
WELL, I SURE AM EXCITED.
YIPPEE.
WHAT COULD POSSIBLY GO WRONG?

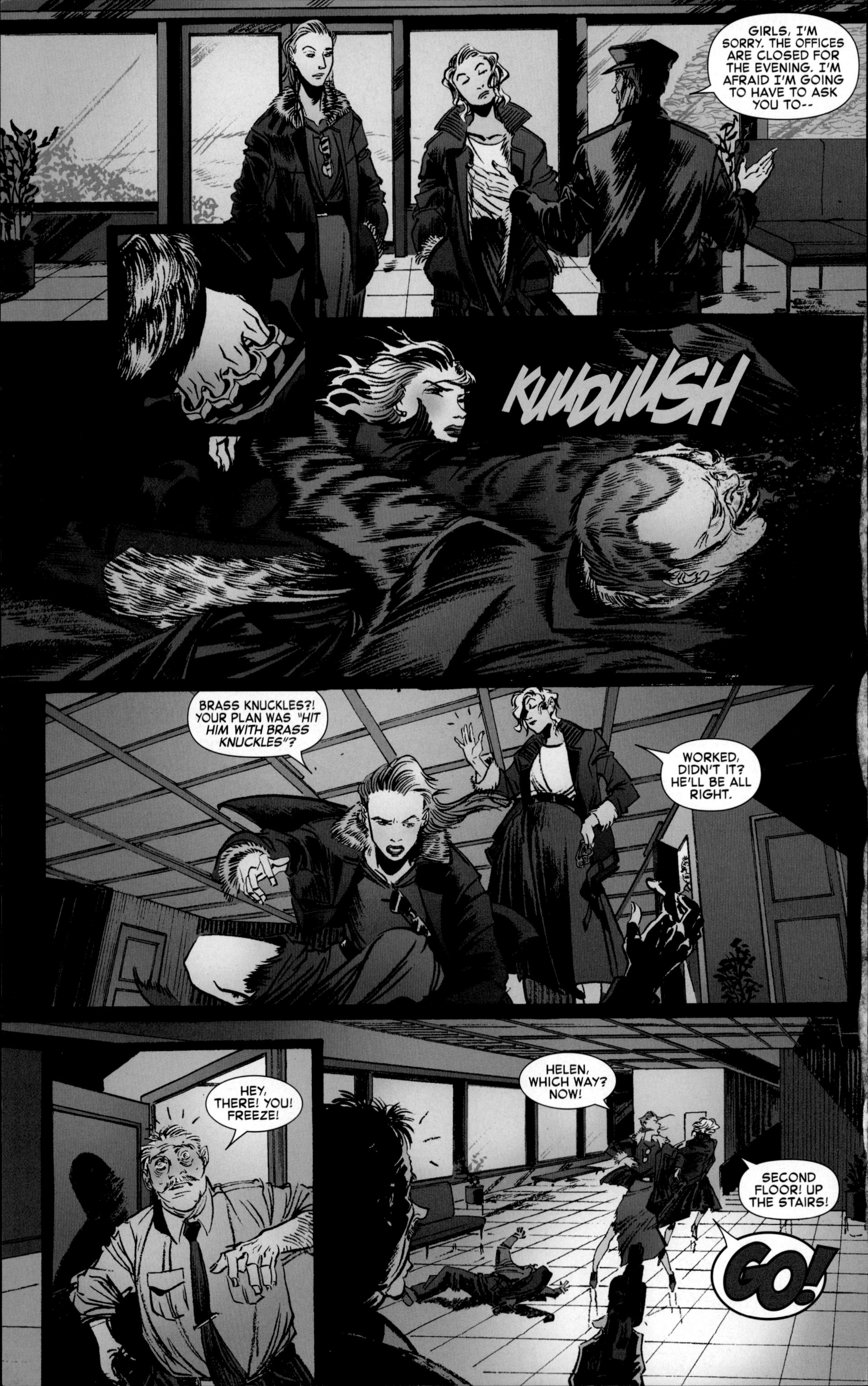
GIRLS, I'M SORRY. THE OFFICES ARE CLOSED FOR THE EVENING. I'M AFRAID I'M GOING TO HAVE TO ASK YOU TO--
KUUDUUSH
BRASS KNUCKLES?! YOUR PLAN WAS "HIT HIM WITH BRASS KNUCKLES"?
WORKED, DIDN'T IT? HE'LL BE ALL RIGHT.
HEY, THERE! YOU! FREEZE!
HELEN, WHICH WAY? NOW!
SECOND FLOOR! UP THE STAIRS!
GO!

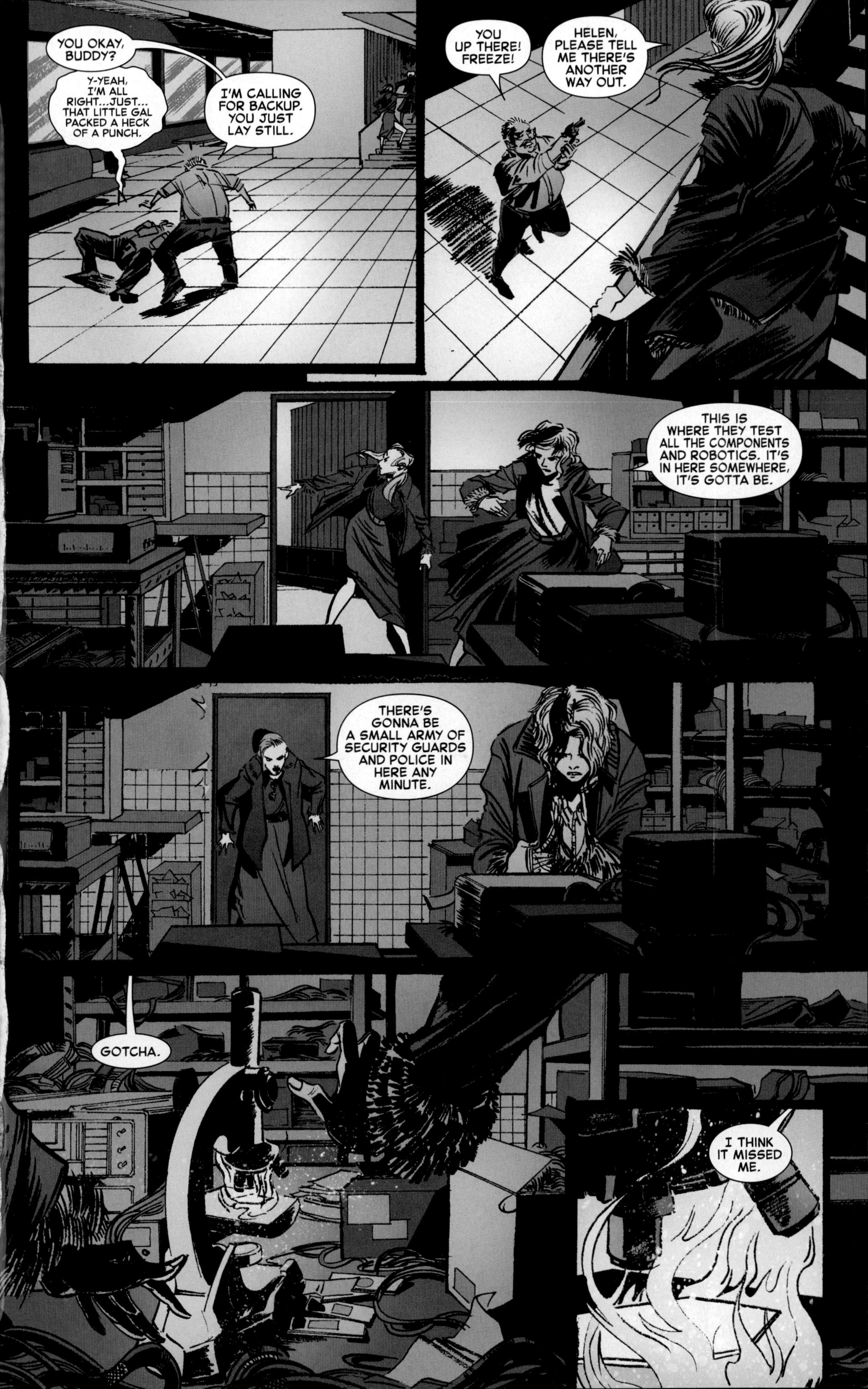
YOU OKAY, BUDDY?
Y-YEAH, I'M ALL RIGHT...JUST... THAT LITTLE GAL PACKED A HECK OF A PUNCH.
I'M CALLING FOR BACKUP. YOU JUST LAY STILL.
YOU UP THERE! FREEZE!
HELEN, PLEASE TELL ME THERE'S ANOTHER WAY OUT.
THIS IS WHERE THEY TEST ALL THE COMPONENTS AND ROBOTICS. IT'S IN HERE SOMEWHERE, IT'S GOTTA BE.
THERE'S GONNA BE A SMALL ARMY OF SECURITY GUARDS AND POLICE IN HERE ANY MINUTE.
GOTCHA.
I THINK IT MISSED ME.

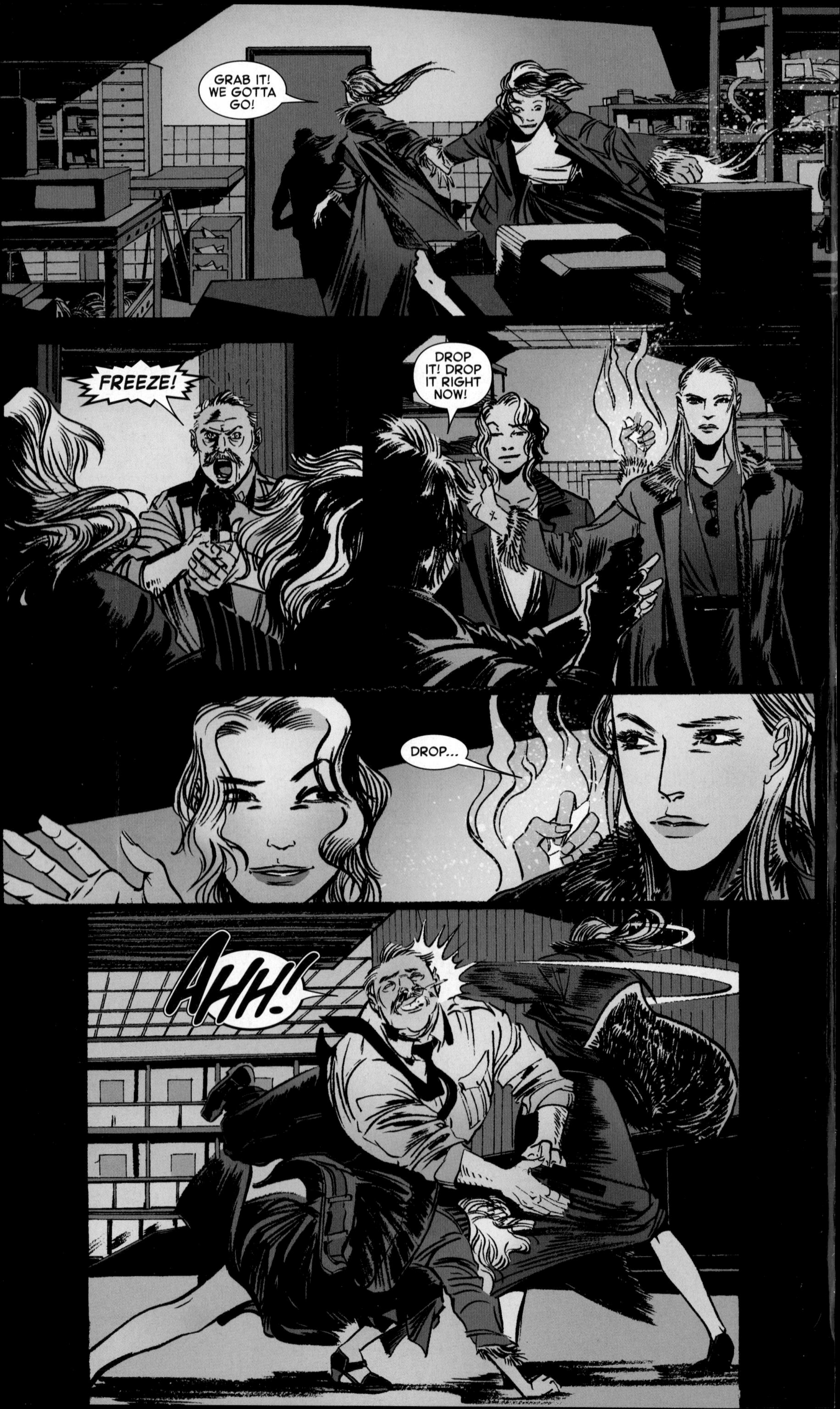
GRAB IT! WE GOTTA GO!
FREEZE!
DROP IT! DROP IT RIGHT NOW!
DROP...
AHH!

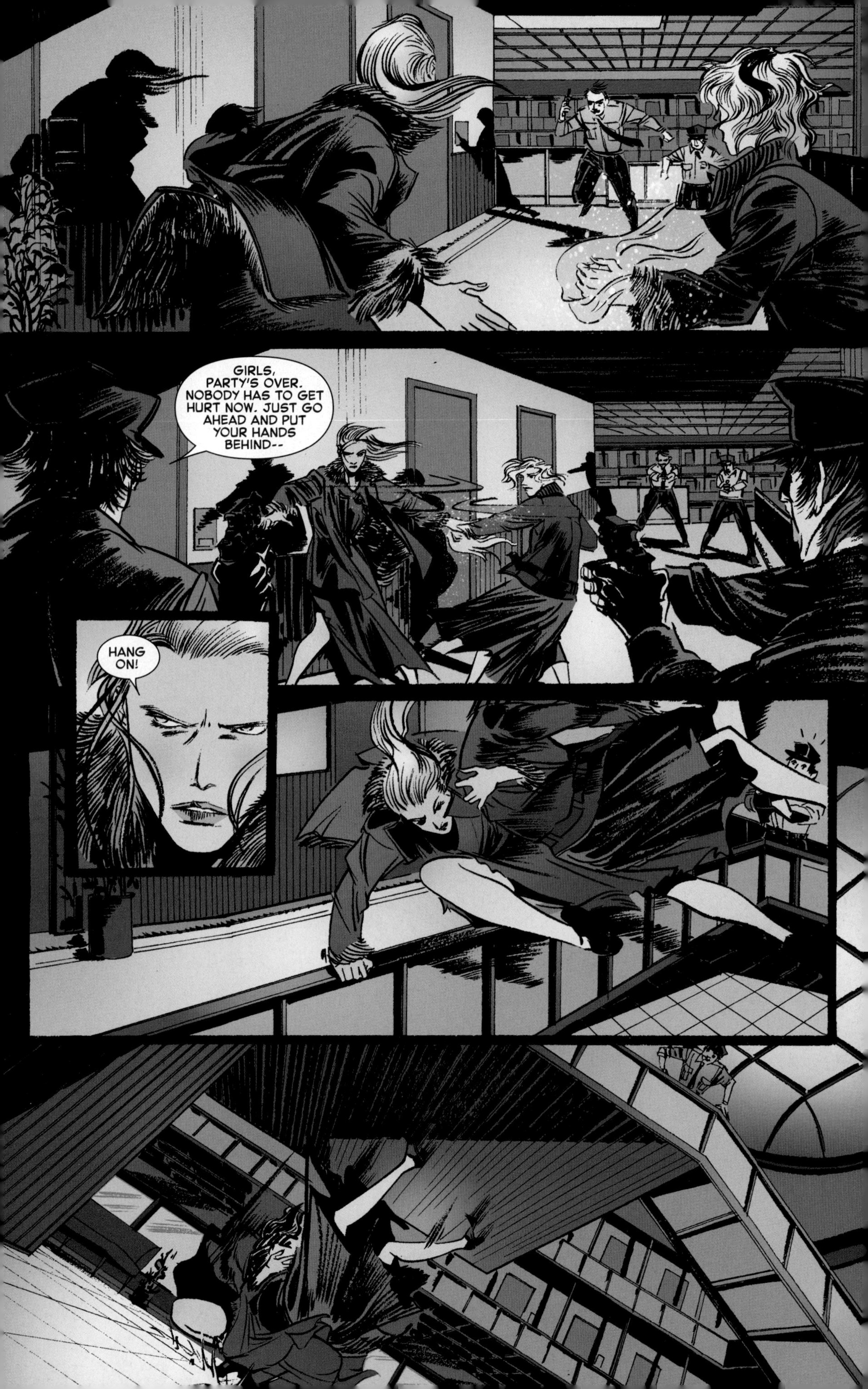
GIRLS, PARTY'S OVER. NOBODY HAS TO GET HURT NOW. JUST GO AHEAD AND PUT YOUR HANDS BEHIND--
HANG ON!

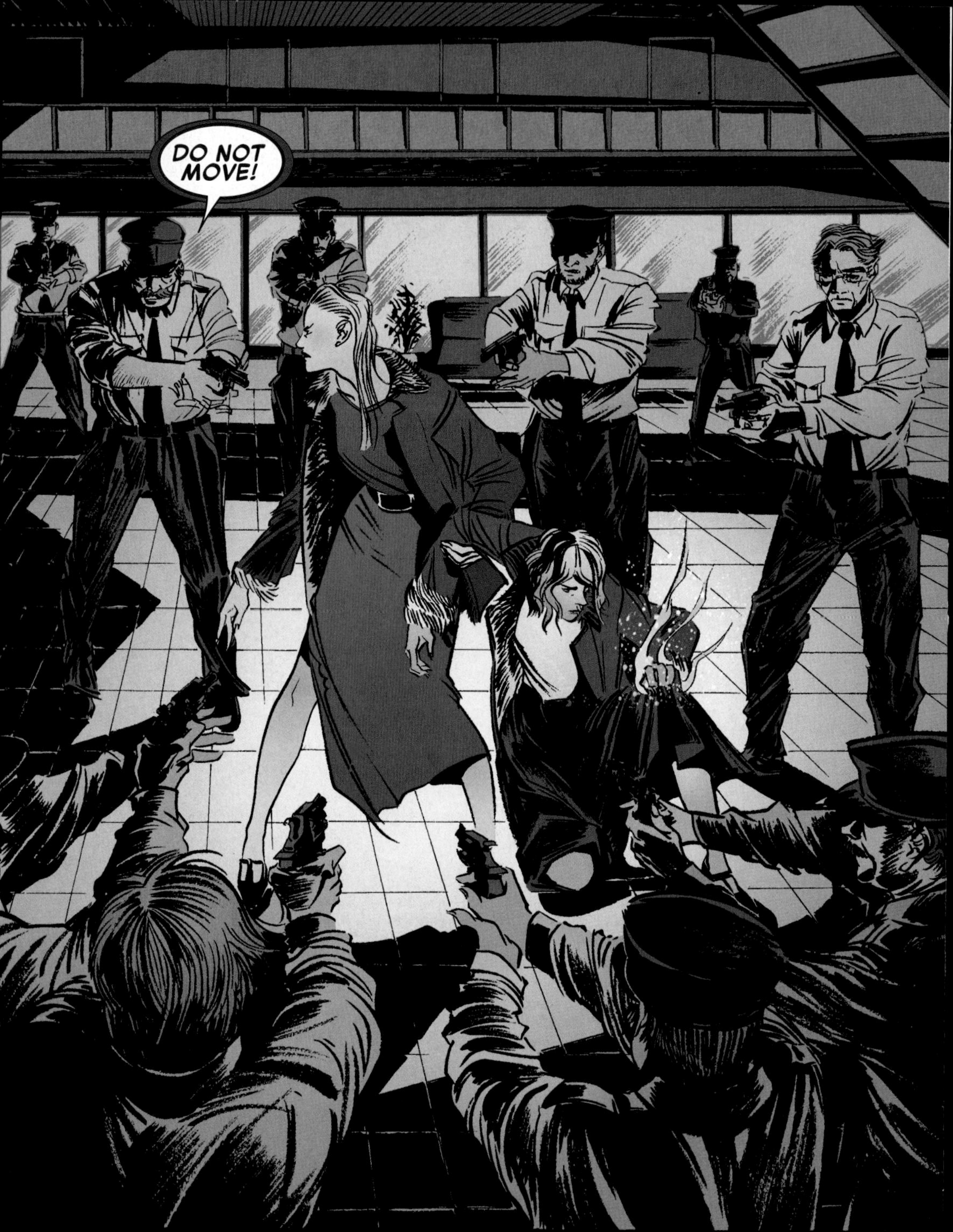
DO NOT MOVE!

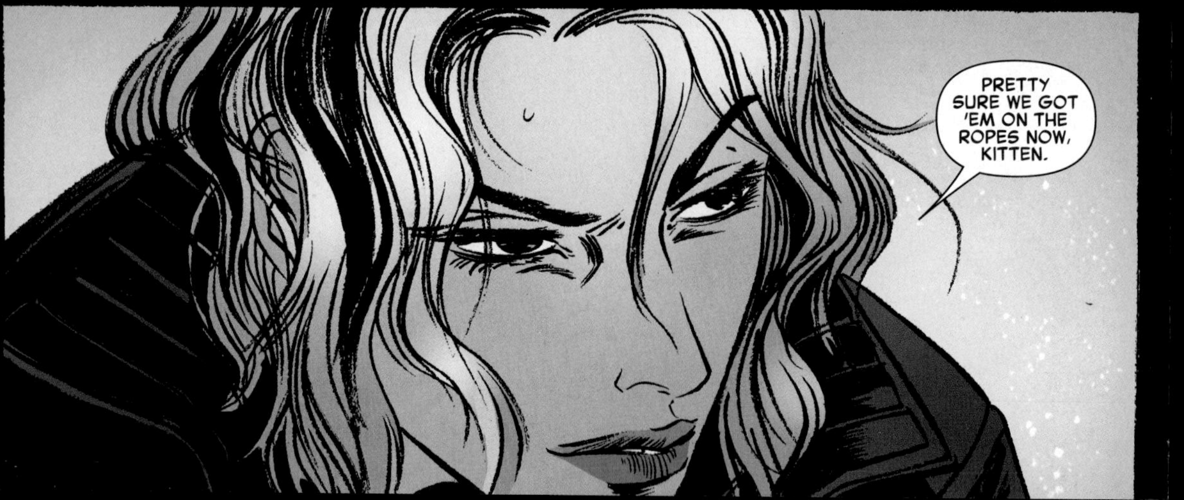
PRETTY SURE WE GOT 'EM ON THE ROPES NOW, KITTEN.

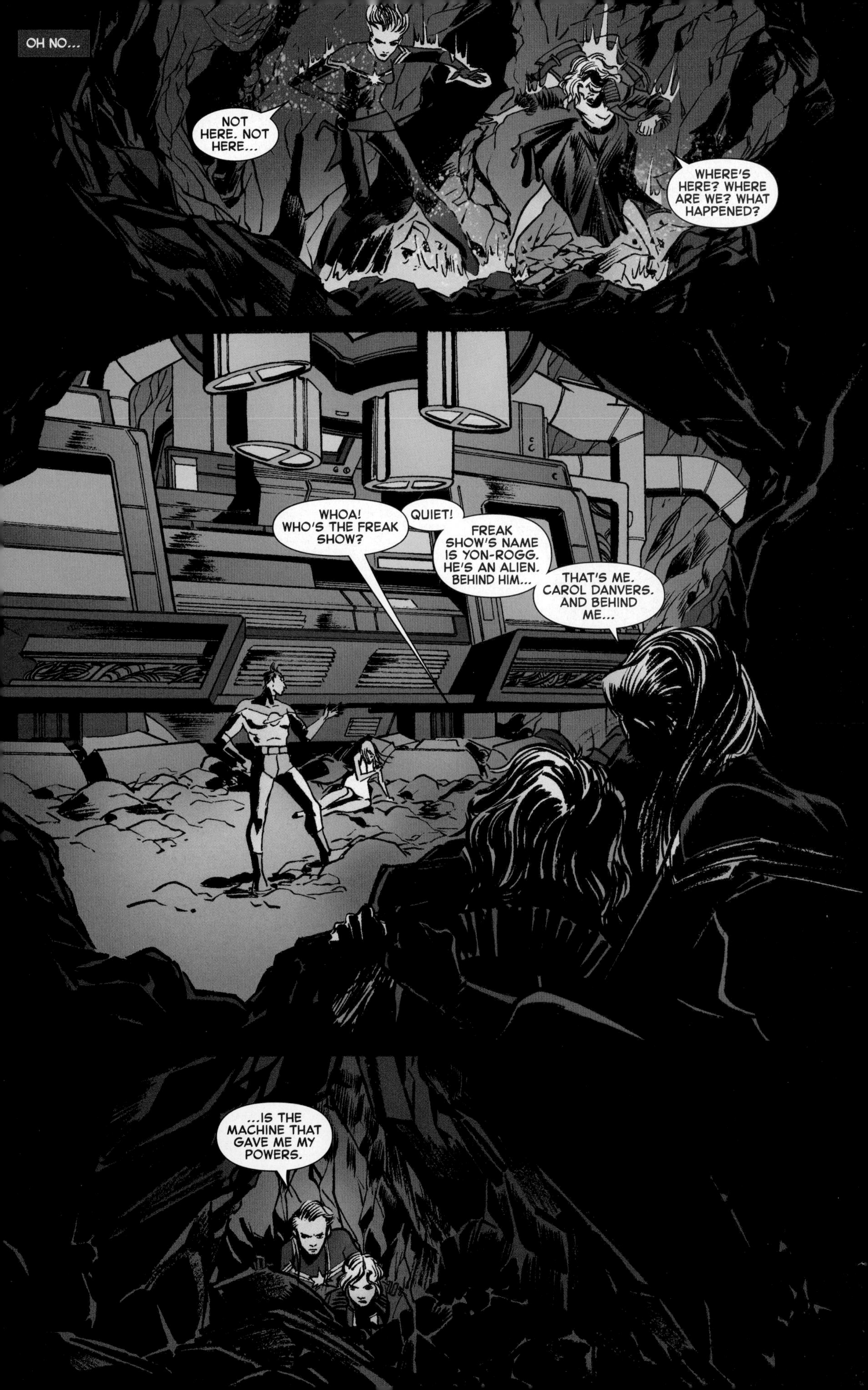
OH NO...
NOT HERE. NOT HERE...
WHERE'S HERE? WHERE ARE WE? WHAT HAPPENED?
WHOA! WHO'S THE FREAK SHOW?
QUIET!
FREAK SHOW'S NAME IS YON-ROGG. HE'S AN ALIEN. BEHIND HIM...
THAT'S ME. CAROL DANVERS. AND BEHIND ME...
...IS THE MACHINE THAT GAVE ME MY POWERS.

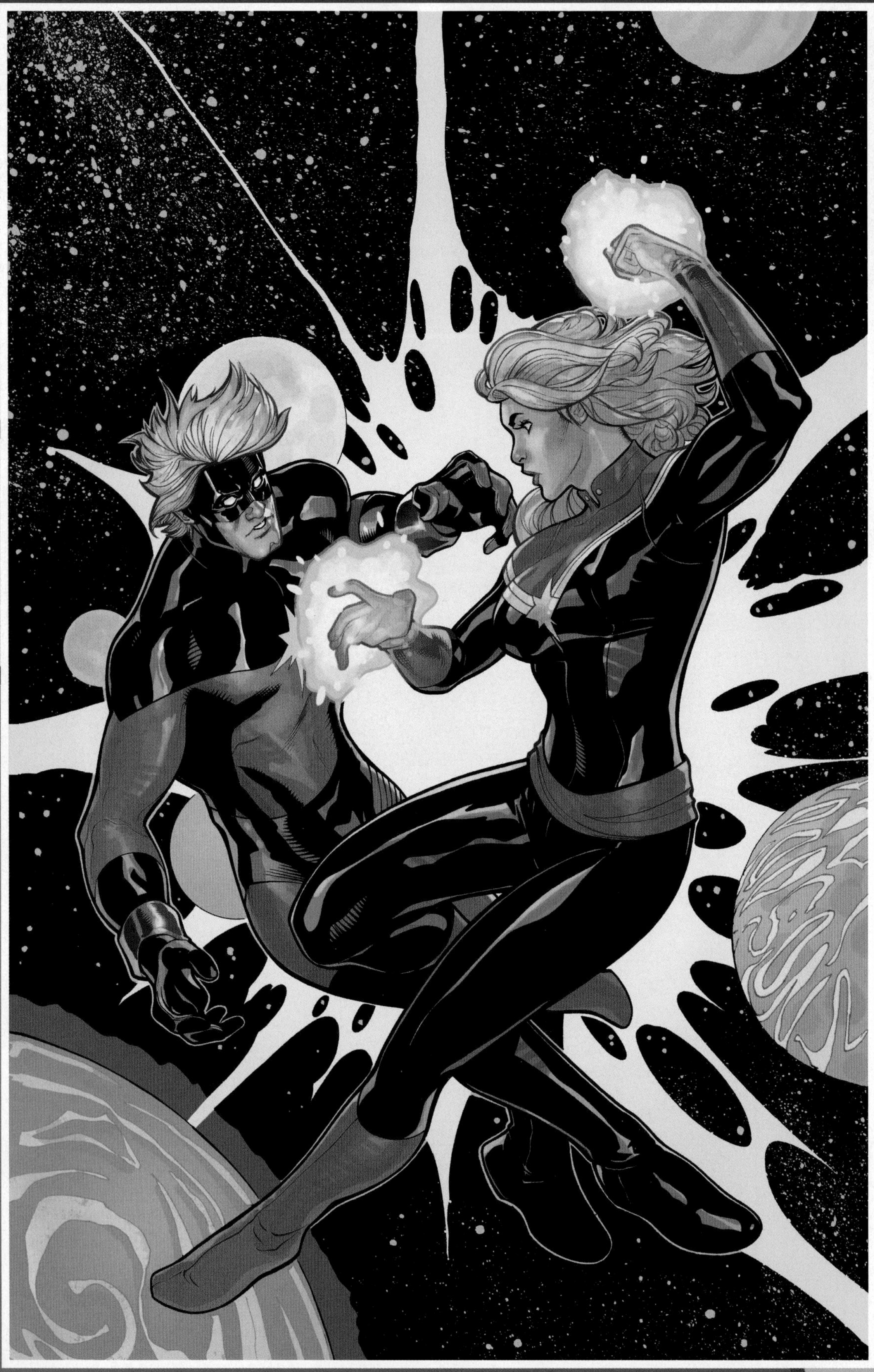

SIX

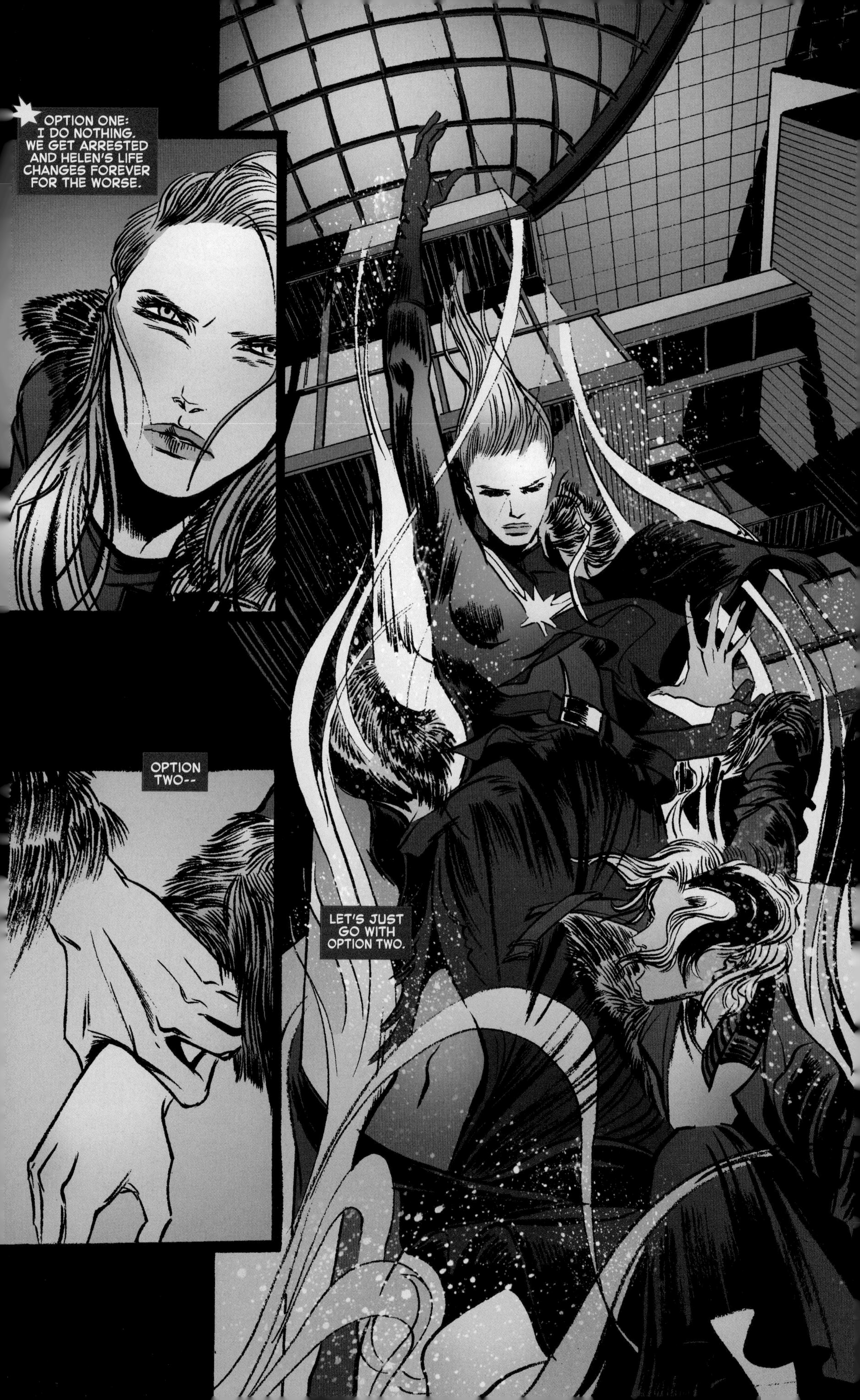
OPTION ONE:
I DO NOTHING.
WE GET ARRESTED
AND HELEN'S LIFE
CHANGES FOREVER
FOR THE WORSE.
OPTION
TWO--
LET'S JUST
GO WITH
OPTION TWO.

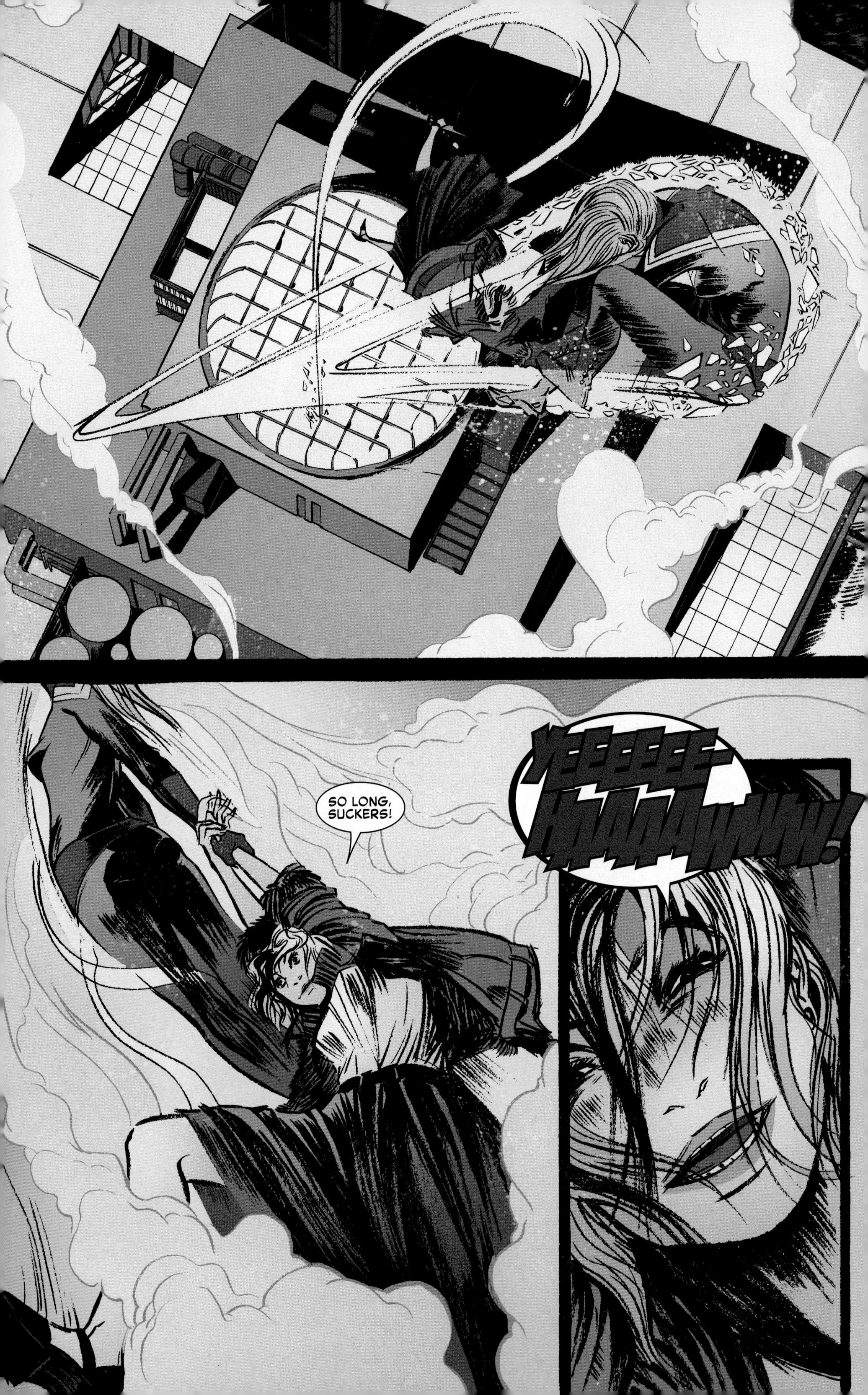
SO LONG, SUCKERS!
YEEEEEE-HAAAAWWW!

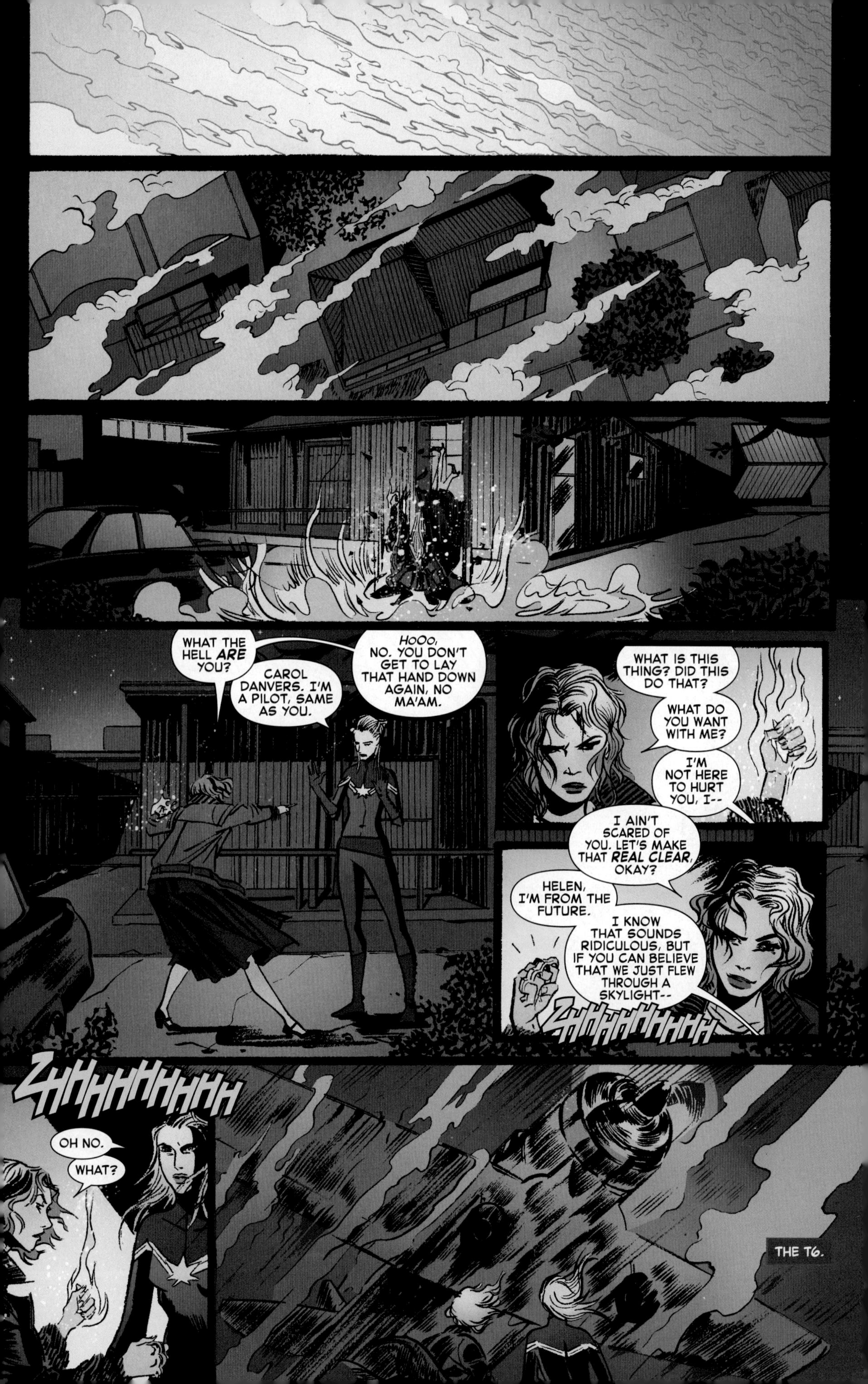
WHAT THE HELL *ARE* YOU?
CAROL DANVERS. I'M A PILOT, SAME AS YOU.
HoOo, NO. YOU DON'T GET TO LAY THAT HAND DOWN AGAIN, NO MA'AM.
WHAT IS THIS THING? DID THIS DO THAT?
WHAT DO YOU WANT WITH ME?
I'M NOT HERE TO HURT YOU, I--
I AIN'T SCARED OF YOU. LET'S MAKE THAT *REAL CLEAR*, OKAY?
HELEN, I'M FROM THE FUTURE.
I KNOW THAT SOUNDS RIDICULOUS, BUT IF YOU CAN BELIEVE THAT WE JUST FLEW THROUGH A SKYLIGHT--
ZHHHHHHHHHH
ZHHHHHHHHHH
OH NO.
WHAT?
THE T6.

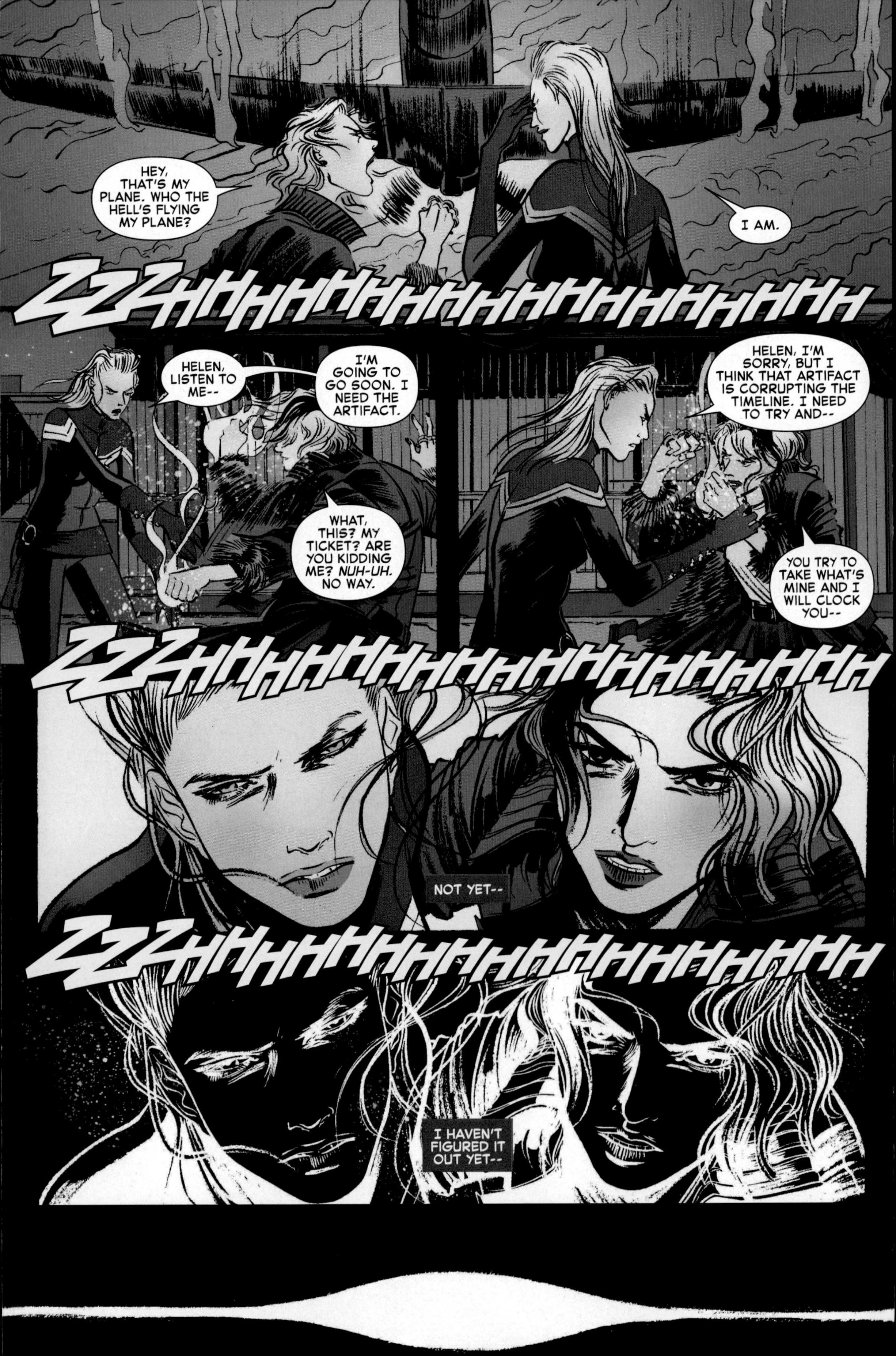
HEY, THAT'S MY PLANE. WHO THE HELL'S FLYING MY PLANE?
I AM.
ZZZHHHHHHHHHHHHHHHHHHHHHHHHH
HELEN, LISTEN TO ME--
I'M GOING TO GO SOON. I NEED THE ARTIFACT.
WHAT, THIS? MY TICKET? ARE YOU KIDDING ME? *NUH-UH.* NO WAY.
HELEN, I'M SORRY, BUT I THINK THAT ARTIFACT IS CORRUPTING THE TIMELINE. I NEED TO TRY AND--
YOU TRY TO TAKE WHAT'S MINE AND I WILL CLOCK YOU--
ZZZHHHHHHHHHHHHHHHHHHHHHHHHHH
NOT YET--
ZZZHHHHHHHHHHHHHHHHHHHHHHHHH
I HAVEN'T FIGURED IT OUT YET--

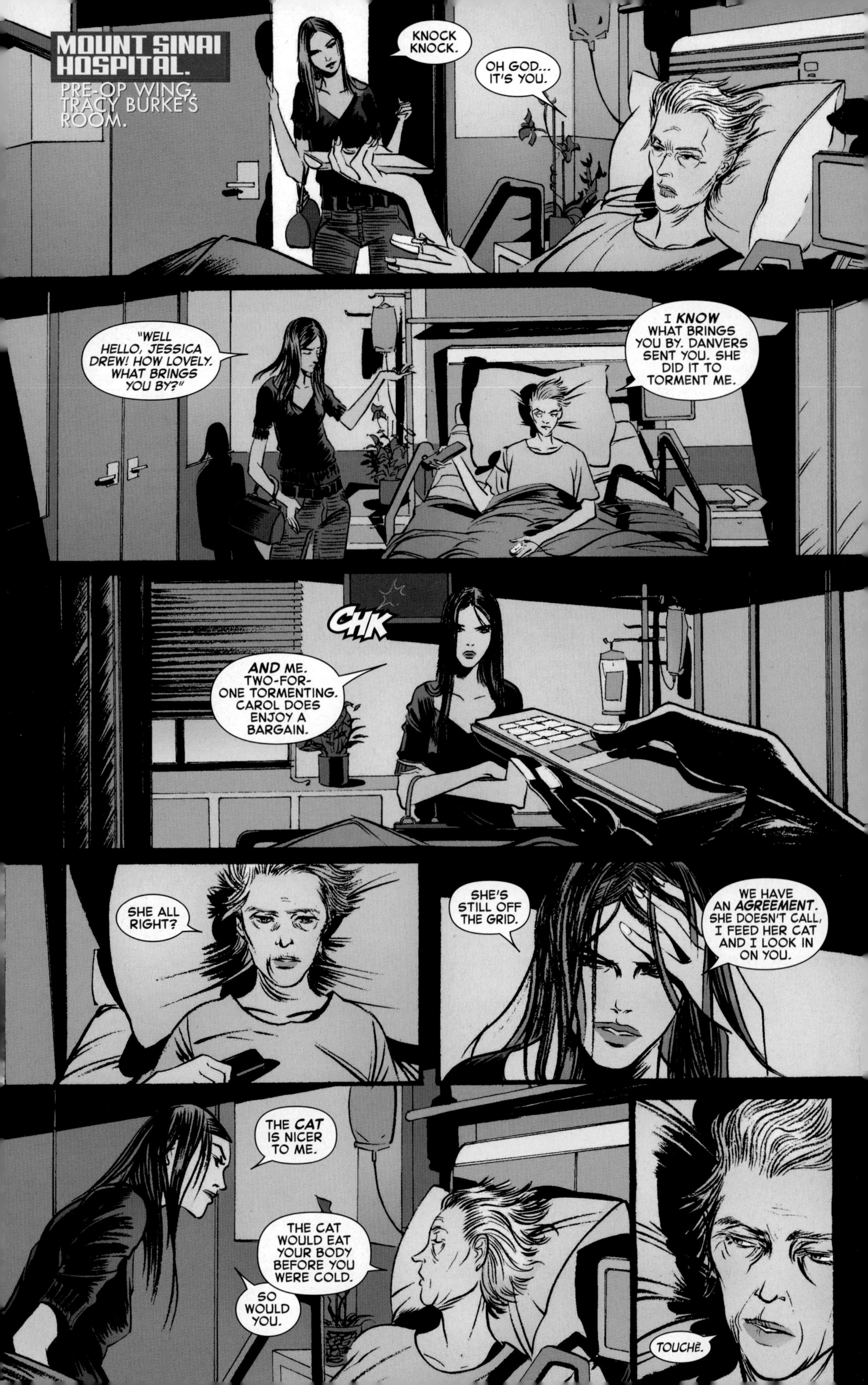
MOUNT SINAI HOSPITAL.
PRE-OP WING, TRACY BURKE'S ROOM.
KNOCK KNOCK.
OH GOD... IT'S YOU.
"WELL HELLO, JESSICA DREW! HOW LOVELY. WHAT BRINGS YOU BY?"
I KNOW WHAT BRINGS YOU BY. DANVERS SENT YOU. SHE DID IT TO TORMENT ME.
CHK
AND ME. TWO-FOR-ONE TORMENTING. CAROL DOES ENJOY A BARGAIN.
SHE ALL RIGHT?
SHE'S STILL OFF THE GRID.
WE HAVE AN AGREEMENT. SHE DOESN'T CALL, I FEED HER CAT AND I LOOK IN ON YOU.
THE CAT IS NICER TO ME.
THE CAT WOULD EAT YOUR BODY BEFORE YOU WERE COLD.
SO WOULD YOU.
TOUCHÉ.

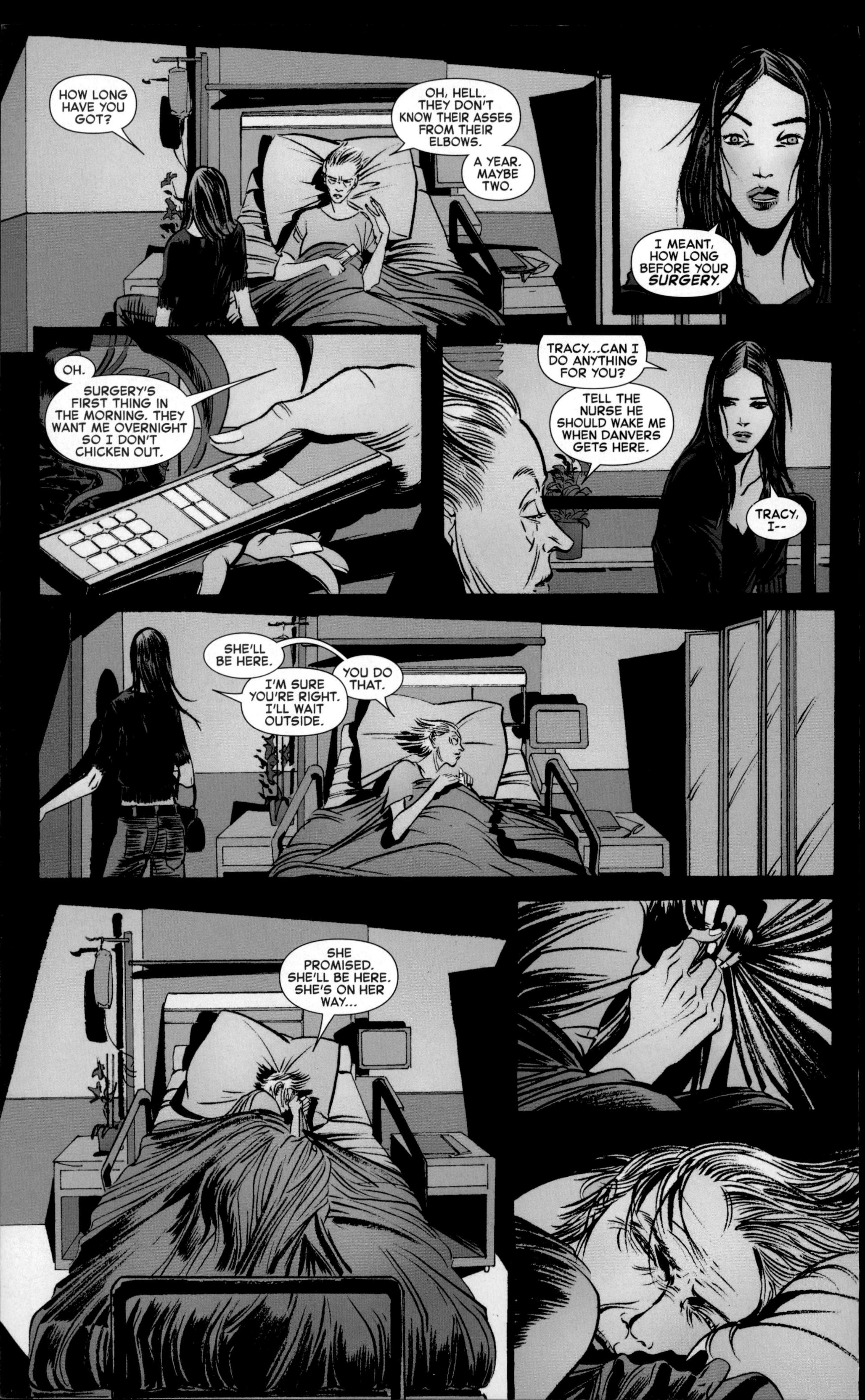
HOW LONG HAVE YOU GOT?
OH, HELL. THEY DON'T KNOW THEIR ASSES FROM THEIR ELBOWS.
A YEAR. MAYBE TWO.
I MEANT, HOW LONG BEFORE YOUR SURGERY.
OH.
SURGERY'S FIRST THING IN THE MORNING. THEY WANT ME OVERNIGHT SO I DON'T CHICKEN OUT.
TRACY...CAN I DO ANYTHING FOR YOU?
TELL THE NURSE HE SHOULD WAKE ME WHEN DANVERS GETS HERE.
TRACY, I--
SHE'LL BE HERE.
YOU DO THAT.
I'M SURE YOU'RE RIGHT. I'LL WAIT OUTSIDE.
SHE PROMISED. SHE'LL BE HERE. SHE'S ON HER WAY...

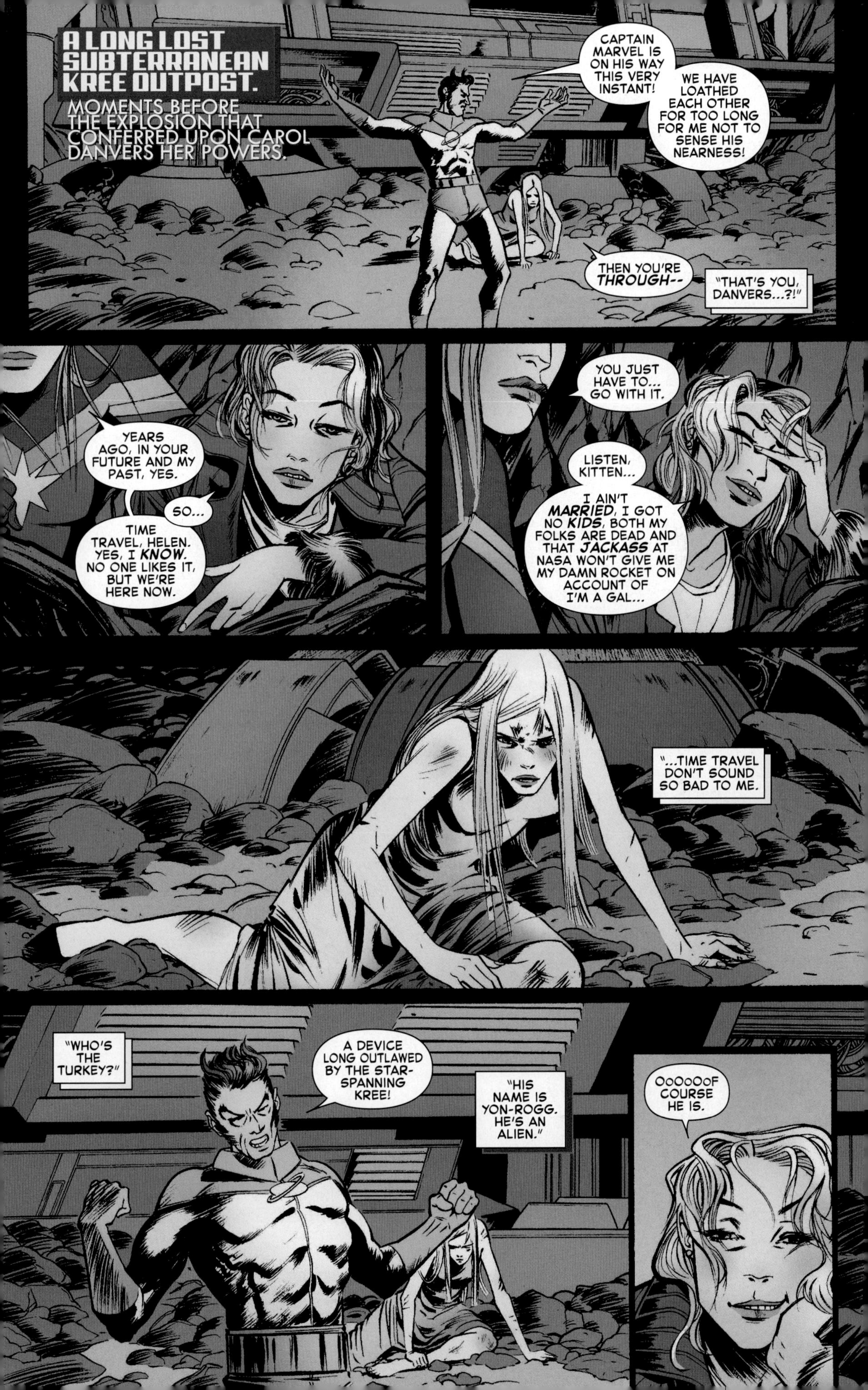
A LONG LOST SUBTERRANEAN KREE OUTPOST.
MOMENTS BEFORE THE EXPLOSION THAT CONFERRED UPON CAROL DANVERS HER POWERS.
CAPTAIN MARVEL IS ON HIS WAY THIS VERY INSTANT!
WE HAVE LOATHED EACH OTHER FOR TOO LONG FOR ME NOT TO SENSE HIS NEARNESS!
THEN YOU'RE THROUGH--
"THAT'S YOU, DANVERS...?!"
YEARS AGO, IN YOUR FUTURE AND MY PAST, YES.
SO...
TIME TRAVEL, HELEN. YES, I KNOW. NO ONE LIKES IT, BUT WE'RE HERE NOW.
YOU JUST HAVE TO... GO WITH IT.
LISTEN, KITTEN...
I AIN'T MARRIED, I GOT NO KIDS, BOTH MY FOLKS ARE DEAD AND THAT JACKASS AT NASA WON'T GIVE ME MY DAMN ROCKET ON ACCOUNT OF I'M A GAL...
"...TIME TRAVEL DON'T SOUND SO BAD TO ME.
"WHO'S THE TURKEY?"
A DEVICE LONG OUTLAWED BY THE STAR-SPANNING KREE!
"HIS NAME IS YON-ROGG. HE'S AN ALIEN."
OOOOOOF COURSE HE IS.

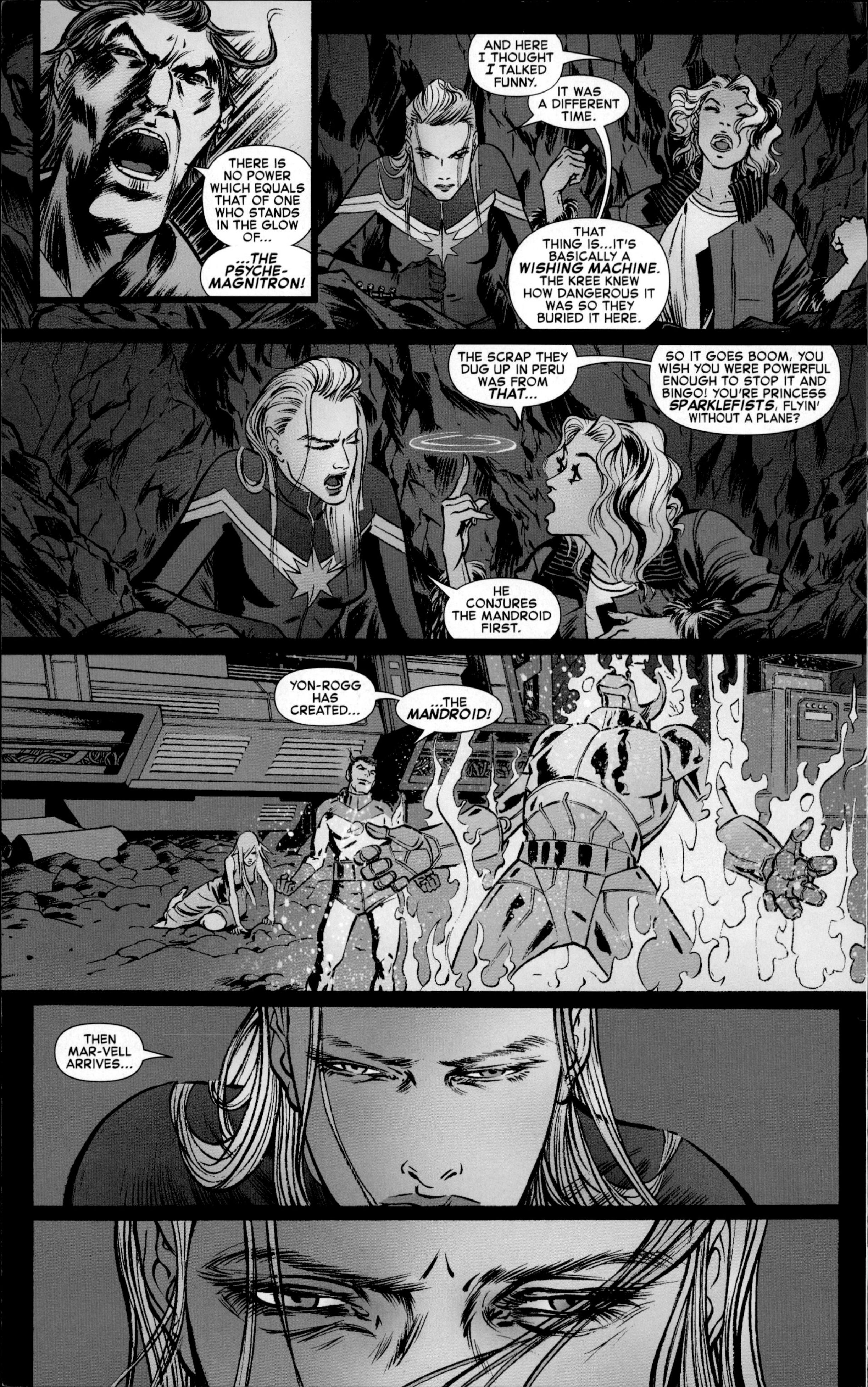
THERE IS NO POWER WHICH EQUALS THAT OF ONE WHO STANDS IN THE GLOW OF...
...THE PSYCHE-MAGNITRON!
AND HERE I THOUGHT I TALKED FUNNY.
IT WAS A DIFFERENT TIME.
THAT THING IS...IT'S BASICALLY A WISHING MACHINE. THE KREE KNEW HOW DANGEROUS IT WAS SO THEY BURIED IT HERE.
THE SCRAP THEY DUG UP IN PERU WAS FROM THAT...
SO IT GOES BOOM, YOU WISH YOU WERE POWERFUL ENOUGH TO STOP IT AND BINGO! YOU'RE PRINCESS SPARKLEFISTS, FLYIN' WITHOUT A PLANE?
HE CONJURES THE MANDROID FIRST.
YON-ROGG HAS CREATED...
...THE MANDROID!
THEN MAR-VELL ARRIVES...

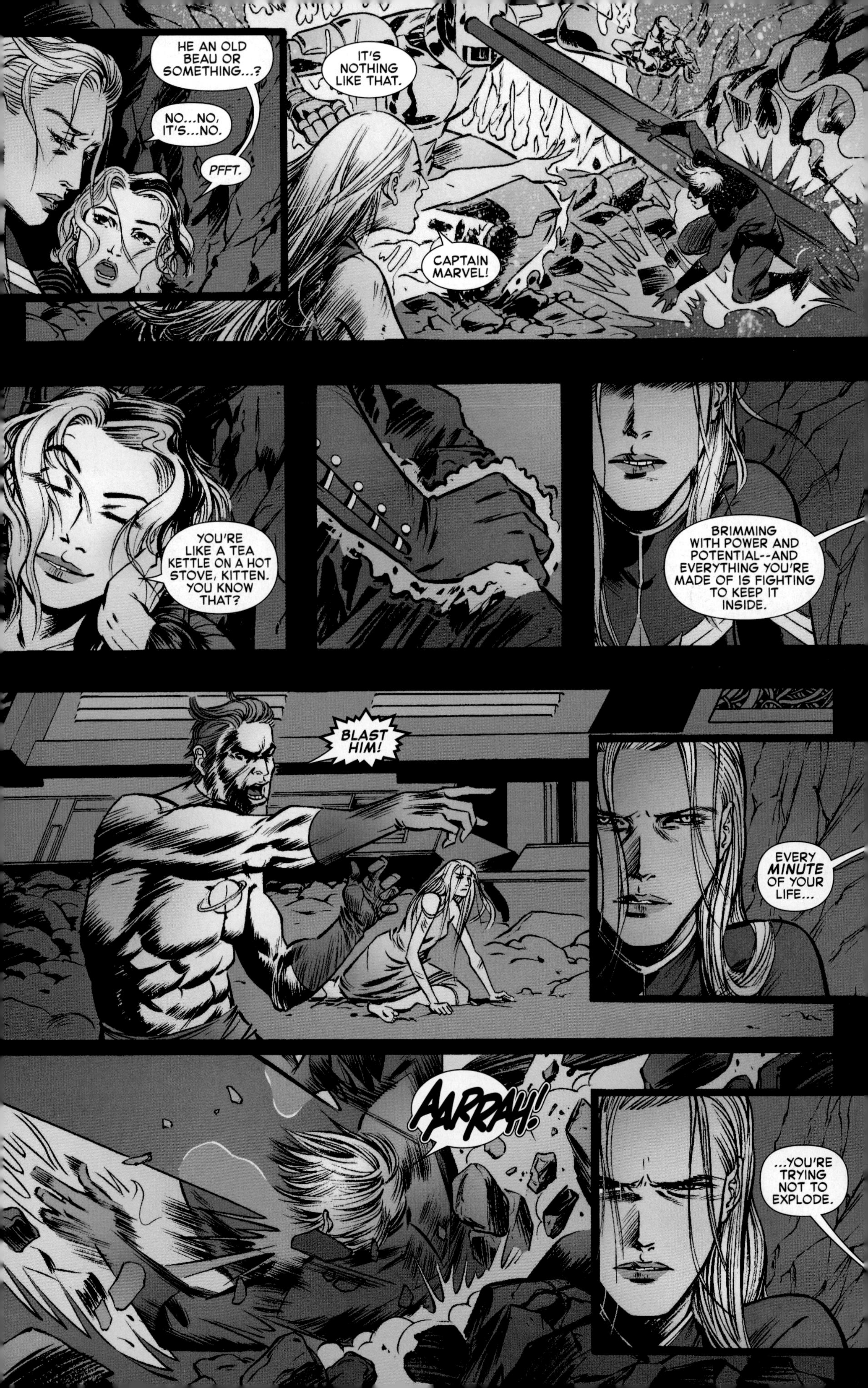
HE AN OLD BEAU OR SOMETHING...?
NO...NO, IT'S...NO.
PFFT.
IT'S NOTHING LIKE THAT.
CAPTAIN MARVEL!
YOU'RE LIKE A TEA KETTLE ON A HOT STOVE, KITTEN. YOU KNOW THAT?
BRIMMING WITH POWER AND POTENTIAL--AND EVERYTHING YOU'RE MADE OF IS FIGHTING TO KEEP IT INSIDE.
BLAST HIM!
EVERY MINUTE OF YOUR LIFE...
AARRAH!
...YOU'RE TRYING NOT TO EXPLODE.

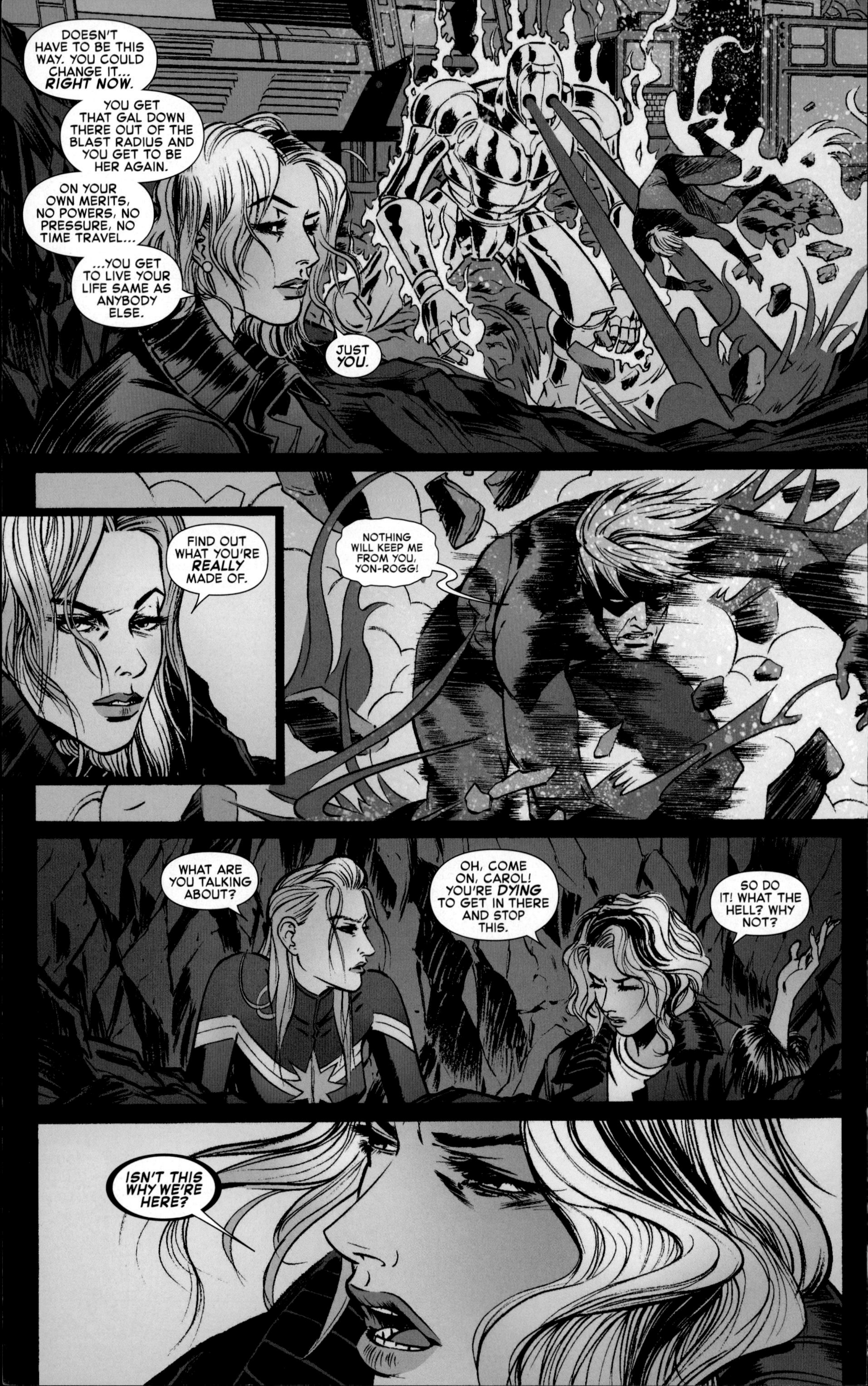
DOESN'T HAVE TO BE THIS WAY. YOU COULD CHANGE IT... RIGHT NOW.
YOU GET THAT GAL DOWN THERE OUT OF THE BLAST RADIUS AND YOU GET TO BE HER AGAIN.
ON YOUR OWN MERITS, NO POWERS, NO PRESSURE, NO TIME TRAVEL...
...YOU GET TO LIVE YOUR LIFE SAME AS ANYBODY ELSE.
JUST YOU.
FIND OUT WHAT YOU'RE REALLY MADE OF.
NOTHING WILL KEEP ME FROM YOU, YON-ROGG!
WHAT ARE YOU TALKING ABOUT?
OH, COME ON, CAROL! YOU'RE DYING TO GET IN THERE AND STOP THIS.
SO DO IT! WHAT THE HELL? WHY NOT?
ISN'T THIS WHY WE'RE HERE?

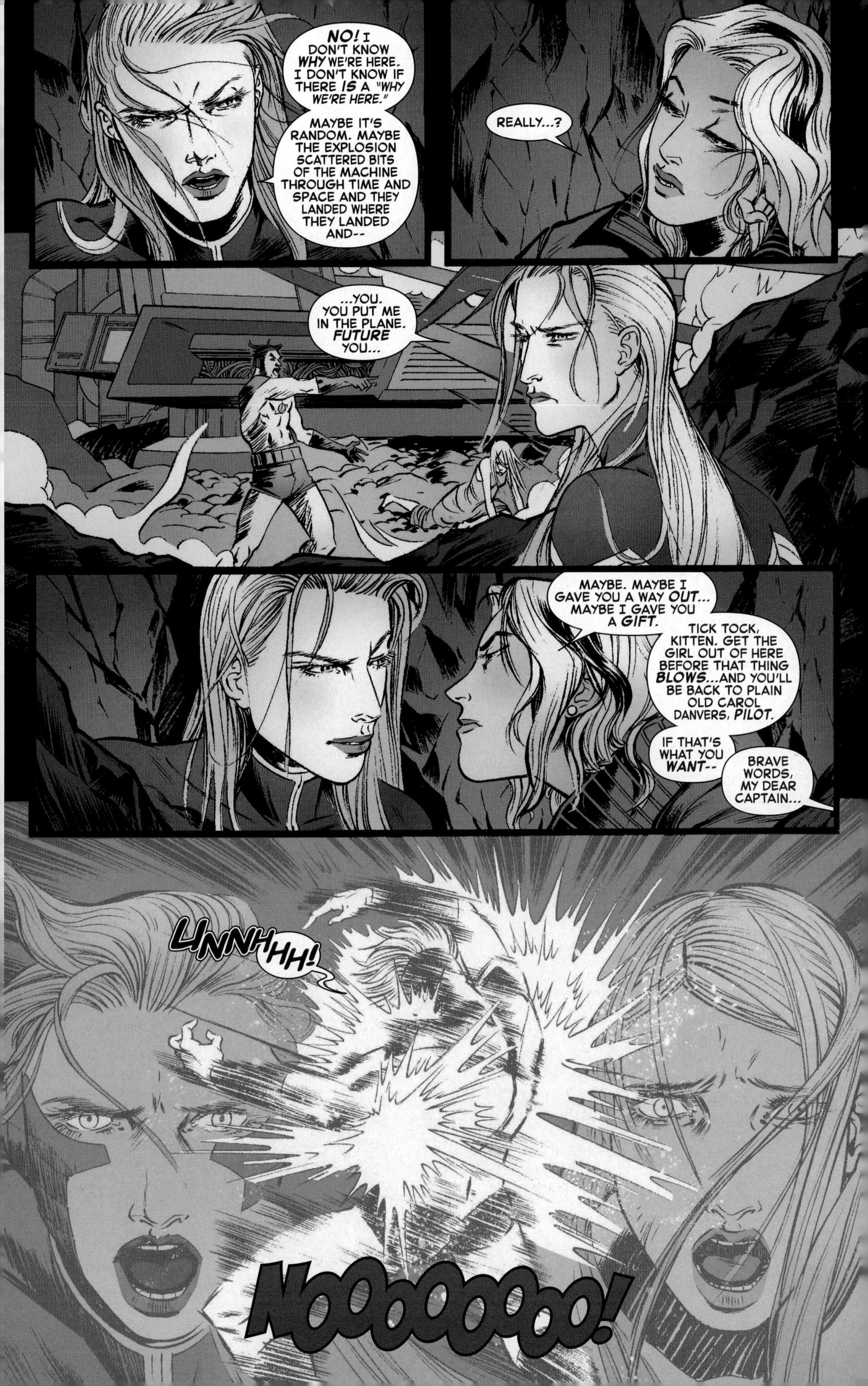
NO! I DON'T KNOW WHY WE'RE HERE. I DON'T KNOW IF THERE IS A "WHY WE'RE HERE."
MAYBE IT'S RANDOM. MAYBE THE EXPLOSION SCATTERED BITS OF THE MACHINE THROUGH TIME AND SPACE AND THEY LANDED WHERE THEY LANDED AND--
REALLY...?
...YOU. YOU PUT ME IN THE PLANE. FUTURE YOU...
MAYBE. MAYBE I GAVE YOU A WAY OUT... MAYBE I GAVE YOU A GIFT.
TICK TOCK, KITTEN. GET THE GIRL OUT OF HERE BEFORE THAT THING BLOWS...AND YOU'LL BE BACK TO PLAIN OLD CAROL DANVERS, PILOT.
IF THAT'S WHAT YOU WANT--
BRAVE WORDS, MY DEAR CAPTAIN...
UNNHHH!
NOOOOOOOO!

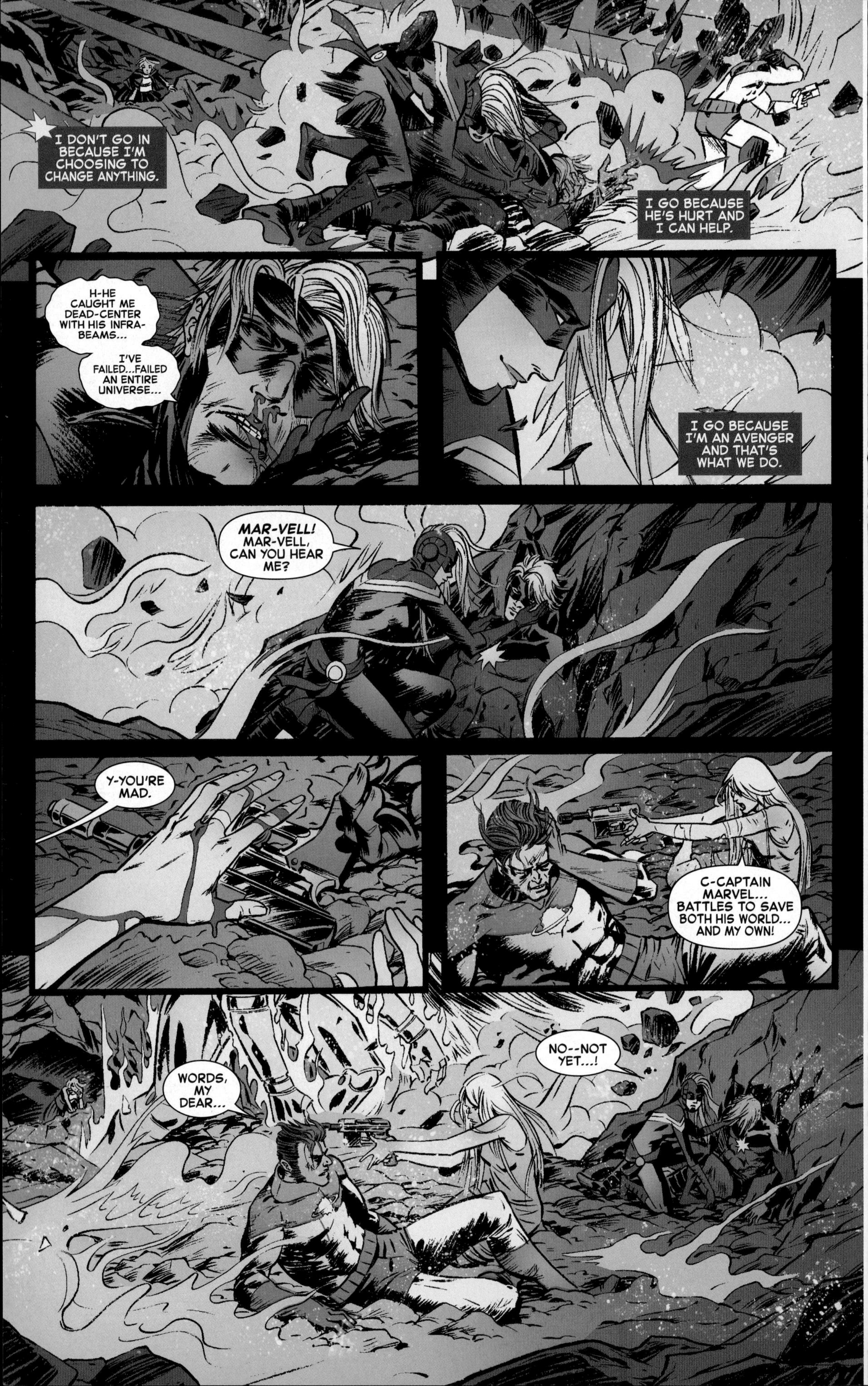
I DON'T GO IN BECAUSE I'M CHOOSING TO CHANGE ANYTHING.
I GO BECAUSE HE'S HURT AND I CAN HELP.
H-HE CAUGHT ME DEAD-CENTER WITH HIS INFRA-BEAMS...
I'VE FAILED...FAILED AN ENTIRE UNIVERSE...
I GO BECAUSE I'M AN AVENGER AND THAT'S WHAT WE DO.
MAR-VELL! MAR-VELL, CAN YOU HEAR ME?
Y-YOU'RE MAD.
C-CAPTAIN MARVEL... BATTLES TO SAVE BOTH HIS WORLD... AND MY OWN!
WORDS, MY DEAR...
NO--NOT YET...!

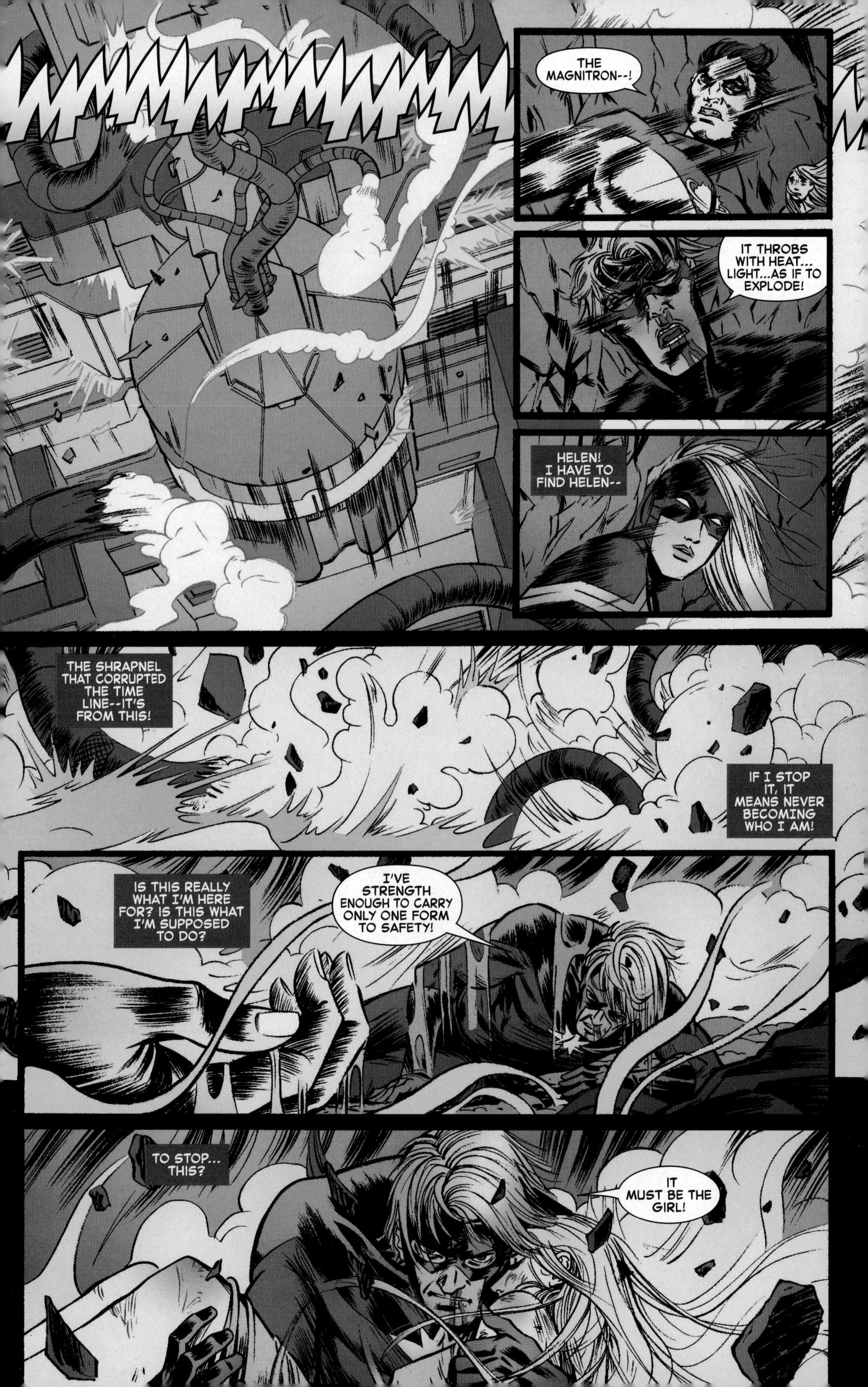
THE MAGNITRON--!
IT THROBS WITH HEAT... LIGHT...AS IF TO EXPLODE!
HELEN! I HAVE TO FIND HELEN--
THE SHRAPNEL THAT CORRUPTED THE TIME LINE--IT'S FROM THIS!
IF I STOP IT, IT MEANS NEVER BECOMING WHO I AM!
IS THIS REALLY WHAT I'M HERE FOR? IS THIS WHAT I'M SUPPOSED TO DO?
I'VE STRENGTH ENOUGH TO CARRY ONLY ONE FORM TO SAFETY!
TO STOP... THIS?
IT MUST BE THE GIRL!

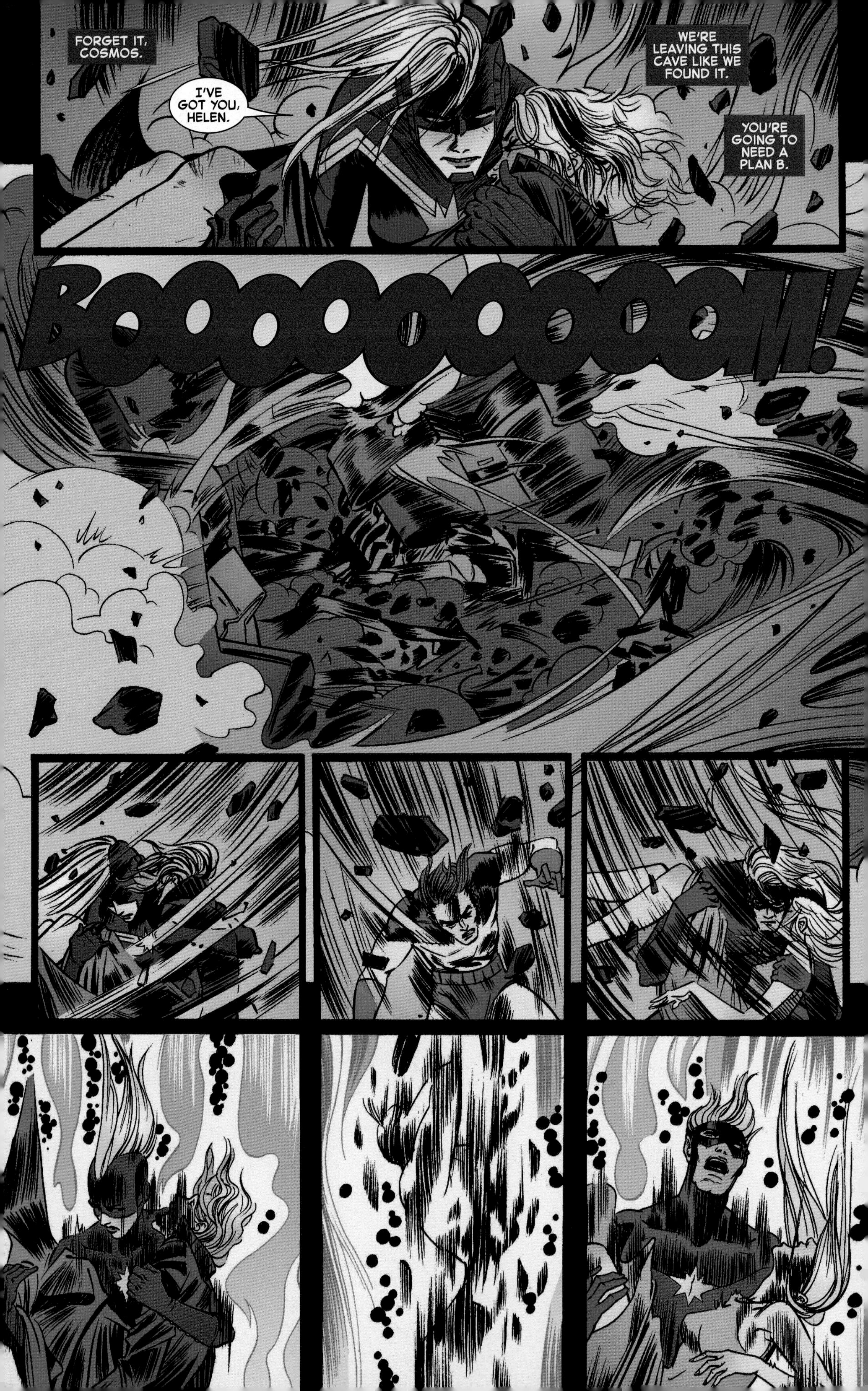

FORGET IT, COSMOS.
I'VE GOT YOU, HELEN.
WE'RE LEAVING THIS CAVE LIKE WE FOUND IT.
YOU'RE GOING TO NEED A PLAN B.
BOOOOOOOOOM!!

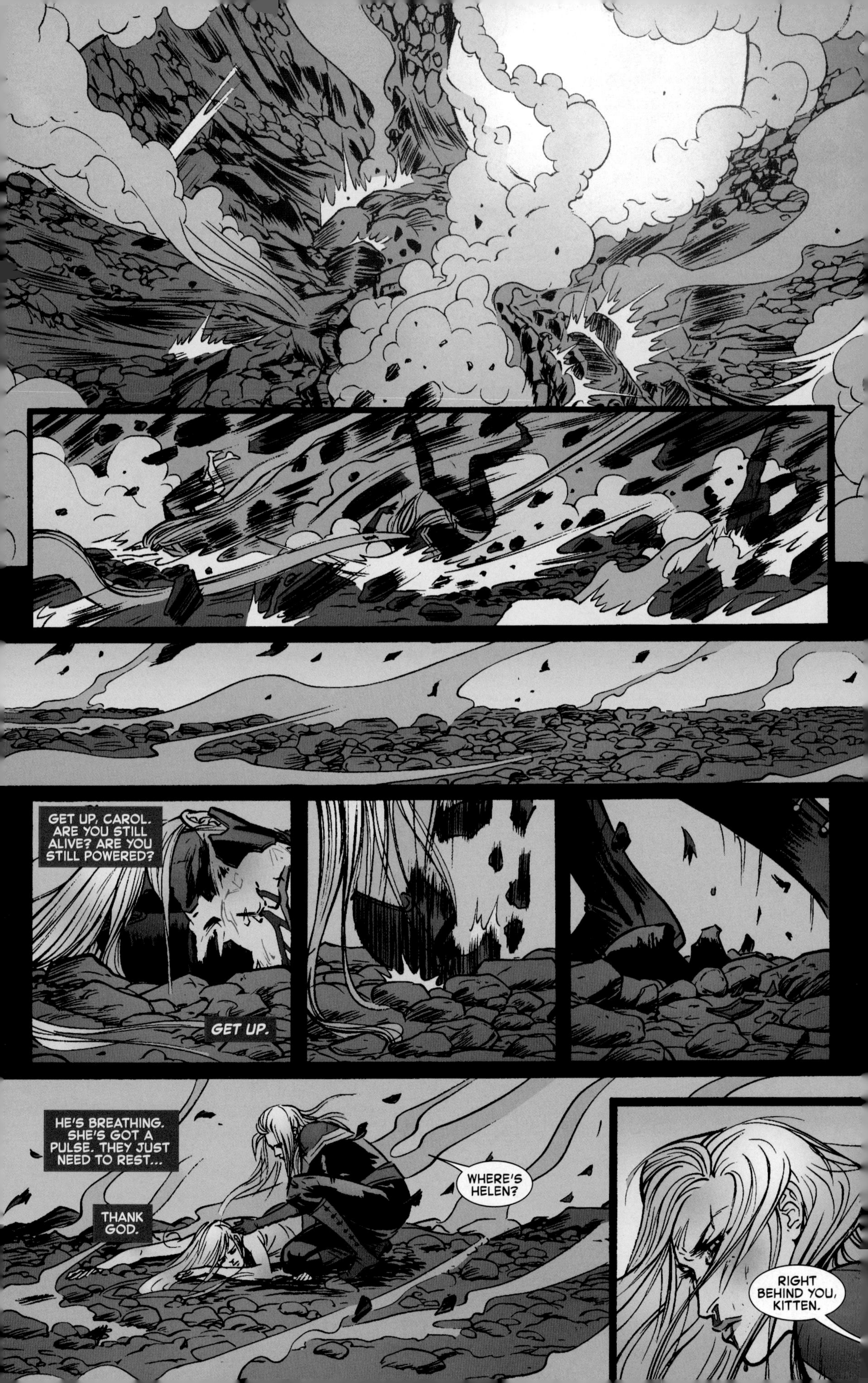
GET UP, CAROL. ARE YOU STILL ALIVE? ARE YOU STILL POWERED?
GET UP.
HE'S BREATHING. SHE'S GOT A PULSE. THEY JUST NEED TO REST...
THANK GOD.
WHERE'S HELEN?
RIGHT BEHIND YOU, KITTEN.

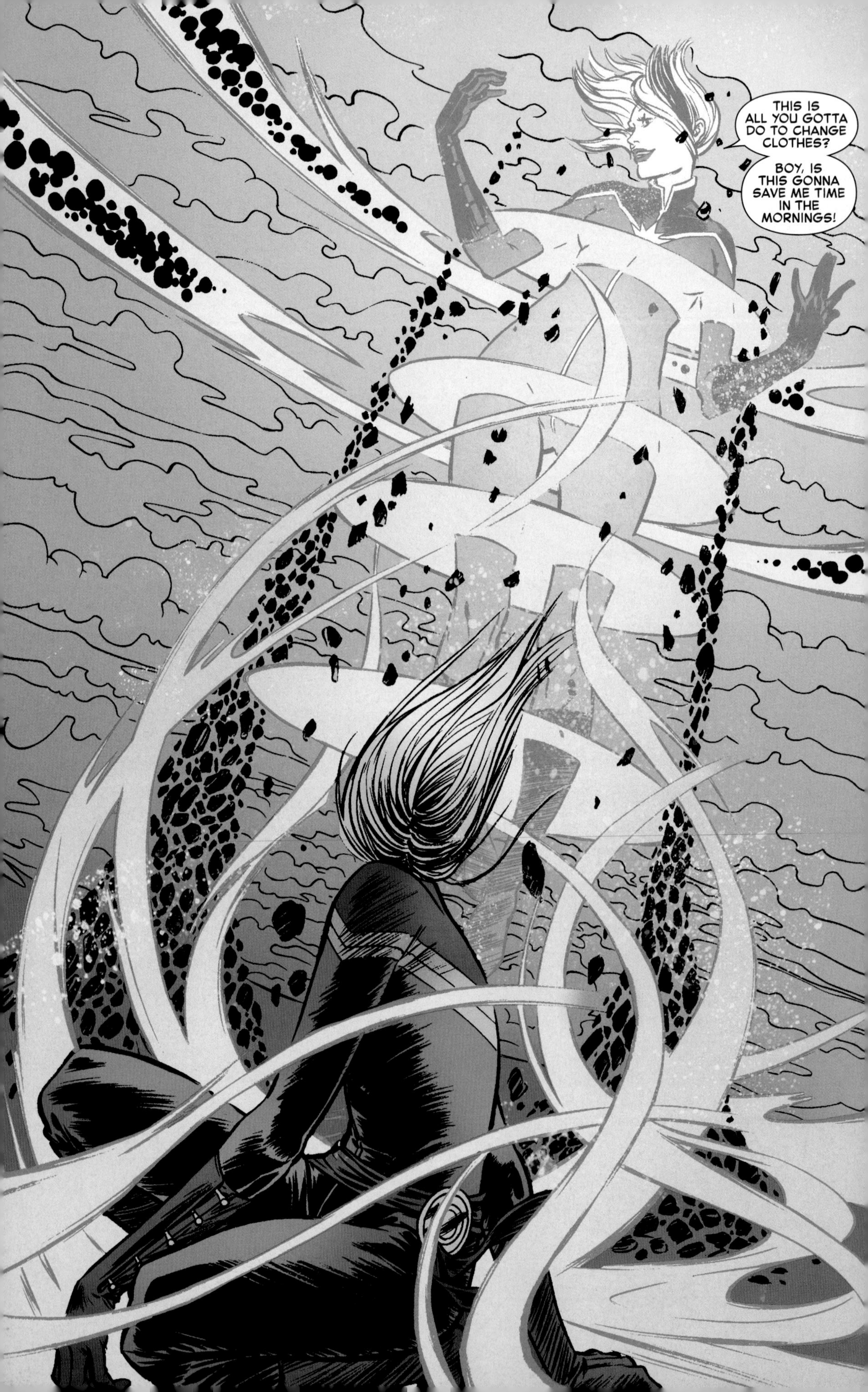
THIS IS ALL YOU GOTTA DO TO CHANGE CLOTHES?
BOY, IS THIS GONNA SAVE ME TIME IN THE MORNINGS!

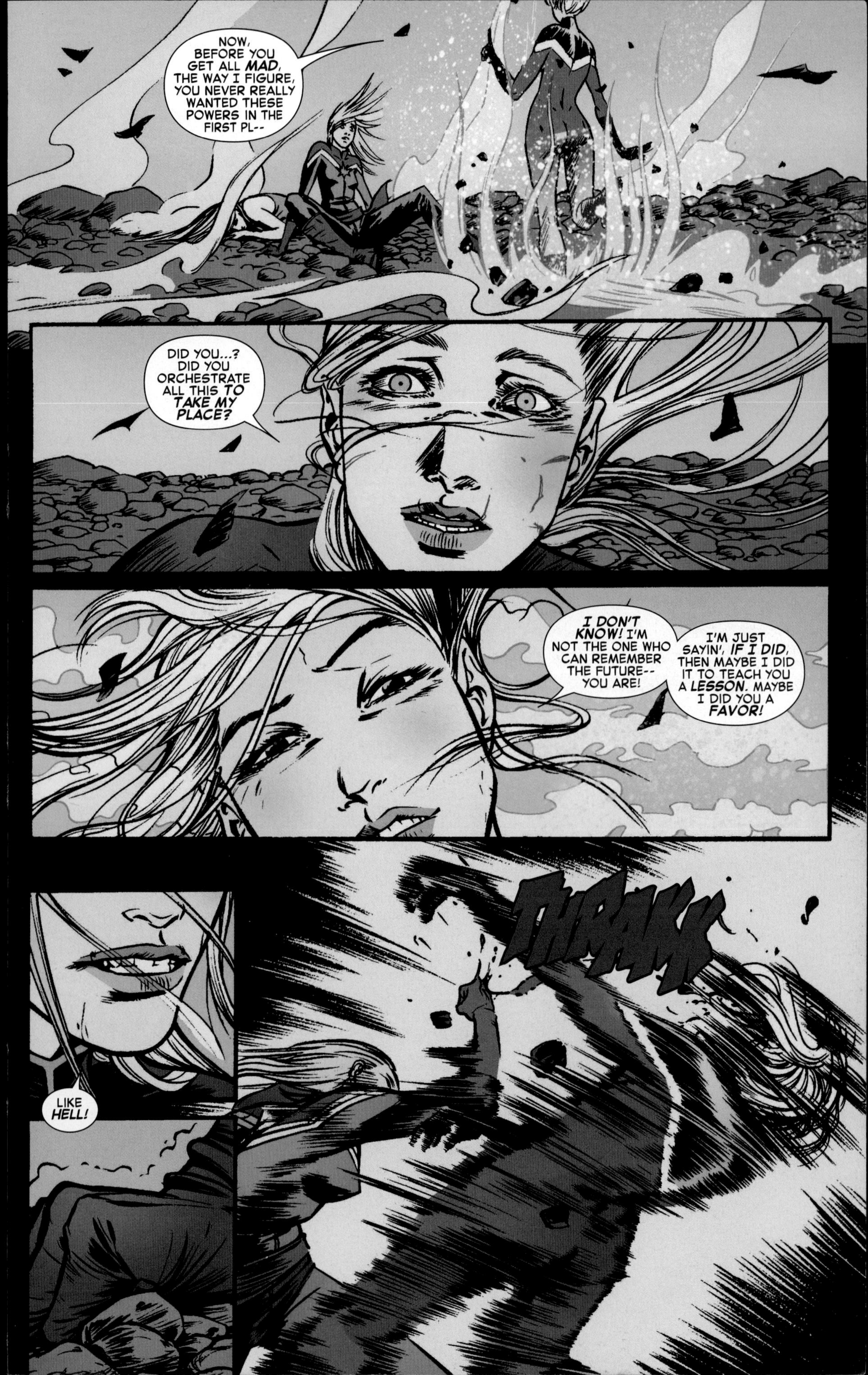
NOW, BEFORE YOU GET ALL MAD, THE WAY I FIGURE, YOU NEVER REALLY WANTED THESE POWERS IN THE FIRST PL--
DID YOU...? DID YOU ORCHESTRATE ALL THIS TO TAKE MY PLACE?
I DON'T KNOW! I'M NOT THE ONE WHO CAN REMEMBER THE FUTURE-- YOU ARE!
I'M JUST SAYIN', IF I DID, THEN MAYBE I DID IT TO TEACH YOU A LESSON. MAYBE I DID YOU A FAVOR!
LIKE HELL!
THRAKK

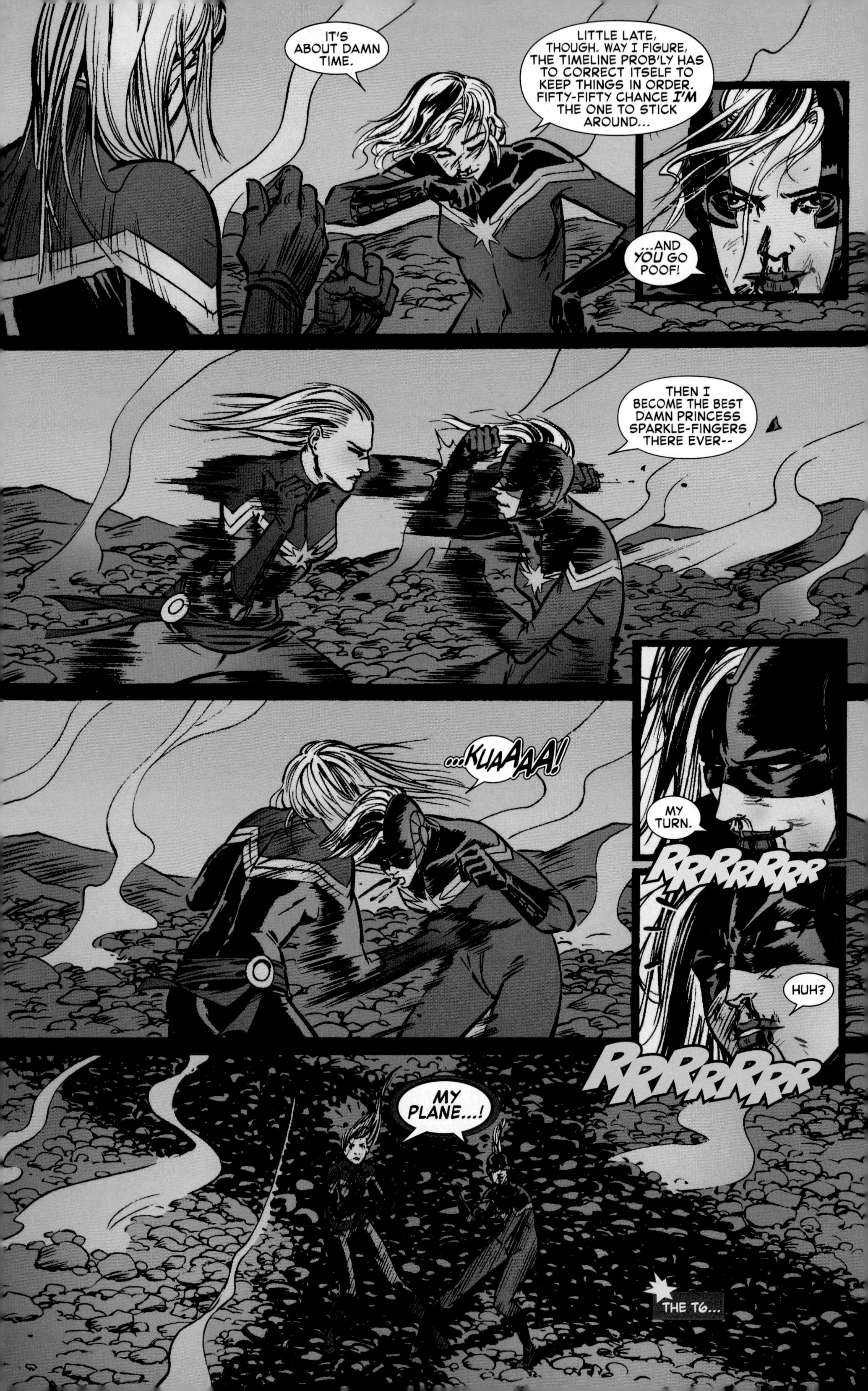
IT'S ABOUT DAMN TIME.
LITTLE LATE, THOUGH. WAY I FIGURE, THE TIMELINE PROB'LY HAS TO CORRECT ITSELF TO KEEP THINGS IN ORDER. FIFTY-FIFTY CHANCE I'M THE ONE TO STICK AROUND...
...AND YOU GO POOF!
THEN I BECOME THE BEST DAMN PRINCESS SPARKLE-FINGERS THERE EVER--
...KLIAAAA!
MY TURN.
RRRRRRRR
HUH?
RRRRRRRR
MY PLANE...!
THE T6...

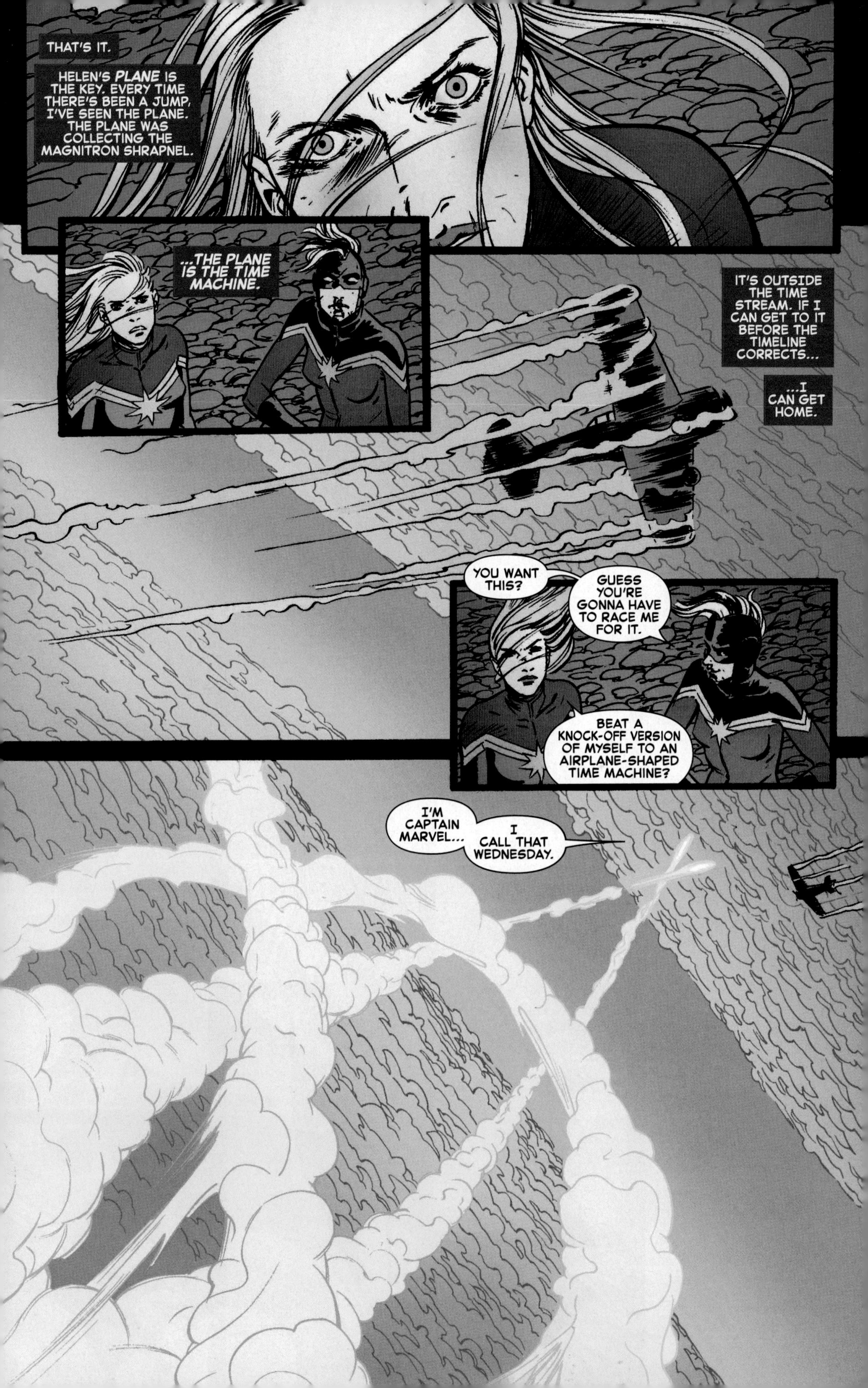
THAT'S IT.
HELEN'S PLANE IS THE KEY. EVERY TIME THERE'S BEEN A JUMP, I'VE SEEN THE PLANE. THE PLANE WAS COLLECTING THE MAGNITRON SHRAPNEL.
...THE PLANE IS THE TIME MACHINE.
IT'S OUTSIDE THE TIME STREAM. IF I CAN GET TO IT BEFORE THE TIMELINE CORRECTS...
...I CAN GET HOME.
YOU WANT THIS?
GUESS YOU'RE GONNA HAVE TO RACE ME FOR IT.
BEAT A KNOCK-OFF VERSION OF MYSELF TO AN AIRPLANE-SHAPED TIME MACHINE?
I'M CAPTAIN MARVEL...
I CALL THAT WEDNESDAY.

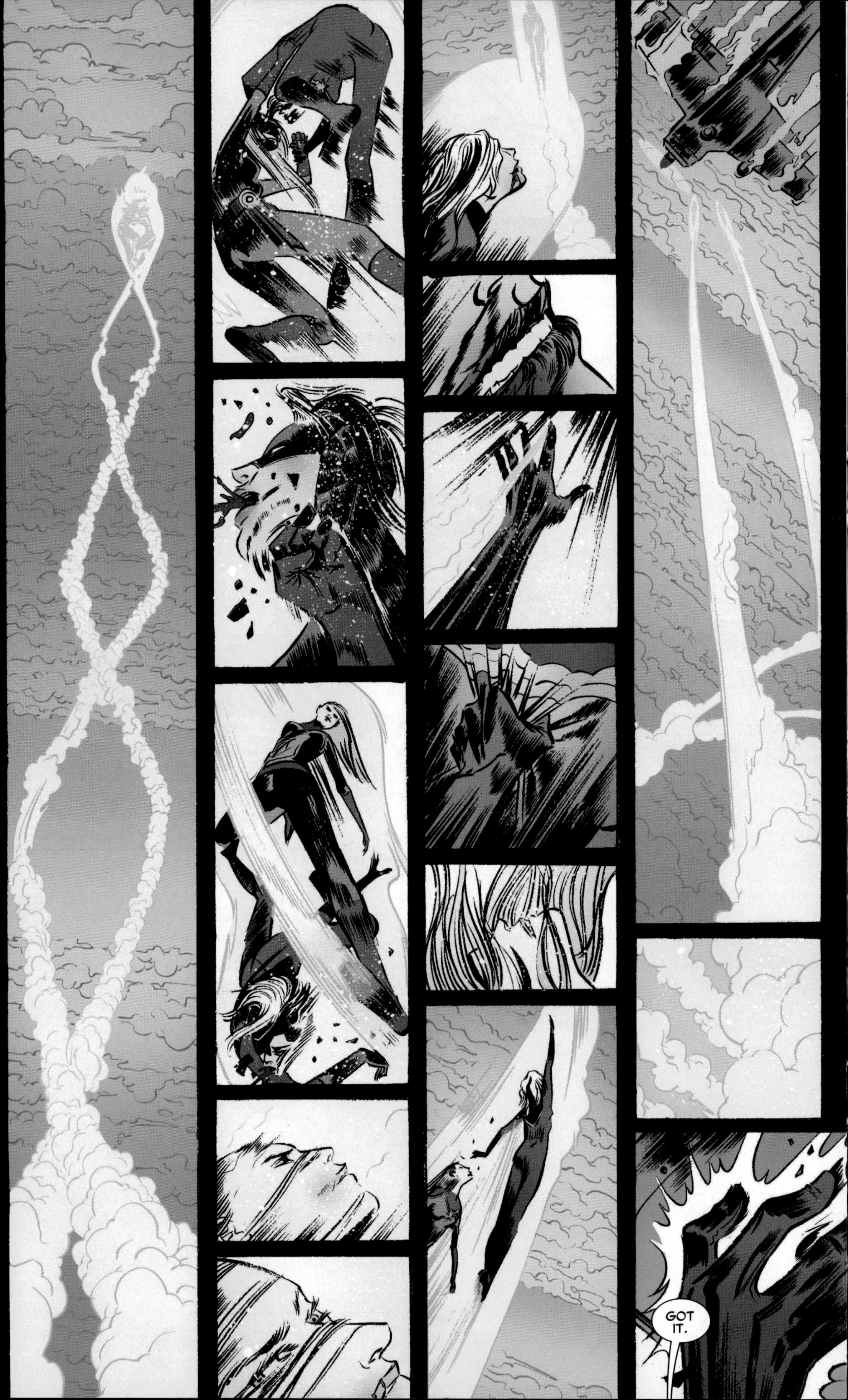
GOT IT.

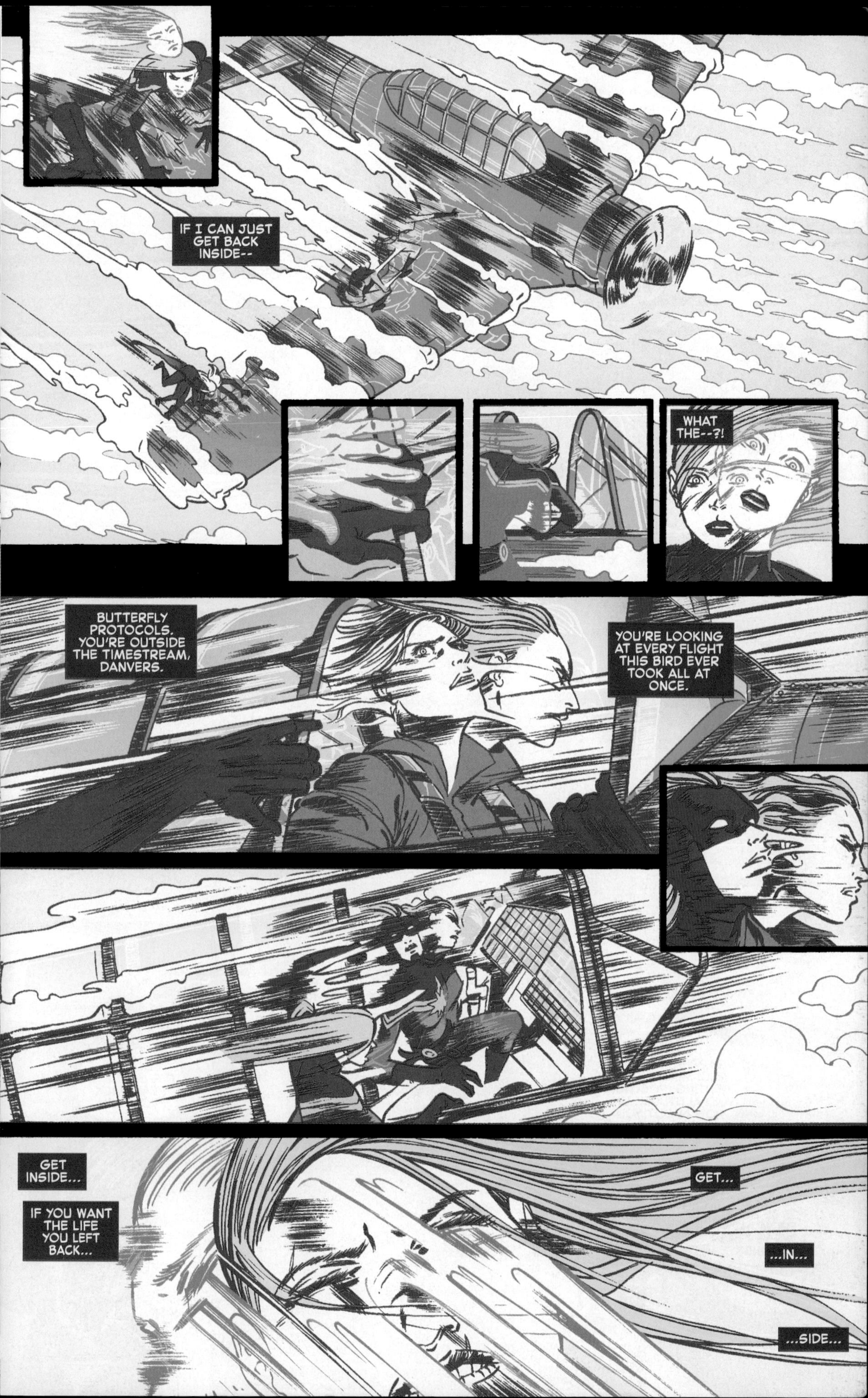
IF I CAN JUST GET BACK INSIDE--
WHAT THE--?!
BUTTERFLY PROTOCOLS. YOU'RE OUTSIDE THE TIMESTREAM, DANVERS.
YOU'RE LOOKING AT EVERY FLIGHT THIS BIRD EVER TOOK ALL AT ONCE.
GET INSIDE...
IF YOU WANT THE LIFE YOU LEFT BACK...
GET...
...IN...
...SIDE...

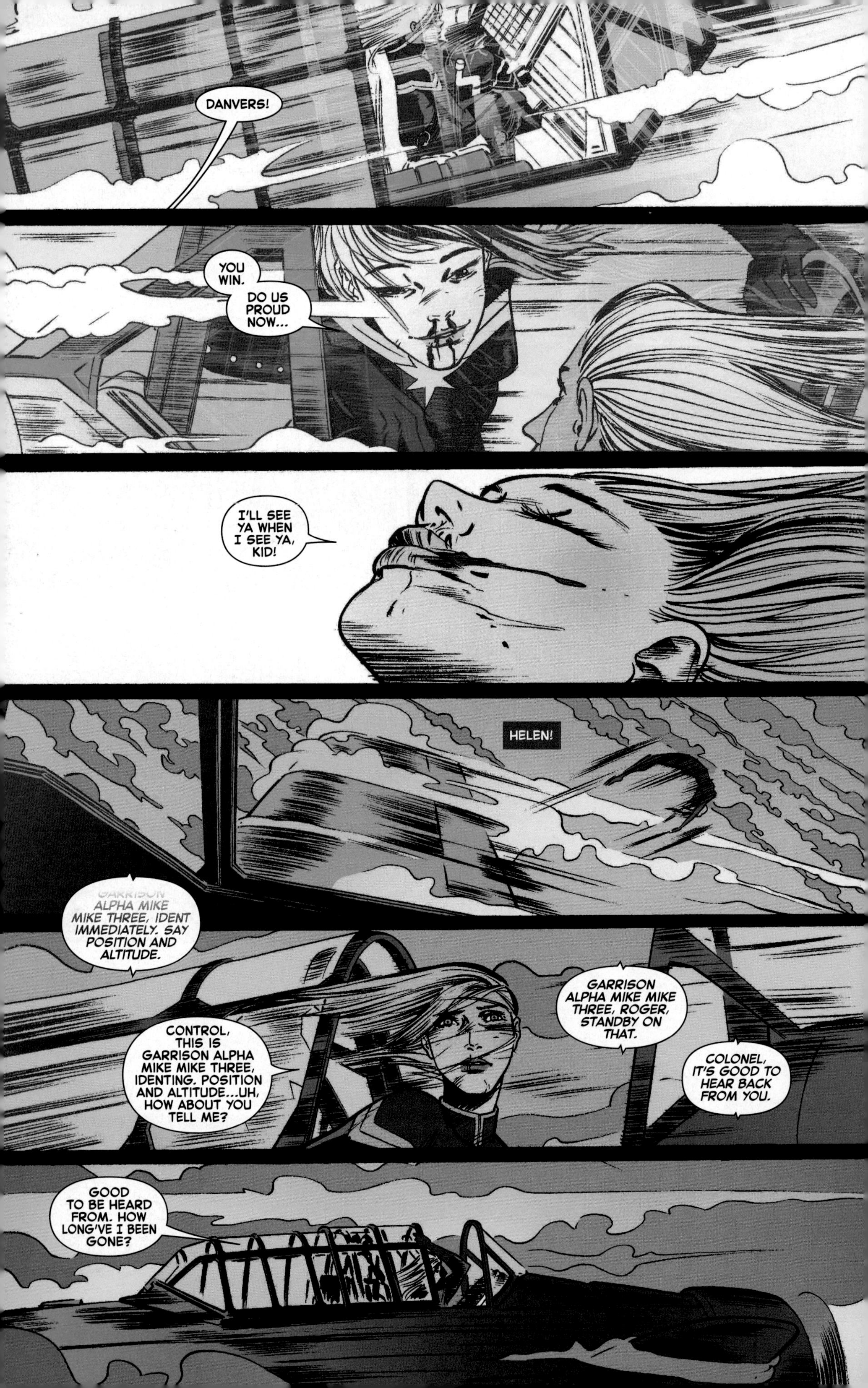
DANVERS!
YOU WIN.
DO US PROUD NOW...
I'LL SEE YA WHEN I SEE YA, KID!
HELEN!
GARRISON ALPHA MIKE MIKE THREE, IDENT IMMEDIATELY. SAY POSITION AND ALTITUDE.
CONTROL, THIS IS GARRISON ALPHA MIKE MIKE THREE, IDENTING. POSITION AND ALTITUDE...UH, HOW ABOUT YOU TELL ME?
GARRISON ALPHA MIKE MIKE THREE, ROGER, STANDBY ON THAT.
COLONEL, IT'S GOOD TO HEAR BACK FROM YOU.
GOOD TO BE HEARD FROM. HOW LONG'VE I BEEN GONE?

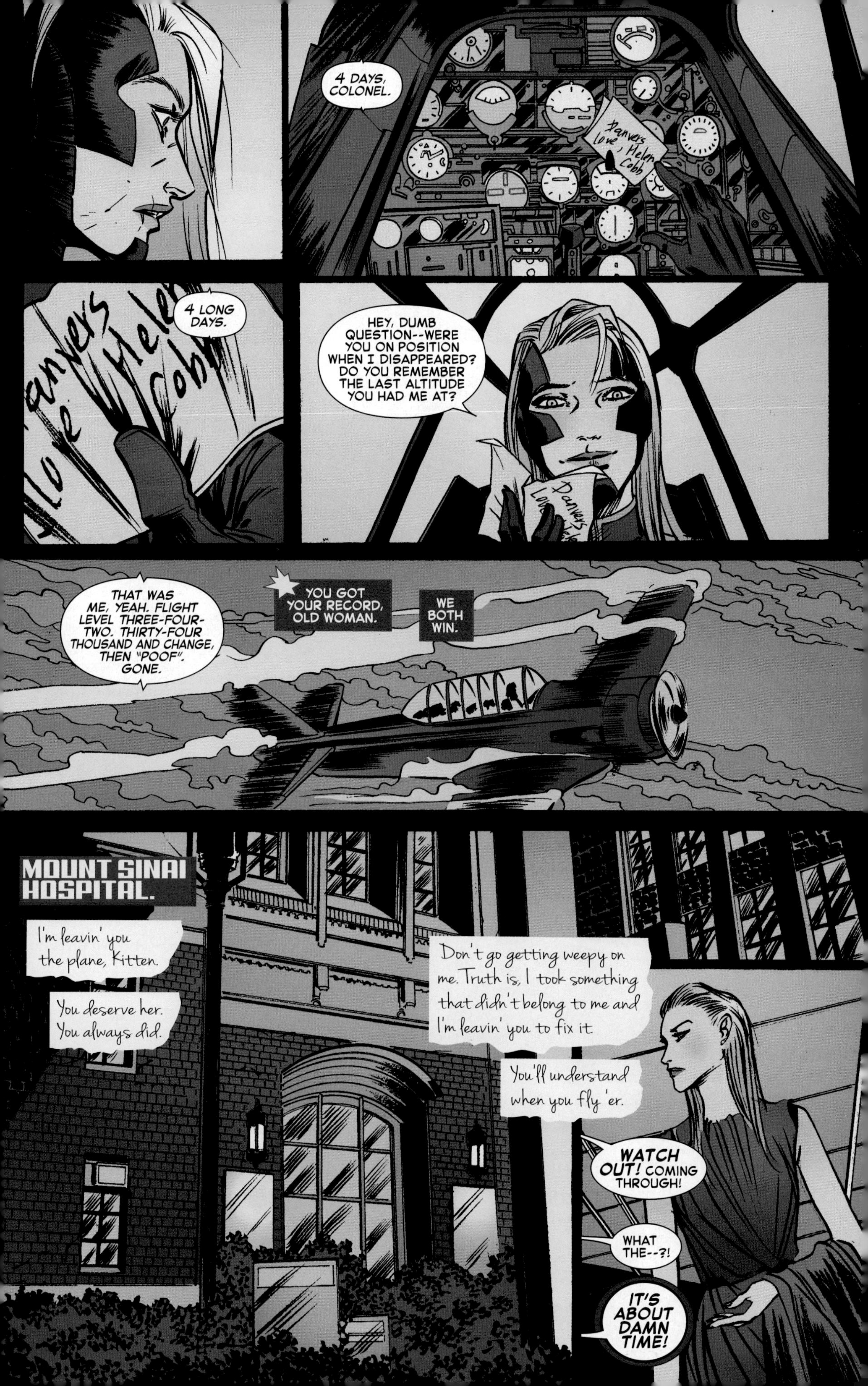
4 DAYS, COLONEL.
Danvers Love, Helen Cobb
4 LONG DAYS.
HEY, DUMB QUESTION--WERE YOU ON POSITION WHEN I DISAPPEARED? DO YOU REMEMBER THE LAST ALTITUDE YOU HAD ME AT?
THAT WAS ME, YEAH. FLIGHT LEVEL THREE-FOUR-TWO. THIRTY-FOUR THOUSAND AND CHANGE, THEN "POOF". GONE.
YOU GOT YOUR RECORD, OLD WOMAN.
WE BOTH WIN.
MOUNT SINAI HOSPITAL.
I'm leavin' you the plane, Kitten.
You deserve her. You always did.
Don't go getting weepy on me. Truth is, I took something that didn't belong to me and I'm leavin' you to fix it.
You'll understand when you fly 'er.
WATCH OUT! COMING THROUGH!
WHAT THE--?!
IT'S ABOUT DAMN TIME!

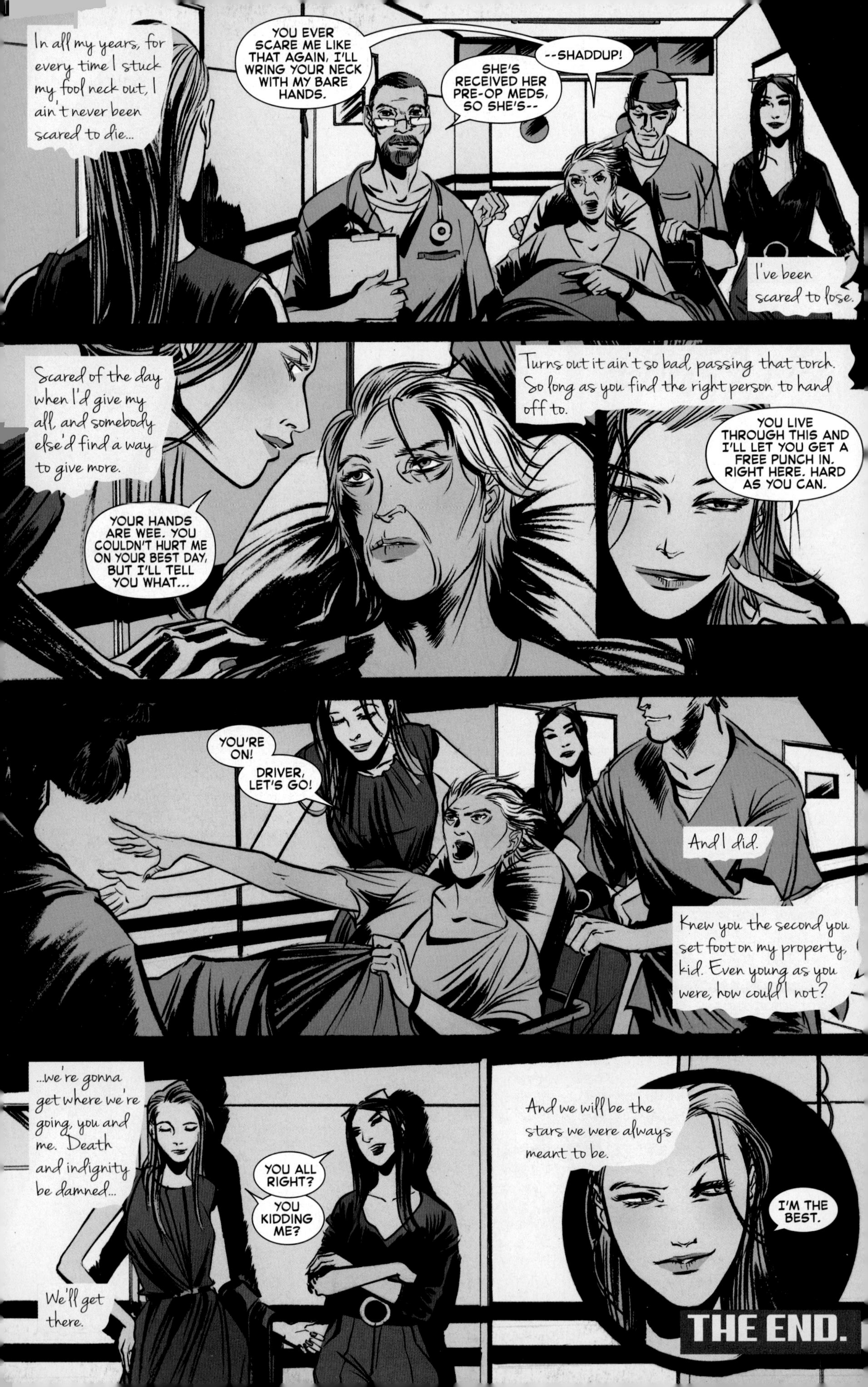

In all my years, for every time I stuck my fool neck out, I ain't never been scared to die...
YOU EVER SCARE ME LIKE THAT AGAIN, I'LL WRING YOUR NECK WITH MY BARE HANDS.
SHE'S RECEIVED HER PRE-OP MEDS, SO SHE'S--
--SHADDUP!
I've been scared to lose.
Scared of the day when I'd give my all, and somebody else'd find a way to give more.
YOUR HANDS ARE WEE. YOU COULDN'T HURT ME ON YOUR BEST DAY, BUT I'LL TELL YOU WHAT...
Turns out it ain't so bad, passing that torch. So long as you find the right person to hand off to.
YOU LIVE THROUGH THIS AND I'LL LET YOU GET A FREE PUNCH IN. RIGHT HERE. HARD AS YOU CAN.
YOU'RE ON!
DRIVER, LET'S GO!
And I did.
Knew you the second you set foot on my property, kid. Even young as you were, how could I not?
...we're gonna get where we're going, you and me. Death and indignity be damned...
YOU ALL RIGHT?
YOU KIDDING ME?
We'll get there.
And we will be the stars we were always meant to be.
I'M THE BEST.
THE END.

CAPTAIN MARVEL

HISTORY: Carol Danvers grew up the oldest child of three in a traditional Boston home, with a contractor father who believed in hard work. When he built their Cape Cod summer home, Carol insisted on working as hard as her younger brothers, trying to make herself the equal of both in her father's eyes. A voracious reader, she dreamed of becoming an astronaut and visiting distant planets; as a teen she even hitchhiked to watch a launch at Cape Canaveral. Her father, however, could not accept women as men's equals, and when financial troubles meant he could send only one child to college, he chose middle child Steve despite Carol's superior grades. Having been moved ahead in school as a child, Steve graduated a year before Carol and chose to enlist in the military at age 17 with his father's permission; at some point, Steve introduced Carol to one of her heroes, pioneering pilot Helen Cobb, the two bonded over a kindred adventurous spirit. When Steve was killed shortly thereafter, the tragedy initially brought the family closer together, Carol's father blamed himself for Steve's death and drank heavily, verbally taking his guilt out on Carol. Carol graduated from high school first in her class and took a summer sales job. A few months later, the day after she turned 18, Carol turned her back on her father and joined the Air Force, intending to get a college degree via the military while pursuing her love of flying.

Rising quickly to the top of her Air Force class, Carol became one of the Force's best fliers and was selected to pilot the new Stark S-73 stealth surveillance jet on its first mission. While taking holographic images of Afghanistan, the plane was shot down, presumably by insurgent Ghazi Rashid's men. Carol survived the crash with an open leg fracture, was captured and repeatedly tortured. After three days, she escaped, killing several of her captors; though Carol believed Rashid was among the slain, he survived. She also stole some of her captors' computer disks, which implied Rashid may have had CIA ties, before limping to a safe house. Air Force Special Operations Colonel Michael Jonathan Rossi debriefed her there. Impressed by Carol, he had her pilot status revoked and enlisted her into Special Operations. While undergoing months of physical rehabilitation for her injuries, Carol trained beside Rossi as a spy, and the pair investigated Rashid's CIA contact (code-named Vitamin). They tracked Vitamin to Berlin only to see his apartment bombed by freelance operative Rick Mason (the Agent), who then escaped. Unbeknownst to Carol, Rossi secretly was Vitamin, and was initially plotting to eventually recruit Carol as his CIA mole in Air Force Special Operations.

Carol became romantically involved with her now partner/mentor Rossi, whom she nicknamed "Ace" on their first Russian mission. Their mission record proved excellent, but their romance eventually faded. She later became friends with Canadian agent Logan (James Howlett, later Wolverine); they faced underworld ninjas in Madripoor, and Logan saved Carol's life when her cover was blown while investigating Jacques Preen, a dangerous Canadian arms dealer. Carol was later drawn into New York's Hellfire Club's plot to conceal the existence of mutants while privately exploiting them. After killing four agents who tried to murder her in her hotel room, Carol helped Logan protect Dr. Perry Edwards, who intended to expose the so-called "mutant hierarchy." Edwards died when the Hellfire Club's Victor Creed seemingly killed himself while detonating a bomb, hospitalizing Carol for a month. Following her recovery, she took her information on the underground mutants to up-and-coming Senator Robert Kelly, setting him on a path that would define his career.

Carol later teamed with the CIA's Colonel Nick Fury; posing as scientist Myron MacLain's secretary, she again encountered Logan, now an amnesiac, when he came to MacLain for Adamantium information. Carol and Fury witnessed a conflict involving Logan, a team of Hydra agents, operative Victor Creed (later Sabretooth) and Russian Natalia Shostakova (later the Black Widow/Natasha Romanoff). Fury soon sent Carol, pilot Ben Grimm (later the Fantastic Four's Thing) and Logan into Russia to investigate the top-secret Red Storm espionage project; shot down by Russians, Carol escaped capture, stole a plane, rescued

REAL NAME: Carol Susan Jane Danvers
ALIASES: Ms. Marvel, Warbird, Lady Marvel, Binary, "Ace," Cheeseburger; pseudonyms used have included Carol Daniels, Karolya Danilovska, Linda Danvers, Catherine Donovan, others.
IDENTITY: Publicly known
OCCUPATION: Adventurer; former licensed super hero, instructor in "Training Day" program, author, Department of Homeland Security chief of tactical operations, freelance writer, NASA security chief, Woman Magazine chief editor, US Air Force Special Operations intelligence agent, pilot, salesgirl (Note: Carol's intelligence work required her to claim to be working for several agencies, including the CIA, the Department of Defense, and the Defense Intelligence Agency. Though she did work with many of these agencies, she was a USAF employee.)
CITIZENSHIP: USA
PLACE OF BIRTH: Boston, Massachusetts
KNOWN RELATIVES: Joseph "Joe" Danvers (father, deceased), Marie Danvers (mother), Steven J. Danvers (brother, deceased), Joseph "Joe" Danvers, Jr. (brother), Benny (uncle)
GROUP AFFILIATION: Avengers; formerly Operation: Lightning Storm, Initiative, Queen's Vengeance, Starjammers
EDUCATION: Extensive military training, acquired BA while in military
FIRST APPEARANCE: (Danvers) Marvel Super-Heroes #13 (1967); (Ms. Marvel) Ms. Marvel #1 (1977); (Binary) Uncanny X-Men #164 (1982); (Warbird) Avengers #4 (1998); (Captain Marvel, Reality-58163) Secrets of the House of M (2005); (Captain Marvel, Reality-616) Avenging Spider-Man #9 (2012)

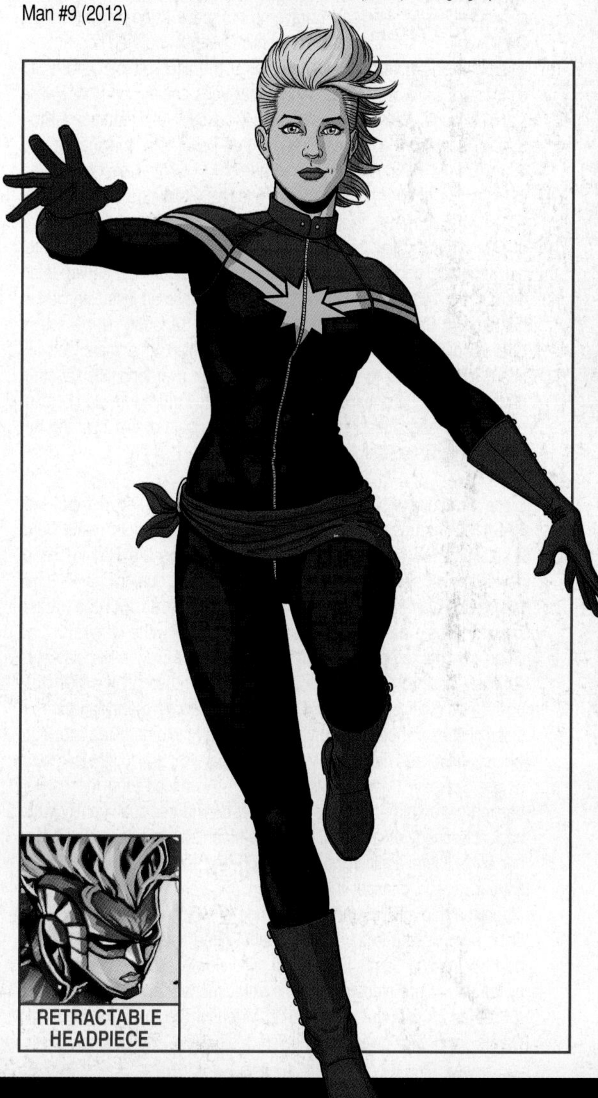
RETRACTABLE
HEADPIECE

Art by Jamie McKelvie & Dexter Soy (inset)

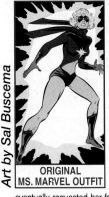

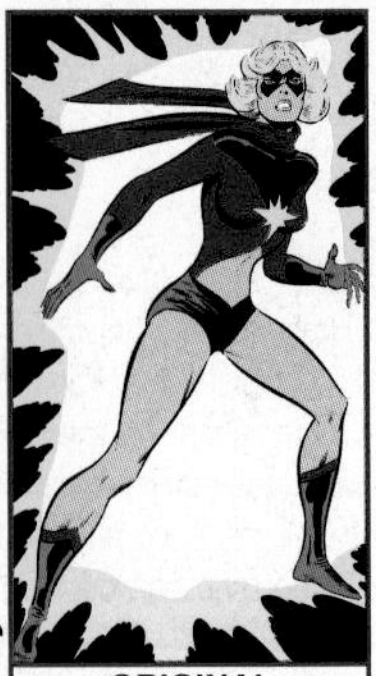
ORIGINAL MS. MARVEL OUTFIT

Art by Sal Buscema

Grimm and Logan (despite a dogfight with Shostakova), and completed the mission. As all this was classified top secret, she and her fellows would later publicly pretend not to recognize each other.

When Carol was captured and held in Russia's Lubyanka prison, Rossi and Logan went rogue to break her out. Shortly thereafter, a position as head of security at NASA's Kennedy Space Center opened up, and Carol's old dreams of space led her to call in her markers as she exploited the many contacts she had made in NASA over the years to lobby for that job. NASA eventually requested her for the position and she resigned from the Air Force, bumping to full colonel at retirement. Now the youngest security captain in NASA's history, she became embroiled in the schemes of the interstellar Kree Empire. She was present when the robotic Kree Sentry 459 was transported to NASA for study, and got caught in the middle when Kree soldier Captain Mar-Vell battled it after it awoke. During her NASA stint she led an investigation into Mar-Vell's assumed alter ego, Dr. Lawson, which proved beneficial when the Super-Skrull (Kl'rt) briefly also impersonated Lawson and was exposed. On another occasion, Carol singlehandedly recovered a shuttle stolen by a Skrull agent and in doing so finally achieved her dream of traveling into space. In the coming months Carol would be kidnapped by the robotic Cyberex and then hospitalized when a villain-controlled Iron Man (Tony Stark) attacked the Center. Still concussed, Carol was kidnapped by Mar-Vell's enemy Yon-Rogg; while Mar-Vell fought Yon-Rogg, Carol was knocked into a damaged Kree Psyche-Magnitron, a powerful device that could turn imagination into reality. Carol's dreams of flight and her envy of Mar-Vell's powers led the machine to alter her genetically, effectively making her a half-Kree superhuman; however, this change was gradual, and Carol was unaware of it for months. After the Sentry reactivated and damaged the Center before departing in pursuit of the Avengers, Earth's premier superhuman team, Carol's continued inability to control superhuman incursions led to her removal. She was reassigned to a minor NASA facility near Chicago. After Nitro raided that base, Carol was demoted to a mere security guard and returned to Kennedy Space Center. Not long after another alien incursion, Carol learned of Rossi's reported death in a plane crash, unaware he had actually survived. In the aftermath of this loss and her plummeting career, Carol resigned from NASA.

Living off accumulated salary, Carol wrote an angry tell-all exposé of NASA, burning many bridges. The best-selling book briefly made Carol a celebrity, and she wrote for national magazines like Rolling Stone; however, she also developed a dual personality due to the Psyche-Magnitron's alterations. She would black out and become a Kree warrior, instantaneously donning a costume which the Psyche-Magnitron had created for her to ease her body's changes. These fugue-like blackouts seriously alarmed Carol, but didn't stop her from accepting a New York position as chief editor at the Daily Bugle's new Woman Magazine. In times of stress, she would continue to transform into her Kree alter ego, who soon took the name Ms. Marvel after Mar-Vell. She fought foes such as the Scorpion (Mac Gargan) and AIM (Advanced Idea Mechanics) before before Carol discovered the truth behind her dual identity while back at Kennedy on a story; the Psyche-Magnitron was destroyed during her battle there against the Destructor, and the explosion completed Carol's genetic change; the explosion apparently sent shards of the Magnitron through time and space, one of which was found by Helen Cobb, who used it to transform a plane into a time machine. Over the next few months Carol's fragmented mind slowly recovered, first pushed by the benevolent interference of the extradimensional Hecate, and when a Kree attack with the mind-altering Millennia Bloom device backfired, Carol's mind was completely healed. Meanwhile, she became one of New York's premier heroines, Woman Magazine profiling her while she worked with Spider-Man (Peter Parker), the Defenders, the Avengers and others, and became friendly with the Avengers' Wonder Man (Simon Williams). Abandoning her Mar-Vell-derived costume, she donned her own original costume and became a full-fledged Avenger, replacing an absent Scarlet Witch. Carol reveled in her new status, aiding the team against foes like Chthon, the Absorbing Man and the Grey Gargoyle (Paul Duval), and fitting in personally as well, even joining the Avengers' regular poker games; however, things began to grow bleak when Carol was fired from her editorial job due to her frequent disappearances. She rescued her astronaut friend Salia Petrie from the alien Faceless One, but Salia was severely traumatized. Carol's psychiatrist and close friend, Michael Barnett, was murdered by mutant shape-shifter Mystique, whose precognitive associate Destiny (Irene Adler) had warned her that Carol would hurt Mystique's foster-daughter Rogue (Anna Marie). Barnett's murder pulled Ms. Marvel into conflict with the Hellfire Club and Mystique's Brotherhood of Evil Mutants. Before she could track down Mystique, Carol's extradimensional admirer Marcus, the son of time-traveler Immortus, kidnapped Carol to timeless Limbo, wooed her with a "subtle boost" from mind-influencing devices, impregnated himself into her, and returned her to Earth with no memory of this. Finding herself seemingly impossibly pregnant, Carol came to term in less than two days, and she delivered the child, Marcus, who grew to adulthood in one day; however, Marcus continued to age quickly towards death. Still under the lingering mental influence of his devices, Carol told the Avengers she loved Marcus and accompanied him back to Limbo. Once there, his rapid aging unexpectedly continued and he soon died, leaving Carol trapped in Limbo. She eventually found her way home and, resenting the Avengers for not seeing through Marcus, gave up her Ms. Marvel identity and secretly settled down in San Francisco.

Mystique continued plotting Carol's downfall, however, and Rogue decided to remove this thorn from her foster-mother's side, attacking Carol herself. Their fierce battle atop the Golden Gate Bridge ended when Rogue's absorption of Carol's powers, memories and emotions accidentally became permanent. Thrown from the bridge, Carol was rescued by Spider-Woman (Jessica Drew), who brought the powerless and near-amnesiac Carol to Professor Charles Xavier for treatment. He restored most of her memories, though her emotional ties to them remained lost. After a bitter confrontation with the Avengers, Carol remained with Xavier and his X-Men, working to restore her mind. Aiding the X-Men for weeks, Carol led them in infiltrating the Pentagon to delete their governmental records. She encountered Rogue and Mystique there for the first time since their attacks on her; while the X-Men defeated Rogue, Carol captured Mystique and turned her over to the authorities. Soon after, the alien Brood captured Carol and the X-Men. Fascinated by her genetic structure, they manipulated Carol's physiology up and down the evolutionary scale before Wolverine freed her. These manipulations transformed Carol into the energy-wielding Binary, and she helped defeat the Brood, destroying their homeworld and the outworld of Madrizar, and freeing the Brood's slave race, the Acanti. She returned home with the X-Men, but her childhood dreams of space travel beckoned. After learning of Mar-Vell's death by cancer and holding an emotionless farewell with her parents, she left the X-Men on bad terms upon learning they had allowed the troubled Rogue to join their group, Destiny's prediction coming true as Carol's stolen memories had come to torment her. After punching Rogue through their roof, Carol departed Earth and joined the space-faring Starjammers.

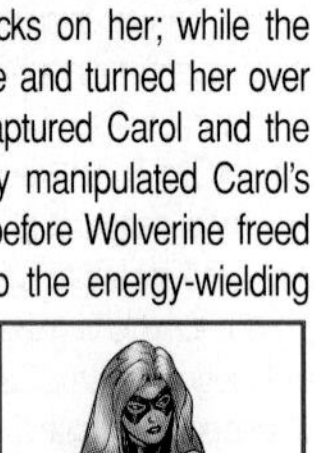
2ND MS. MARVEL OUTFIT

Art by Aaron Lopresti

Alongside the Starjammers, Carol traveled with exiled Shi'ar ruler Lilandra Neramani and aided

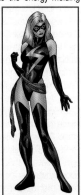

her when she and her embittered sister Deathbird (one of Ms. Marvel's early foes) fought to use the cosmic Phoenix Force's power to increase their positions. When the Kree-Shi'ar War menaced Earth's sun, Carol nearly burned out her own powers in saving the sun and was hospitalized in Avengers Headquarters for weeks, during which time she made peace with her past as an Avenger. When Starjammer Raza was coerced by Kree into trying to kill the Avengers' Black Knight (Dane Whitman) for his actions during the war, Binary ended the conflict and falsely claimed Raza had been mind-controlled to protect him; afterward she decided to remain on Earth, feeling that she had been running from her problems. She moved into her parents' Beverly, Massachusetts home and began a semi-autobiographical science fiction novel titled "Binary." She also worked with Peter Corbeau of Starcore in orbital projects, as well as with other heroes. When the alien Skeletron pushed the Moon out of orbit, Binary was among those who opposed him, pursuing Skeletron to the Stranger's World alongside Quasar (Wendell Vaughn) and other heroes; wanting full-strength allies against Skeletron, the Stranger restored Carol's damaged psyche, briefly giving her full access to her lost memories and buried emotions, though they soon faded. When another alien plot destabilized the wormhole from which Carol drew her powers, she worked with the X-Men to restore it; weeks later, she realized this had failed when her Binary powers ceased replenishing themselves. Troubled by her apparently fading powers and memories of her short-lived emotional reconnection to her past, Carol began drinking heavily. When the disbanded Avengers re-formed while facing Morgan Le Fay, Carol rejoined the team as Warbird. Though her powers had stabilized at her old Ms. Marvel levels, she kept the loss of her Binary-level powers secret. Her drinking led to bad judgment calls against Kree enemies, and the Avengers called a special tribunal to investigate Warbird's actions. When it looked like Carol would be demoted to reserve status, she quit before a decision was reached. She moved to Seattle and resumed writing while her first novel successfully saw print; a contract for several others followed. Meanwhile, Avengers founder Iron Man had also relocated to Seattle, and the recovered alcoholic Stark tried to offer Carol guidance despite her resistance. She bottomed out when, during an alcoholic blackout, she threw Iron Man through the wing of a passenger jet. She and Iron Man saved the passengers, but Carol finally realized she had a problem and began attending AA meetings. She revealed her identity to governmental authorities and took responsibility for the crash; much to her surprise, the judge gave her a suspended sentence, demanding that she rejoin the Avengers and that they supervise her.

Back with the Avengers and sober, Carol thrived. She drew the standoffish Triathlon closer into the team, helped end the Shi'ar conversion of Earth into a "prison planet," led an Avengers contingent against a Deviant army in China, and led a mission to find the Master (Eshu) during Kang's invasion of Earth. On the latter mission she encountered Kang's son Marcus, a virtual duplicate of the Marcus who had once kidnapped her (as Kang is an alternate temporal counterpart to Immortus). Like his predecessor, this Marcus was smitten with Carol, who was in turn both intrigued and disturbed by him. Reluctantly accepting aid against the Master's forces from Marcus, Carol ultimately killed the Master in combat (Carol would later demand she be court-martialed for this "murder," eventually being declared innocent of wrongdoing). Carol played a key role in the destruction of Kang's orbital Damocles base, helping defeat Kang's invasion. The Avengers' seizure of the Master's technology made this victory possible, and Kang ultimately slew Marcus for disloyalty since he knew his son had secretly aided Carol against the Master. Later, after the Avengers helped contain the "Red Zone" disaster, the US president offered Carol a position as chief tactical officer for the Department of Homeland Security (DHS); she accepted, leaving the Avengers.

Carol recruited the Thunderbolts' Dallas Riordan to work with her at the DHS, but chafed at the deskwork and kept slipping into costume — she teamed with Wolverine and Captain America (Steve Rogers) against Rapture and Project Contingency (a renegade SHIELD anti-mutant operation), with the Thunderbolts against Fathom Five and Baron Strucker's Hydra forces, and with several heroes against Titannus. The Commission on Superhuman Activities (CSA) cornered her into approving an assault by the Thunderbolts on the Avengers, and her discontent grew. Eventually, the mad Scarlet Witch altered Earth to create the mutant-ruled Reality-58163 ("House of M") where Carol, despite her non-mutant status, was that world's greatest hero as Captain Marvel. When the world was restored to normal, Carol retained her Captain Marvel memories, and decided she was wasting her time in a desk job. She resigned from the DHS, resolving to make herself into the hero she now knew she could be. Carol hired an agent, Sarah Day, to help with her public image, and readopted her Ms. Marvel name at Day's suggestion. Carol subsequently defeated a Brood army and the Brood-hunting Cru, aided the Avengers against the Collective, attended the birth of close friend Jessica Jones' baby, and served as the maid of honor at Jessica's wedding. She battled Warren Traveler, a dimension-lost foe from Reality-58163, and battled Titannus again, all while conducting TV interviews and maintaining a very public blog. When the Superhuman Registration Act passed, Carol became one of its strongest supporters and an early recruit of the government's new super-hero army, the Initiative. She and fellow Initiative agents apprehended anti-registration heroes like the Prowler (Hobie Brown), Shroud and fellow Avenger Arachne (Julia Carpenter), and trained would-be heroes like Araña, who regarded Carol as a surrogate mother.

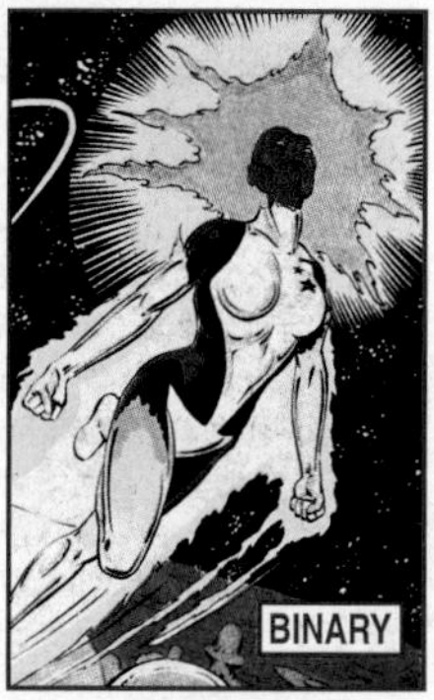
BINARY
Art by Paul Smith

Asked by Initiative founder Iron Man to lead a new government-backed Avengers group, Carol reluctantly agreed. She personally selected Wasp (Janet Van Dyne), Wonder Man and Ares for her team, and at Stark's request also included Black Widow, Sentry (Robert Reynolds) and Iron Man himself. The balance of power within the group between Carol and Iron Man was uneasy. He had recruited Sentry and later added Spider-Woman over Carol's objections, and often ignored her opinions. Still, the team performed well against the Mole Man, Ultron, an invasion of Venom-like symbiotes, Tiger Shark, and the BAD Girls, and even brought Dr. Doom (Victor von Doom) to trial for his terrorist activities. As a condition of accepting the Avengers leadership, Carol had demanded her own elite SHIELD strike force, known as Operation: Lightning Storm; she hoped to use this force to right what she saw as the world's wrongs, undertaking missions too quiet or too questionable for the Avengers. After initially using the strike force for personal reasons to try to mend fences with Arachne, Carol defeated AIM forces who had unleashed a genetic bomb in Indianapolis, Lightning Storm suffering serious casualties in the process. She began recruiting her core agents from the Initiative rather than SHIELD thereafter, working with Machine Man (X-51) and Sleepwalker to end the Puppet Master (Phillip Masters)'s slave ring and stop a Brood invasion. During this time, Carol also honored the Initiative's Ultragirl with a copy of her earlier Ms. Marvel costume, although administrators would later confiscate that from her. When a Skrull imposter impersonated her and her sometime boyfriend, William Wagner, the succeeding investigation resulted in the Skrulls blowing up Lightning Storm's minicarrier headquarters, killing many of Carol's support personnel as well as civilians on the ground. Suffering the aftermath of the Skrulls' actions, Lightning Storm has not yet been reconstituted.

On the personal front, Carol's romantic interest Wagner, possibly a Kree spy, was later apparently kidnapped by AIM and Carol had an ill-advised fling with Wonder Man. Amidst this, Carol believed she was failing at her mission to become a true hero and regretted her work with the Initiative and Lightning Storm resulted in betrayal of friends and operative deaths.

The more responsibility Carol took on, the more she doubted her own abilities and looked back fondly on the times when she only relied on herself. She also learned that her parents and brother had relocated to the more agreeable climate of the Maine coast, but that her father was dying of lung cancer. Carol began losing control of her powers during a full-blown Skrull invasion of Earth, having apparently burned herself out while fighting the invaders. She aided friend Jessica Jones in recovering her baby (kidnapped by the Skrulls), and during that process she returned to Avengers Tower and found corrupt businessman Norman Osborn assuming control of the Avengers. Carol angrily quit rather than serve under him, and Osborn replaced Carol with a new Ms. Marvel: Moonstone (Karla Sofen). Carol joined a renegade Avengers team in opposing these "Dark Avengers," but her destabilizing power set led to her vowing to cut back on use of her powers; at some point during this time, Carol's father passed away.

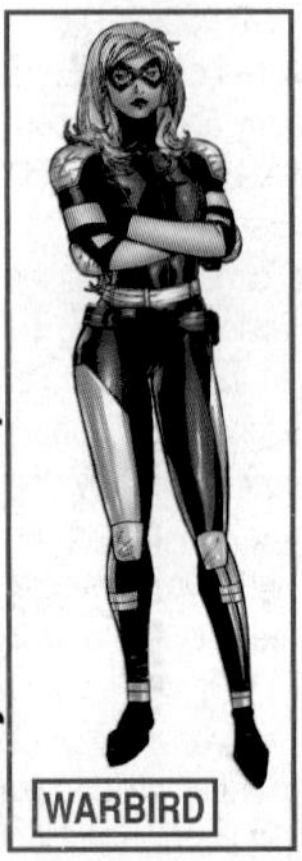
WARBIRD

Art by Olivier Coipel

Osborn saw Carol as a major threat, and decided to eliminate her. Investigating, he uncovered her early history with Ghazi Rashid and Michael Rossi, and recruited Rossi to treat Rashid with the Ascension serum, empowering Rashid. Rossi finally revealed his survival to Carol by summoning her and Rick Mason to a secret meeting at his own grave, where he told them that Rashid was still alive and in possession of a very powerful weapon. Eagerly grasping this link to what she regarded as a more successful time in her life, Carol agreed to help bring Rashid down. After trading with the information siphon known as Essential for a complete dossier on Osborn and confronting a new Captain Marvel (the Kree Noh-Varr, later called Protector), Carol faced down Ghazi in Hong Kong. Confronting the now super-powered Rashid and being reminded of her hate for him finally triggered an unlocking of Carol's lost emotions, but Carol's power use also further destabilized her. She defeated Rashid, but her powers overcharged and she explosively detonated over Hong Kong's Victoria Harbor, apparently disintegrating in a cosmic light explosion. Following Carol's seeming death, Rossi turned Ghazi over to Osborn, and Rick Mason swore to avenge her, apparently killing Rossi. As her dispersed energies coalesced, Carol returned in multiple forms, including one as Ms. Marvel and a civilian guise as successful writer Catherine Donovan, but her mental energies and physical substance eventually merged back into a complete Carol Danvers. As Ms. Marvel, Carol handed her would-be successor Moonstone a painful and humiliating defeat, sparing her life in the hopes it might motivate Sofen to change her ways. Later, happily reunited with Rick Mason, Carol exposed Mystique as the killer behind a murder spree supposedly committed by Mar-Vell.

Later, Carol assisted the Avengers when they defeated and discredited Osborn during his siege of Asgard, but was briefly possessed by the Venom symbiote when she separated it from its host, Mac Gargan (formerly the Scorpion). Carol rejoined the Avengers after their reorganization and became particularly close with Spider-Man. When the cosmic Phoenix Force went on a destructive journey through the universe, Carol and a contingent of Avengers left Earth to contain it. While pursuing the Force on Kree world Hala, Carol was affected by megalomaniacal Kree leader Minister Marvel's control of the Kree (via his son Marvel Mind's psychic powers) and was compelled to turn on her teammates alongside Captain Marvel (Mar-Vell), resurrected by the Minister and a portion of the Force. When the Phoenix Force approached Hala, Carol rejected Marvel Mind's influence and tried to absorb the Force, but Mar-Vell sacrificed his life to save Carol and Hala. Soon after, Carol was deeply upset by now-teammate Protector siding with the Kree against the Avengers, despite his later repentance, and told him he was not welcome on Earth. On Earth, Carol later adopted a new costume and claimed the Captain Marvel name, inspired by Mar-Vell's sacrifice. She inherited a vintage plane from Helen Cobb upon her death, which sent Carol through time; first, to World War II, where she fought alongside the Banshee Squad, a Women Air Force Service Pilot squad, against a platoon of Japanese pilots armed with Kree technology; to 1961, where she met Cobb, who joined her time-spanning journey; and to her own empowerment with the Psyche-Magnitron. During the latter adventure, Cobb usurped Carol's powers, challenging her to reach the plane first and return to the present; Carol succeeded, learning that Helen had apparently orchestrated the entire adventure to repair the damage she'd done to history by stealing the Psyche-Magnitron shard.

HEIGHT: 5'11"
WEIGHT: 145 lbs.
EYES: Blue
HAIR: Blonde

ABILITIES/ACCESSORIES: The Psyche-Magnitron transformed Carol into a peak human, athletically as fit as humanly possible, and also modified her DNA with Kree genes. It gave her the powers of flight, superhuman strength (sufficient to press 70 tons following subsequent genetic alterations) and greatly enhanced durability, as well as "seventh-sense" precognitive flashes and the ability to change into her costume instantaneously. Six months after her transformation, the Psyche-Magnitron produced a suit that enabled her to survive in space and was designed to ease her body's continuing transformation; however, this suit was eventually destroyed. After Carol lost her powers to Rogue, she maintained her "peak human" status though she lacked super-powers, save apparently the ability to change instantaneously into costume. Carol currently wears a costume made from Tony Stark-designed impervious fabric that features a retractable protective headpiece. As Binary, Carol channeled the energies of a white hole (also known as a wormhole) through her body to release any form of radiation or gravity. The white hole boosted her strength and endurance levels far beyond her old Ms. Marvel levels, and she could survive indefinitely in space. Losing access to the white hole didn't change her Binary powers, merely the level at which they function — she can still fly, can still project photonic energy blasts, and still possesses extreme strength and durability approximating her original Ms. Marvel levels. These powers are maintained by ambient energy absorbed from her environment, and as a result she can have negative effects on sensitive machinery and raises the temperature around her 2-3 degrees. She can temporarily augment her powers by absorbing energy forms, most notably electromagnetic radiation, plasma and sonics; however, unless she is prepared, her energy absorption is rarely instantaneous, so she draws only miniscule power from many energy attacks and can still be damaged by them. Without energy sources, Carol can no longer survive unaided in space. If she absorbs particularly high levels of energy, her old Binary energy corona may surround her hands, head or body. Carol is fluent in English, Russian and another unrevealed Earth language, as well as Kree and Shi'ar languages. She speaks passable Rajaki and has a limited vocabulary in many other languages, including Arabic. Carol is an accomplished pilot, having extensive experience with USAF planes as well as with Kree, Shi'ar and other alien starships. She has extensive training in military tactics, espionage, armed and unarmed combat, including numerous martial arts. Carol is an accomplished author and editor, is immensely strong-willed,able to endure incredible physical pain and is a recovering alcoholic.

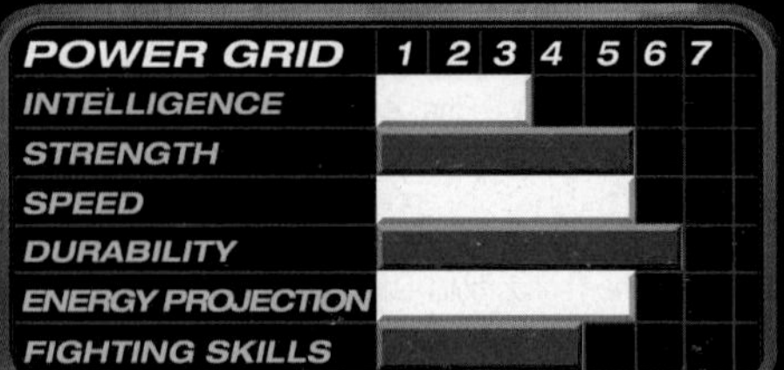
POWER GRID
1 2 3 4 5 6 7
INTELLIGENCE
STRENGTH
SPEED
DURABILITY
ENERGY PROJECTION
FIGHTING SKILLS

Text by Mark O'English & Rob London with Mike O'Sullivan